The *Working Woman's* Cookbook & Entertainment Guide

by Pat McMillen

with a Foreword by Phil Donahue

THE BOBBS-MERRILL COMPANY, INC., INDIANAPOLIS/NEW YORK

Published by The Bobbs-Merrill Co., Inc.
Indianapolis/New York
Manufactured in the United States of America
First Printing
Designed by Mary A. Brown

Library of Congress Cataloging in Publication Data

McMillen, Pat.
The working woman's cookbook and entertainment guide.

  Includes index.
  1. Entertaining. 2. Cookery. I. Title.
TX731.M395 1983   641.5'55   83-3814
ISBN 0-672-52708-1

CONTENTS

Foreword
by
Phil Donahue

I know a lot more about Pat McMillen than I do about cooking.

As the senior producer of the DONAHUE Show, Pat has been responsible for more program ideas than anyone else on our extremely gifted staff. During the fifteen-year life of my program she has been the whirlwind who has booked guests, fought for their airline seats, gotten them into overcrowded hotels, arranged for their makeup and hair styling, presented me with reams of her own research, warmed up the audience on the day of the program, and then finally, *finally* gone home to prepare dinner for herself and her loved ones. The woman does not have time to chew gum.

Pat is more than aware of the daily grind of millions of women who over the last decade have found themselves with two jobs — one at work and one at home. She has produced countless shows featuring these players in this modern-day drama. Like her, they are determined not to let their own health or their interest in good meals diminish under the pressures of their challenging life-style.

If you have discovered that life's responsibilities do not end at the conclusion of the eight-hour work day, this book is for you. It is also for anyone who wishes to avoid the guilt-ridden system that I resorted to while I was a single parent: steak on Monday, TV dinners on Tuesday, steak on Wednesday, etc.

What follows is a collection of practical ideas and delicious recipes for the woman who wants variety and nutrition in her weekly menu but who has neither the funds to attend the Cordon Bleu nor the time to prepare its complicated menus. While chicken canneloni with skinned and seeded tomatoes is a great idea, it doesn't marry well with the real-life day-after-day needs of the busy woman whose loved ones often greet her — after she's had a near riotous day at the office — by asking, "What's for dinner and how soon will it be ready?"

If you've heard these questions a million times, read on. In these pages you'll find interesting and time-saving answers to the problem that modern American women have to face.

To working women everywhere

ACKNOWLEDGMENTS

Those Who Took Time to Fill Out My Questionnaire

Kathie Berlin
Erma Bombeck
Grace Brewer
Shirley Drexler
Barbara Kauffman
Carol Kleiman
Jude Lujack
Mary McFadden

Suzanne McFarlane
Kathy Ann Mitchell
Carol Mix
Judith Ann Nielsen
Susan O'Connell
Patricia A. Straus
Angie Urbano
Cindy Lee Walker

Those Who Shared Their Favorite Recipes

Mabel Baker
Ruth Baker
Alene Drexler
Mabel Hastings
Sandy Hastings
Darlene Hayes

Marie Kauffman
Bernice Priest
Elyse Mach
Jane Rawnsley
Sheri Singer

Those Who Supported and Contributed

Herman Baker
Phil Donahue
Maxine Joachim

Shirley Mueller
Helen Snyder

Editing, Expertise, and Friendship

Rosalyn T. Badalamenti

Stefanie Woodbridge

Photography, Recipe Testing, Patience, and Understanding
During the Writing of This Book
Bob Hastings

A Classic Question

"What am I going to fix for dinner?"

You've asked that question; every woman has. It's a classic. You've probably also experienced the sinking feeling that can accompany it, the one Victorians used to call "a pang." I call it "a panic."

Scene: It's about four o'clock in the afternoon, and you are tired. You've been working hard all day, concentrating, coping with one thing after another. The phone. The mail. An unexpected problem. Then you hear someone talking about plans for the evening, or perhaps you check the time and realize that five o'clock is in sight. Suddenly you think, "Dinner! What are we going to have for dinner?"

If you're like many working women I know, you then have a conversation with yourself that sounds like this:

YOU:	Chicken.
YOURSELF:	No, we had that last night.
YOU:	Lamb stew?
YOURSELF:	Too much work, and anyway the kids hate it.
YOU:	I know, spaghetti!
YOURSELF:	No, no, Bob requested that for his birthday tomorrow night. (How am I ever going to lose weight?)
YOU:	There's always steak.
YOURSELF:	But it's so expensive!
YOU:	Fish has too many bones. . . . An omelet.
YOURSELF:	No.
YOU:	I give up. Hamburgers.
YOURSELF:	God, am I tired of hamburgers!

The Syndrome

This conversation is a symptom of The What-to-Have-for-Dinner Syndrome. It is the result of unpreparedness, the lack of an idea or interest or inspiration, a heavy, sluggish feeling of duty. Unless you love to cook and look forward to time in the kitchen, it can be depressing to think of going home and facing yet another chore. Some days you may be so preoccupied with work that dinner doesn't matter much. On other days you may not feel like cooking because you're simply too tired. Worst of all, perhaps, are the days when you just run out of ideas, when you're bored with every dish you can think of and life seems like eternal February.

One woman used to recite this rhyme under her breath:

> Pork-lamb-veal, chicken-turkey-beef,
> Turkey-veal-pork, lamb-chicken-beef,
> Six different suppers —
> Then I come to grief.

The Syndrome hits wives and mothers and singles alike. (Families and couples are not the only ones who eat dinner.) No one is immune. Today, even men are no longer completely protected from it, although, let's face it, women still carry the major responsibility for cooking. Buying take-out food, especially fast food, is a quick cure, but as a steady solution it is expensive and may not offer the dietary balance you prefer.

Actually, The Syndrome has to do with more than just food. It's part of the larger, more subtle problem of making a smooth transition from day to evening so that your time away from work is pleasant and you can look forward to the next day. Like all periods of transition, those hours between four and seven can be tricky. You have to switch gears, from job life to home life. If you carry job problems with you, if your commute is one long hassle, or you face an empty evening alone, if your kids greet you at the door with six crises each, you may wish you'd stayed at work. Dinner is part of this tricky time. It is the final hurdle you have to clear before you get to evening and time for yourself. In my experience, evening can be significantly affected by dinner.

Daily Pressure

The women of previous generations may have faced the inescapability of dinner, just as we do, but life was probably gentler in the past.

It was structured differently. Most women didn't work outside the home, and the pace of life was more relaxed. The eighties, by contrast, are a fast track. Women have become a significant part of the work force, and everybody is on the go. Ours is a high-tech, high-energy, career-conscious world.

Look at some of the jobs women now do and the hours they put in. As vice-president of the All-American Bank in Chicago, Shirley Drexler works a minimum of ten hours a day overseeing bank operations. Cindy Lee Walker, program manager for WBBM(CBS)-TV in Chicago, is responsible for selecting and placing all syndicated and locally produced programs, and for the station's appearance on the air. She is on call from eight o'clock in the morning until nine at night. The well-known dress designer Mary McFadden works seven days a week, as do journalists like Carol Kleiman of the *Chicago Tribune.* Suzanne McFarlane puts in twelve hours a day as executive assistant to Henry Kissinger in Washington, D.C. And then there's Judith Ann Nielsen, who is an evening supervisor for a telephone counseling service called LifeLine in upstate New York. Judy works an eight-hour shift three nights a week. That's not a lot, you say? Well, she spends the rest of her time at home, looking after her family, which numbers one husband and fourteen children living at home — count 'em, fourteen. (For more information about these working women and others, see Chapter 7.)

Schedules like these leave little time for meal planning and food preparation. No wonder fast food is so popular today. No wonder specialty food shops and delicatessens package food that working people can buy on their way home. Thank goodness, because such foods can bail you out of a jam. But as I've said, buying prepared foods is only a temporary solution. Short of hiring a cook, as the rich do (which, by the way, isn't without its problems), is there any way out?

A New Approach

I think there is a solution.

I know what it is to be busy, what it is to get tired. I get up at 5:00 A.M., and I arrive at work some mornings by 7:00 A.M. because we're doing the DONAHUE Show live at 9:00, so I put in a long day. But I don't suffer from The Syndrome. I know that dinner is already solved.

Let me illustrate (and hint at the solution). Those of us who work in television face all types of emergencies, which can be either unpleasant or pleasant. It all depends. This year we had a particularly memorable emergency. We rushed to Los Angeles on less than twenty-four hours' notice to tape a show with Tom Selleck, the handsome star of *Magnum, P.I.,* whose looks have provoked comment — shall we say? — from the women of America. I was still at home one Friday morning when I got a call saying that Mr. Selleck would do the show. In less than two hours I was packed and ready and at work. I left on a plane a few hours later. The only thing I had time to do at home was leave a note for Bob, the man in my life. It said, "Off to L.A. to tape a show with Tom Selleck. See you Sunday evening." Food was the furthest thing from my mind. In fact, I didn't think of the food situation at home until Sunday evening when I walked in to find Bob enjoying ham and applesauce for dinner. On Friday night he had had spaghetti; on Saturday evening, vegetable lasagne. No problem at all. He had simply eaten from the food supply in the freezer while I was gone. I suppose I might have thought of food sooner, but I'm so used to having plenty of it on hand that I'm free to forget about it.

How did I achieve such freedom? My life as a cook changed dramatically some years ago when Bob and I and his two children went to Greenwich, Connecticut, to visit my friend Carol Mix and her family for a four-day weekend, part of which we planned to spend sailing. There were eight of us all together at breakfast, lunch, and dinner every day. If you've had weekend guests, you know how dizzying it can be to spend time with them, provide three meals a day, and still have enough energy to go to work on Monday morning. If you're not careful, you've no sooner cleaned up after breakfast than it's time to start lunch.

Carol's food and her culinary management that weekend were a revelation to me. She and her husband met us at the airport, and she insisted we go to their home for dinner rather than stop at a restaurant. The food seemed to prepare itself magically while we had drinks. The next morning Carol had the food for the boat ready to go. On the boat, all we had to do was add a few finishing touches, and heat up our meals. She had even planned a cooking project in the galley for the kids. They made brownies, which provided our dessert that evening and at the same time saved them from boredom. When we returned from sailing, Carol again insisted we have dinner at her home before going to the plane. And again she provided a full-course meal with only minor assistance. Carol works outside the home forty hours a week and has no domestic help, so I marveled at how she managed. Finally I said, "You must be some kind of Superwoman. How do you do it?"

She explained that she planned ahead. "I have company often, and when I invited you three weeks ago, I made a list, purchased everything I needed, cooked and froze the food. I always do it that way so that I can enjoy my guests."

The modest speech planted an idea in my head.

How I Came to Write This Book

After my visit to Carol's I found myself thinking a lot about what she had said. If organizing meals ahead of time worked when guests arrived, it seemed to me it would also work for everyday living. In fact, it might work wonders. Just as Carol had time to be with her guests, I would have time to spend on things I enjoyed, with my friends or with my family. And I would be spared from working as a cook all evening after working all day. The more I thought about organizing, the better it seemed.

Starting with Carol's basic premise, I evolved the ideas I present here. I have used them for several years. As a result, I no longer dread the transition from day to evening.

One afternoon Sheri, one of the former producers in my office, remarked, "Pat, you always seem to know what you're going to fix for dinner. You're so prepared!" We had talked about my approach before, but this time I sat down and explained it to her. Soon afterward Sheri arrived at the office on Monday morning and announced proudly that she wasn't going to have to worry about dinner all week because she had used my plan. Now *she* was prepared, and she felt good. So did I, because I had helped her and because her experience showed me that my approach wasn't just an idiosyncrasy, something that happened to suit my personal ways. It occurred to me then that this approach could perhaps help other working women, too. So I decided to write this book.

Who Is a Working Woman?

To me, a working woman is one who holds down a job, whatever and wherever the job may be. Kathie Berlin, senior vice-president of Rogers and Cowan, an international public relations company, has a visible, glamorous position; but as I see it, that doesn't make her more of a working woman than Grace Brewer of New Milford, Connecticut, who is a full-time housewife and mother of five children. Today, housewives and mothers do just as much managing as the briefcase-carrying managers in corporations across the country do: they coordinate schedules, administer budgets, make decisions and strategic plans; they also do all the staff work — the shopping, cleaning, and chauffeuring. A woman busy with her household and family in this way is no stranger to The What-to-Have-for-Dinner Syndrome just because she's not in an office.

This book isn't just for family people, for women with husbands and children to think of every evening. If you're single, it's for you, too. Some single people treat dinner as a toss-away meal if they're eating alone. They grab something on the run or make do with a container of yogurt, because cooking for one seems like too much trouble. From the point of view of health, that's unwise. Nutrition is important, and so is the psychological benefit that comes with knowing there's a nice dinner at home at the end of a long day.

Can a Book Solve a Problem?

Yes, I believe so.

In these pages you will find answers to the question of what to have for dinner. Whenever the problem arises, you will be able to avoid those depressing conversations with yourself; in fact, you won't even have to think. You can look up a menu that appeals to you. You will also find a solution to the problem of time and tiredness, an organizational approach that solves The Syndrome. And you will find a section on entertaining that will tell you how to do it graciously, with a staff of one — yourself. The prospect of dinner guests can loom as an awesome chore, the last thing you want after a busy week. So you put off entertaining until the voice of conscience forces you to face it. But it should be and can be fun. I hope this section will help you make entertaining at home less expensive, more enjoyable, and a regular part of your life.

Finally, I hope this book will revise the scenario with which we began so that it will be more like this:

Scene: It's four o'clock on a Thursday afternoon. Your phone has been ringing constantly, and you're tired. The end of the day is coming, thank goodness. Then — dinner.

But at that thought you grin. Because dinner is all planned. You don't have to think about it and you don't have to shop for it. Possibly you don't even have to cook it because you've organized ahead.

"Hey, Mom," you whisper to yourself, "what's for dinner?"

Yourself smiles knowingly.

2

The McMillen Method

Part 1: The Cooking Session

A One-Word Answer

Efficiency. Planning. Order. The solution to the working woman's dinner syndrome is *organization*. But the question is, *how* to organize? How to be a good cook and an efficient one?

The principles of organization are basically a matter of common sense. If most of us could just get around to organizing, we'd be all set. But getting around to it can be hard when you're busy. Think of the closets and papers you intend to put in order as soon as you have a chance. Natural as organization may seem, it does take time, thought, and experience; a certain talent and the right attitude helps, too. As a result, a new breed of consultant is surfacing today: the professional organizer, a person who goes into homes and offices to organize everything from financial records to clothes closets to elaborate file systems. These people provide a much-needed service, and their growing numbers prove it.

Perhaps what I offer is the culinary equivalent — an efficient approach to meal preparation so that you don't have to figure one out for yourself. My approach is meant to be flexible. You can use it all the time or some of the time. You can adapt it to your own situation. You can use it to prepare your favorite dishes as well as my recipes. Once you get the hang of it, you can make it your own.

First, let's see how organized you already are. Try this quiz and rate yourself.

7

Are You a 10 in the Kitchen or a 3 on KP?

Answer the following questions yes or no. The correct answers and a key for scoring can be found below.

1. Are your appliances, both small and large, located conveniently?
2. Do you sometimes prepare dinner in a haphazard fashion — for example, fixing vegetables before putting the meat on or setting the table partially and then going back to cooking?
3. Do you keep basics like chopped onion in the freezer ready for use when you're cooking?
4. When you make a casserole, do you make only enough for one meal?
5. Do you have to stand on your head or a chair or crawl into a cupboard to reach things you use in cooking?
6. Are your recipes readily available and readable?
7. Are you always running to the store for something you forgot to buy?
8. Do you go to the store more than twice a week other than for bread and milk?
9. Do you fix several complicated dishes for one meal?
10. Do you spend most of a meal running in and out of the kitchen while the rest of the family is eating?

Scoring yourself on the quiz: Give yourself 1 point for each correct answer.

If your score is:

    10:    Perfect! You'll have an easy time adapting my approach.

    6—9: You've got the basic idea, but you're not practicing it enough.

    3—5: You've made a small beginning; try to extend it.

    0—3: You need to get organized. You're wasting precious time and energy in the kitchen when you could be enjoying yourself.

Here are the correct answers:

1. Yes. 2. No. 3. Yes. 4. No. 5. No. 6. Yes. 7. No. 8. No. 9. No. 10. No.

Getting Started

To get the full benefit of this book, first read it through to understand the basic ideas and to learn where everything is discussed so that you can use it as a reference book. Then think about how you want to tailor the basic ideas to fit your circumstances. To put the plan into action, you'll need to choose the scale on which you want to begin. I recommend that you start small. If at first you save measurable time one or two nights a week, you will begin to enjoy the benefit, and you can proceed from there as your time and interest allow.

Be sure you heed the time-saving procedures in the next Helpful Habits section. They will make a great difference in your efficiency.

You will find that, to follow this plan, you will need to keep certain basic items on your kitchen shelves. So before you begin to use this plan, consult the "Stocking Up" section.

Helpful Habits, or "How Can You Do So Much in 2 Hours?"

How did you score on the quiz? If your score was less than 9, you should pay more attention to organization. One important way to be organized is in your approach to small things. I'm going to start with these because my approach to cooking assumes them; it works best if you operate efficiently with basics. These small things are tricks to make your kitchen time go further.

Keep components ready. Never peel a small onion or chop half of a larger one only to throw the other half away (or plop it into the refrigerator to be thrown out later). Choose a large onion. Chop or slice the whole thing. Use what you need. Then put the rest in a plastic freezer container with an airtight lid, label it, and place it in the freezer. The next time you make chili, meat loaf, omelets, spaghetti, pizza, or anything else that calls for onion, you'll have it ready, chopped and waiting for you in the freezer. No more tears. You will have saved time, and maybe even money, because onions spoil if held too long.

Apply the same approach to all the foods on the following list. You can prepare and freeze these foods when you're cooking; or you can periodically set aside some time to stock your freezer. The following foods should be in your freezer at all times: onions; green peppers, chopped and sliced; celery; bread crumbs; cracker crumbs; mozzarella cheese, grated; Cheddar, grated; fried bacon slices, whole or chopped; chocolate or anything else you use frequently and spend time grating, slicing, or chopping. Keep in mind that chopped raw onion becomes more potent in the freezer; if a recipe calls for four tablespoons of onion, you may want to decrease the amount to three and a half tablespoons. Black pepper and garlic seem to become more potent in a casserole that is frozen, so you may want to use less than usual in food you plan to freeze.

If you rarely use some of these items, of course, delete them from the list. Again, it saves time and money to prepare a large quantity at once. This is something your children can do for you if they are old enough to handle a knife. Even very young children can have fun making the bread and cracker crumbs. Allowing them to do simple things will save you time and teach them valuable lessons about food. Time spent together in the kitchen can also be cozy and pleasant. You'll find more about kids in the kitchen in Chapter 6.

It is important to label everything before you put it in the freezer. (See more about freezing and labeling in Chapter 3.) Once, when I ran out of labels, I put some food in the freezer intending to label it later, and I ended up one night serving Sloppy Joes over spaghetti because they looked so much like my spaghetti sauce. I keep peel-off labels and a smudgeproof pen in a drawer beside the freezer. You won't mind the labeling process if you keep the materials in a convenient spot.

There is a psychological benefit to having even a few of the dinner chores done ahead of time. If you haven't made your meat loaf ahead, you'll feel better knowing that all you have to do is open that package of ground beef, take from the freezer a tablespoon or two of chopped onion, green pepper, and celery, throw it all into a bowl, stir and roll in cracker crumbs (also from the freezer). This makes the whole process much less of a chore. No tiresome peeling, chopping, and rolling. Your meat loaf, from front door to oven, is only 3 to 5 minutes away instead of half an hour or more; and you can relax with the family or take a bath while it is cooking.

Prepare meals in an organized manner, not helter-skelter. For instance, if you do need to mix your meat loaf when you get home, do the meat loaf and dinner preparations systematically. It will save you much time and effort. If it seems to take you forever to get dinner on the table, consult the following list of do's and don'ts to find out where you may be wasting time.

DO	DON'T
Turn oven to correct temperature.	Get out ground beef.
Fix meat loaf and place in oven.	Put plates on table.
Fix salad and refrigerate.	Get out vegetables and place on counter.
Get vegetables ready to cook.	Put silver on table.
Prepare dessert.	Mix meat loaf.
Set table.	Get out salad fixings.
Rest while meat loaf cooks.	Put napkins on table.
Cook vegetables while dishing up remainder of meal.	Prepare vegetables.

DO

Turn oven to correct temperature.

Fix meat loaf and place in oven.

Fix salad and refrigerate.

Get vegetables ready to cook.

Prepare dessert.

Set table.

Rest while meat loaf cooks.

Cook vegetables while dishing up remainder of meal.

Total 1½ hours

(Think of the time you would have saved if you had prepared the meat loaf ahead of time.)

DON'T

Get out ground beef.

Put plates on table.

Get out vegetables and place on counter.

Put silver on table.

Mix meat loaf.

Get out salad fixings.

Put napkins on table.

Prepare vegetables.

Make salad and place in refrigerator.

Put drinking glasses on table.

Plan dessert.

Put meat loaf in pan.

Turn on oven.

Place meat loaf in cold oven (because you forgot to turn oven on to preheat).

Now everything is ready except the meat loaf. You spent about 45 minutes of your evening just getting dinner together (and it still isn't ready) when *you could have done it in 15 to 20 minutes* and relaxed for a while.

Total: 2½–3 hours

The Cooking Session

The magic that solves the dinner problem and puts a secret smile on your face at four in the afternoon is the cooking session.

For the purposes of this book, a cooking session is any time spent in the kitchen preparing *food for more than one meal.* That means cooking in larger quantities than you need for a particular meal, and freezing the extra amounts for the future. When you prepare a casserole, for example, you make two, three, or four times as much as you need — depending on how much freezer space you have.

Although that's basic, and many people do it as a matter of course, I stress it because it is a simple, straightforward way of saving time. You get two or three or four meals for little more than one meal's work.

Once you get used to this simple form of the cooking session, you can move on to a more sophisticated level. A real cooking session is even more efficient: you make *more than one recipe for more than one meal.* For example, you sauté hamburger while you're roasting a chicken. I sometimes prepare two or three dishes to cook in the oven while one or two more are cooking on top of the stove. (This may sound intimidating at first, but you'll find that it becomes easier with time and practice.) It isn't necessary to do any particular number of dishes at once. *The main point is not to cook each meal separately, but to cook as much as you can, comfortably, each time you cook.*

The basic trick to the cooking session is to know what recipes can be prepared together so that you can cook the most food in the time available. Pick foods that are prepared similarly or that are easy to do between fixing other recipes. For instance, once you get a soup started, it has to simmer for a long time. While it's simmering, you can be getting another dish — say, a pot roast — ready to cook. While the pot roast is simmering, you can attend to the soup or mix a batch of cookies.

As I've said, you choose dishes that use the top of the stove and the oven at the same time. If you have a microwave oven and a crock pot and an electric skillet, you can do even more — but they are not necessary.

Let me illustrate. Here is a cooking session that yields the basics for approximately eight to ten meals, depending on the size of your family. These meals are not meant to be eaten all in one week, of course, but to be stockpiled in the freezer to be used as needed:

- Chicken and Noodles
- Creamed Chicken and Egg Slices over Biscuits
- Chunky Chicken Salad or another baked chicken casserole
- Quick Sloppy Joes
- Irish Spaghetti
- Spaghetti Sauce
- Taco Meat Base
- Chicken Cacciatore (2 dinners)
- Baked Chicken in Chicken Sauce

Using crock pot. Put 2–3 whole or cut-up chickens in the crock pot. Add 1–1½ cups water and turn the crock pot on. Now that's out of the way for the time being. Use this for Chicken and Noodles and Creamed Chicken over Biscuits. Any extra chicken can be used for chicken salad or other chicken recipes.

On top of the stove. Brown five or six pounds of ground beef with chopped onion. Use this later to make Chili, Quick Sloppy Joes, Irish Spaghetti, Spaghetti Sauce, and Taco Meat Base. (Recipes for the above are listed in the meat section.)

In the oven. Put 1 or 2 cut-up chickens in two glass baking dishes. Cover with tomatoes or tomato sauce, sprinkle with cheese, oregano, onion, green pepper, spices, and bake (for Chicken Cacciatore).

Put 1 cut-up chicken in baking dish, pour over 1 or 2 cans of condensed cream of chicken soup, and bake. This recipe can be easily increased by adding more chicken. Depending on the size of your family and how heartily they eat, this can be turned into one or two meals. Recipe on page 145.

Procedure for a Cooking Session

To have a cooking session, follow these basic steps:

1. Choose entrées that you and your family like and that can be prepared in quantity. You may wish to begin by following the sample cooking session above or those given later in this chapter.
2. Make a shopping list.
3. Shop. If you have food coupons on hand, use them now.
4. When your schedule permits, do the cooking.
5. Package the prepared food; label and freeze it.

Do *not* try to do all of this — or even steps 3, 4 and 5 — on the same day — it can be too tiring.

A Note on Portions

After a cooking session, serve your family part of what you have cooked. Then divide the rest into meal sizes and freeze. To get the right single-portion size, fill one dinner plate as you normally would to serve one person. Then put the portion in a freezer container and freeze it. If there are five in your family, put all five portions in one container. You can separate them again when you reheat. For soups, know how many ladlefuls it takes to fill one bowl, and then count as you are filling the soup container. After a little practice, you will be able to tell automatically how many ladlefuls you'll need without measuring.

A fringe benefit of the cooking-ahead plan, especially for those who are diet conscious, is that when you freeze individual dinners, you'll eat only what's thawed out and prepared for that meal. You won't take second or third helpings just because the food is sitting in front of you. The second and third helpings are frozen solid in the freezer for a second or third meal later on.

Many of us eat entirely too much. I certainly do. So I decided the best way to cut down was to stop serving the food in bowls, family style. Instead, I filled the plates at the stove. Most of the time, however, I found I had just enough left to serve one more person. Usually I had the right amount of meat, but with the vegetables, I played the add-on game: a little more to this plate, then a little more to that plate. Gradually, over a year, this added a little more to the body, defeating the whole purpose of individual servings. Now, I freeze that extra food to use later in purees, soups, meat pies, and stews.

I never worry about having half a package, half a cup, or a few pieces of anything left over. If it is perishable, I just figure out a different way to use it within the next day or so, or I freeze it in a lock-top freezer bag. I also keep a plastic container in the freezer for extra vegetables.

Sometimes the extra portion left over from dinner makes an excellent lunch later on. Even if a food can't be put into a sandwich, it can be taken to work in a small container. I use plastic butter or cheese containers. They look small, but they hold a surprising amount in grams and ounces.

Sample Cooking Sessions

Once you get used to cooking sessions, you won't have to follow the steps I outlined earlier. You'll find that the process becomes automatic. You just look at your stock of supplies and create meals from them.

Here are some cooking sessions to get you started. Once you've tried some of these, you'll want to create your own.

• MIXED-ITEM COOKING SESSION

2 chickens in crock pot
1 chicken in oven for Potato
  Chip Chicken
Brownies
Baked Potatoes for freezing
  and stuffing (2 or 3 recipes)

Baked Round Steak
Pork Roast and Beef Roast (or
  both, perhaps eliminating
  one of the other dishes
  above)

1. Put the chickens in crock pot and start cooking.

2. Clean chicken for the potato chip recipe but don't assemble the dish until later in the session. (Just refrigerate it for a little while.) It saves time to clean and wash all the chicken at one time, whether whole or in pieces.

3. If you cook two roasts, brown both lightly in the same large skillet at the same time if your skillet is large enough; if not, brown the roasts separately. Put them in separate baking pans, prepared according to recipe, cover, and bake.

4. Pound, cut up, season, flour, and brown the round steak. Place in a baking dish and bake.

5. Put the potatoes in to bake.

6. Assemble the Potato Chip Chicken and bake.

7. Make the Brownies.

As the food comes out of the oven or crock pot, finish off each dish one at a time. Slice the beef roast, make gravy, and baste the meat with it. Leave the pork roast whole or slice it and make gravy, depending on how you think you might best use it later.

Mash and stuff most of the potatoes. Save one or two for cottage fries (with or without eggs).

The crock pot chicken should be done now. Cool, bone, and prepare for freezing. These chickens will be used to make the following recipes:

Chicken-Filled Pasta Shells
Chunky Chicken Salad
Chicken and Noodles
Chicken Soup

Chicken Pot Pie
Creamed Chicken and Egg
  Slices (or your favorite
  chicken recipe)

Two chickens will not be enough for all of the above recipes, but it should be enough for two or three meals for four people, or obviously more meals for two people. If there are eight in your family, you may want to cook four or five chickens in a large pot on top of the stove instead of two in a crock pot. The recipes will still work, and I'm sure if you have eight in your family you already know how to adjust a recipe.

• GROUND BEEF COOKING SESSION

You will need 8 to 10 pounds of ground beef. Brown all the meat with chopped onions in either large skillets, Dutch ovens, or roasting pans. You may have to brown it in 2 or 3 batches. Drain the grease from all and set aside in a large glass mixing bowl. If you tend to be a little slow in the kitchen, you may want to refrigerate the meat after it cools a little, so the meat doesn't spoil while you are preparing the individual recipes.

Divide the browned meat so that you have:

2 pounds for Chili,　　　　　*1½ pounds for Sloppy Joes*
2 pounds for Spaghetti Sauce,　*1½ pounds for Tacos or Taco*
1 pound for Irish Spaghetti　　　*Salad*

(If you are serving only 2 to 3 people, 2 meals for each can be made from the above meat.)

Prepare the first four dishes after you have browned the meat: first the Chili, then the Spaghetti Sauce, then the Irish Spaghetti. While these simmer, prepare the Sloppy Joes. Simmer until the juice cooks down to the desired thickness your family likes. Everything should be done about the same time.

Cool, package, label, and freeze everything.

Now you have:

2 or 3 meals of Chili,　　　　*family and what you serve*
　depending on what you　　　*with it. (This amount is for*
　serve with it.　　　　　　*4 average eaters or 2 heavy*
2 meals of Spaghetti Sauce.　*eaters.)*
1 or 2 meals of Irish Spaghetti,　*1 or 2 meals of Sloppy Joes.*
　depending on the size of your　*1 or 2 meals of Tacos or*
　　　　　　　　　　　　　Taco Salad.

(Entrées for 8 to 10 meals for 2 to 4 persons in 2 or 3 hours.)

• EASY AND QUICK COOKING-AHEAD SESSION

All-Day Stew

Cut up a beef roast in large chunks or buy chunks of stew meat. Add potatoes, carrots, celery, and onions. Pour tomato soup over everything, cover tightly and bake all day at 225 degrees or for 3 hours at 350 degrees.

Pork Roast

Brown and place in the oven along with the stew. Bake for 1½ to 2 hours at 350 degrees or a little longer at 225 degrees.

Beef Roast with Vegetables

Prepare as for the stew, replacing soup with water and seasoning.

Meat Loaf

Place in oven with stew, Roast, and Pot Roast. Bake for 1 to 1½ hours at 350 degrees or 2 hours at 225 degrees.

Make the gelatin, add the fruit, and refrigerate.

Make the cookie dough, shape it into a long log-like roll, wrap in waxed paper, and refrigerate.

Stir up the box cake mix and bake. Ice the cake with already canned frosting.

Stir the gelatin and fruit occasionally while the other food cooks.

Now sit down and read the Sunday paper while the food for the week finishes cooking.

This whole session was very quick because of organization. First peel and cut all the vegetables to size and put them in bowl of cold water. Then get out a baking pan or dish for each recipe. Put the first three meats in their respective pans, add the vegetables, cover, and put into the oven to bake. Line the meat loaf pan with foil. Mix the meat loaf, roll it in cracker crumbs, put it in the pan, add vegetables, and bake. Then make the gelatin, cookie dough, and cake.

It's very easy for me to prepare these four large dishes because I have two ovens. If you are not so fortunate, you may have to spend a little more time in the kitchen or do these in two sessions.

• ALL AFTERNOON COOKING SESSION

One afternoon while working on this book, I baked a delicious chocolate bundt cake with caramel icing from scratch, using a recipe from a magazine. I froze half of the cake and served the other half for dessert during the next couple of days. While the cake was baking, I made Mexican Chicken for two meals, vegetable soup for three meals, and two batches of double fudge brownies from a mix. I cut one batch into snack-size pieces and the other into dessert-size pieces. Then I froze all of them. When I need the dessert size for snacks, I just cut them in half. I also baked potatoes for two meals. I served two of them for dinner that night with broiled steaks and a salad. I used the remainder of the potatoes later in the week for hash browns.

Here is the order of preparation for that cooking session:

1. Mix cake and put into oven. Put potatoes in oven to bake. Assemble ingredients for icing.

2. Assemble the Mexican Chicken and refrigerate until cake comes out of oven.

3. Cook chunks of beef or beef roast in pressure cooker for vegetable soup.

4. Clean and chop vegetables for soup.

5. Take cake out and put the Mexican Chicken into oven.

6. Finish mixing vegetable soup and cook.

7. Make icing, ice the cake, and mix brownies.

8. Take out chicken and put brownies into oven.

9. Cool, wrap, and freeze everything you won't use within the next day or two.

• SHORT, EASY COOKING SESSION

Put two 2- or 3-pound beef roasts plus 4½ cups of water into a large pressure cooker. Cook until tender.

When the roasts are finished take out one with 1½ cups of broth and use the broth to cook the noodles. You will have 1 or 2 beef and noodle dinners, depending on the size of your family.

With the remaining roast, you can make vegetable soup, Beef and Pot Pie Squares, or hot beef sandwiches with barbecue sauce.

Mix and bake two pumpkin pies using prepared crusts.

Brown 2 to 4 pounds of ground beef with chopped onions to be used later in Tacos, Taco Salad, or Chili.

Note: You are not completing each recipe here, but you are doing the major portion of the cooking. All you have to do when you get home from work is assemble and finish cooking or heating each entrée.

• GROUND BEEF AND RICE COOKING SESSION

5 to 7 pounds of meat
2 pounds for Meat Loaf   *Makes 1 or 2 meals*
2 pounds for Meatballs   *Makes 2 meals*
1 pound for Stuffed Green   *Makes 1 or 2 meals*
   Peppers (or Cabbage Rolls)

Prepare the Meat Loaf first. It's out of the way and baking while you prepare other dishes.

Make the meatballs and brown them. Divide into two portions.

Make Fancy Meatballs in Gravy to go over noodles or rice with half of the meatballs and freeze the other half for appetizers when company drops by. (Just pour on a little sauce and heat and you have a nice warm appetizer. You can put the sauce on and cook before you freeze the meatballs or do it when the company arrives. If you don't put the sauce on before you freeze the meatballs in a pinch instead of using them for appetizers you have the base for a meatball and spaghetti dinner done ahead.)

Put some rice on to cook for Stuffed Green Peppers and Cabbage Rolls unless you have a large supply in the freezer made ahead. This is also a good way to use up rice made ahead so it doesn't sit in the freezer too long. If I were using rice that had already been frozen, I'd use the dish in a day or two without freezing it. I would freeze the stuffed green peppers or cabbage rolls for later use if I were using freshly made rice.

Brown the 1 pound of ground beef with chopped onion. While it is browning, prepare the peppers. Mix the rice, meat, and other ingredients and stuff the peppers. Cover with tomato sauce and bake at 350 degrees for 15 to 20 minutes. Cool and freeze.

By this time the Meat Loaf and Meatballs and Gravy will probably be done. Cool and freeze.

Remember, this is a relatively easy cooking session. It should only take about 2 to 3 hours (even if you are slow), so you might want to get inventive and add in your own recipes to have fixed ahead. It doesn't take long to whip up a batch of brownies from a mix. Just put them into the oven with the meatloaf and they'll all be done at once. Jell-O takes about only 2 minutes. You'll not only have an entrée made ahead but also the dessert. By adding desserts to the cooking sessions yourself, you'll have the basics for four meals here with dessert: plain Jell-O Monday night, brownies with ice cream and chocolate sauce for Tuesday night, Jell-O with whipped topping for Wednesday night, brownies a la mode for Thursday night, and since you've been so creative all week, give yourself a treat on Friday night and go out to eat. If you don't want to serve brownies for dessert twice in the same week, substitute another made-ahead dessert from your freezer.

• CHICKEN, POTATOES, AND JELL-O COOKING SESSION

You will need:

1 package chicken legs
1 package chicken breasts with
  wings
3 whole chickens, cut up
3 to 4 cans cream of chicken
  soup (in this session I used
  3 but if you like more sauce
  use 4)

5 baking potatoes and 2
  medium-sized cooking
  potatoes,
16 ounces mild Cheddar cheese,
  grated
  Milk and butter (if not
  on hand)
4 sweet potatoes
1 package strawberry gelatin

Open, wash, clean, and inspect all the packages of chicken. Put all the cans of soup into 1 container adding ½ to ¾ cans of water for each can of soup. Put the chicken in baking dishes or pans to accommodate your needs. I did mine as follows:

Pan #1: 2 breasts plus 2 medium-sized cooking potatoes, cut in 8 pieces (1 full cup of soup poured over the entire pan)

Pan #2: 2 breasts and wings plus 2 legs (1 full cup of soup poured over the chicken)

Pan #3: 2 legs and thighs, 4 breasts and wings (pour the remaining soup mixture over the chicken)

Put the above 3 pans of chicken in the oven to bake at 350 degrees for 1 hour. Also, put the sweet potatoes and baking potatoes in to bake at the same time. If the potatoes are large, they may have to bake a little more than 1 hour.

Put the remaining chicken into a large saucepan. Cover with salt and peppered water and cook on top of the stove for about 1 hour, or until tender.

Prepare the Jell-O and refrigerate.

Peel and boil enough cooking potatoes for 2 meals of mashed potatoes for your family.

Remove the chicken from the oven and stove and cool it.

Mash the boiled potatoes, put in a container, and freeze.

Mash the baked potatoes, stuff, and freeze.

When the boiled chicken is cool, bone it, and put it in containers for individual meals. I made the following:

1 container chicken meat for Chicken and Noodles.

1 container chicken meat for Chicken-Filled Pasta Shells.

Enough chicken salad for 2 lunches to be used either in sandwiches or stuffed tomatoes or on a salad plate.

Chicken Broth: 2 cups undiluted

2 cups diluted (1 cup broth plus 1 cup water)

½ cup partially diluted

Total Yield for the Cooking Session

Chicken Salad: 2 lunches.

Baked Chicken in Chicken Sauce for dinner guests and Twice-Baked Potatoes.

Baked Chicken in Chicken Sauce for family dinner with Mashed Potatoes.

Chicken and potatoes baked in sauce for family dinner.

Chicken, Noodles, and Mashed Potatoes for family dinner (use 2 cups diluted broth) (use prepackaged noodles or draw from homemade noodles in freezer).

Chicken-Filled Pasta Shells.

Plain Strawberry Jell-O.

2 cups broth to use later in soup, gravy, etc.

1 baked potato (left in skin) to use for hash browns and eggs.

If I had added another chicken or two to boiled chicken in this session, I would have been able to make Chicken Soup and Chicken Pot Pie. With very little more time and work it would have yielded 2 more entrées.

This cooking session took 4½ hours, which is longer than I usually suggest. However, I personally clean, inspect, wash, skin, and drain every piece of chicken before putting it into the pans. I am a fanatic about extremely clean chicken.

Please note, though, that during the 4½-hour cooking session, I was not always cooking and working at the stove. I did the following:

Made 2 long distance calls to friends

Read 3 magazines

Fixed and ate lunch (for 2 people)

Wrote checks to pay bills
Cleaned out the potato basket
Made notes on the cooking session

The only thing not in the above cooking session that you might want to try is browning the chicken slightly before putting it in the pans to bake. I've done it both ways. I would say it depends on your particular taste and how hurried you are.

• ENTRÉE COOKING SESSION

All-Day Stew
Vegetable Soup
Bernie's Chop Suey
2 packages for 2 meals
1 small roast or 1 package of
* stew meat for 2 to 4 meals*

1 pound round steak plus 1 pound pork shoulder or 2 pounds packaged chop suey meat for 4 meals for 2 people or 2 to 3 meals for 4 people.

Some people like more meat in vegetable soup than others, so you may want to increase or decrease the amount of meat. You may also want to adjust the amount of meat used in the vegetable soup depending on whether you plan to serve it as an entrée or as an accompanying soup. Use the amount specified on the recipe for chop suey.

The three entrées above have some of the same items so that is why I choose to cook them in the same cooking session. You don't have to, if you don't want to, but you can save by buying a huge amount of beef and cutting it up yourself. Then all you have to buy is the pork to add to the chop suey.

Peel, cut, and chop the potatoes, carrots, onions (if you don't already have it done in freezer), and celery to the desired size for each of the recipes. Put the vegetables in cold water to hold them.

Put the stew on first to cook or in the oven to bake.

Put beef on to cook for the vegetable soup (I do mine in pressure cooker because it's faster). As soon as the meat is cooked to the desired doneness (if it is a roast, bone, and defat it), cut into pieces and add the vegetables — the carrots, potatoes, and onions prepared while you were readying the stew along with peas, string beans, corn, tomatoes, tomato juice, and any other vegetable you like in soup or happen to have leftover on hand in the freezer. You may also have some frozen broth that you want or need to use. Just add it to the soup. It's much more nourishing and tasty than just adding water to make enough additional broth for your soup. If you use packages of meat already cut up by your butcher it saves time because you don't have to defat or bone the meat. Now cook your soup.

Make the Chop Suey. You already have the celery and onions prepared from the above two recipes, so brown the meat, add the other ingredients and cook.

Remember, to assemble all canned goods and other items for the Chop Suey on the counter top so you aren't running to and fro for each item wasting time and energy.

Cook the rice, if you don't already have rice in your freezer.

• DESSERT COOKING SESSION

Make dough for 3 pies:

1 cherry pie	*2 single pie crusts to be used*
1 apple pie	*for cream pies later*

Assemble pies and bake.

Using two flavors of cake mixes, make one into a cake and the other into cupcakes. Bake and ice.

Time: 3- to 4-hour cooking session.

• COOKIES AND BROWNIES COOKING SESSION

Chocolate Chip	*Oatmeal*
Peanut Butter (with or without	*Double Fudge Brownies (or nut*
chocolate chips)	*Brownies or both)*

I mix all the cookie dough (either one recipe or one package at a time). While the first kind is baking the second is ready. Then if you have space on the pan(s), you can fill it out with the second kind of cookie. Also, if you want to shorten the cooking session, make only two kinds of cookies. I personally prefer the box mixes. If you want to make yours from scratch that's fine, it just takes a little longer. Occasionally, I do make mine from scratch, just for a little taste change. This is also a good time to get the kids involved. If they aren't too interested, let them make faces on the cookies — suddenly it might become a little more fun.

While the last batch of cookies is baking, mix the Double-Fudge Brownies (1 or 2 box mixes), and when the cookies come out of the oven the brownies go in to bake.

When the brownies are done, I divide each pan in half, and wrap, freeze. This gives you options. The first half package may be cut and eaten as brownie snacks. The second half can be cut in larger pieces for a dessert base, topped with a scoop of ice cream, chocolate sauce, and a cherry or chocolate leaf garnish or both.

• A FAVORITE COOKING SESSION

After a while, you'll develop a favorite cooking session once you do a few. In other words, what works best for you and your family in the long term. Sheri, the woman whom I taught to do cooking sessions, called me from Los Angeles the other evening to tell me that she was doing her favorite cooking session, which was almost the same as the first one she had ever done.

Hearty Chicken Soup   *Spaghetti Sauce*
Barbecued Chicken on the Grill   *Salad dressing for the week*
Chili   *from scratch*

Sheri's husband Tom now helps her with the cooking sessions.

1. The chicken for the grill is defrosting while,
2. Sheri cleans, cuts, and cooks the chicken soup
3. The chicken is basted with barbecue sauce and put on the grill
4. The ground meat is browned for Chili and Spaghetti Sauce
5. The chicken is turned on the grill
   Now it is time to wash and recirculate the pots. Tom does the dishes.
6. While all of the above is going on Tom has also been making the salad dressing for the week from scratch.
7. Take the chicken off the grill.
8. Make the Spaghetti Sauce together (one chops and one stirs)

When they are done, they sit down to a dinner of barbecued chicken, salad, and maybe a dessert — while the food they prepared is cooling. Then they package and freeze — and don't worry about dinner for the rest of the week.

Flexibility

A cooking session can be anything you want it to be: all pork, all beef, all pies, all chicken, or a combination, such as pie, cake, turkey, chicken, and pork. You can use a cooking session to prepare a week's meals or to cook up a batch of basics for recipes to be finished later. Or you can cook just to stock your freezer with foods to be defrosted, heated, and served whenever you need them.

Granted, with this approach meals do not magically appear. You are still doing the work. But you're doing it when you choose to, when it's convenient, and when you feel like it.

The weekend is a good time to organize and cook, particularly when you are just beginning to follow this method. You might cook on Sunday afternoon or Saturday morning when you're less rushed than you are during the week. You'll be amazed to see how many meals can result from a Sunday afternoon in the kitchen, and you'll go to work Monday morning feeling way ahead of the game.

How Cooking Sessions Solve
The What-to-Have-for-Dinner Syndrome

If you cook in quantity and freeze meals as you go, you will be stocking your freezer with dinners that are either completely prepared or need only finishing touches. If you cooked enough chicken for four meals and ate only one, you would have three chicken dinners for the future. If you then had a cooking session devoted to spaghetti sauce and baked round steak, your freezer would offer you a choice of chicken, spaghetti, or steak. By having one cooking session a week, in no time you could have five different meals or the bases of five meals in your freezer. That means that if one week you had no time to cook, you'd have five different dinners more or less ready to serve.

An All-Day Cooking Session

So far we've covered two levels of the cooking session: the basic level, at which you make more than one meal's worth of a dish you are cooking; and the more complicated level, at which you prepare different dishes (usually for different meals) at the same time.

For the "black belt" cook — the woman who loves to be in the kitchen, who is experienced, efficient, and very energetic — there is yet another level, even more sophisticated: the cooking session in which you prepare several dishes at a time. In this instance, it takes all day.

As you will see, what follows could almost be called the ultimate cooking session.* It sounds like an exaggeration. The cook who did it is a

---

*If you decide you want to try this, a word of caution. Unless you have become very proficient at other cooking sessions, start with just part of this one — for instance, the hamburger-veal-pork section, yielding two meat loaves, green peppers, Swedish meatballs, and cabbage rolls; then try the rest as another session another day.

definite black belt — Carol Mix, the friend from whom I first got the idea of cooking ahead. Carol does cooking sessions when she's expecting guests. Sometimes she just feels like going on a cooking spree. When I called her to tell her about this book, she was very enthusiastic and wanted to contribute to it. You'll see that besides nonstop energy, she has a wonderful sense of humor. Here's Carol:

"Occasionally the urge will come over me to cook up a storm. When this phenomenon occurs, pots and pans fly, and the family hovers about (along with several feline admirers), sniffing aromas, sneaking a taste, and hoping for a smorgasbord at dusk.

"First, a summary of what I do: I start by frying up a batch of chicken, making potato salad and deviled eggs; while the eggs and potatoes are boiling, and the chicken is simmering in the oven, I start the raw vegetables for soup in another large pot; by this time the eggs and potatoes are finished and this pot can be used to brown hamburger and onion to start the chili; after the potato salad and deviled eggs are made I mix up a batch of hamburger-veal-pork mixture and divide it into two meat loaves; I make up two more batches and prepare Swedish meatballs and stuffed peppers, and use what's left for stuffed cabbage; once this is done, I prepare the veal for veal Parmesan. Now, I know that sounds like a lot of food to fix at the same time, but I have found that these main courses blend together so that you can prepare them all at once. They all end up cooking together while you clean up the mess. Here's how I do it:

"Saturday, 9:00 A.M.: I clean and skin two frying chickens, flour the pieces, and brown them in about 3 tablespoons of vegetable oil in the electric skillet. Once all pieces are browned, I place them in a baking dish and put them in the oven at 350 degrees for about an hour. This makes the crust crispy and keeps the chicken juicy. For seasoning, I use salt, pepper, and paprika.

"While the chicken is frying, I place eight medium-sized potatoes in a pot to boil, and one dozen eggs in another pot to boil. After they have come to a boil, the potatoes take about 45 minutes over low heat and the eggs about 15 minutes. When the eggs are finished, I immediately run cold water over them for about 3 minutes, so that they cool quickly; the cold water also makes them easy to peel.

"Now the chicken is chickening, the potatoes and eggs are bubbling. I place a soup bone in a small pie pan and stick it under the broiler until it is browned. In a large pot I put about 2 quarts of water, 2 celery stalks, 2 carrots, 1 medium to large onion, salt, pepper, garlic powder, and a bay leaf. I bring to a boil and add the soup bone; then I simmer this for about 6 hours.

"Hey, it's starting to smell good: chicken chickening, potatoes and eggs bubbling, soup simmering.

"Soon the eggs and potatoes are cooked and cooling. The chicken is finished and out of the oven.

11:30 A.M.: I brown a pound and a half of hamburger for chili, and two medium-sized chopped onions in an electric skillet; I drain the fat and place the meat in large pot on stove. I add a large can of tomatoes (cut up), 1 medium-sized can of tomato sauce, a bottle of chili sauce, some chili powder, a little salt, and a generous amount of black pepper. I simmer it for one hour and add one can of kidney beans. While this is simmering I boil about 4 more medium-sized potatoes. When potatoes are cooked, I peel them, cut them in quarters, and put them in the chili. They make the chili taste good, and take the gastric quality out of the beans.

"Now it's time to sit down for a few minutes, have a big orange drink, and make the potato salad.

"Woops, I almost forgot the soup. I add 1 pound of uncooked, bite-sized stew beef to soup and a large can of cut-up whole tomatoes, and simmer for another 90 minutes. I add more water if necessary.

"Back to the potato salad. I cut potatoes into bite-sized pieces, chop up one small to medium onion and two stalks of celery in the food processor and add to the potatoes. I peel 7 eggs, chop them in the food processor, and add them to the mixture. I salt it generously, add 1 teaspoon yellow mustard, 2 tablespoons sweet relish, 1 teaspoon sugar, 2 tablespoons cider vinegar and about 3 heaping tablespoons mayonnaise. Then I mix it all up.

"Then I peel the remaining 5 eggs, slice them lengthwise, remove yolks, and arrange the whites on a plate. I puree the yolks in the food processor, add ¼ teaspoon yellow mustard, sweet relish, vinegar, 2 teaspoons mayonnaise, and salt lightly. I taste it: it should be sweet-sour, not too dry, and not too soupy. I fill the cavity of each egg white with the mixture and sprinkle with paprika.

"Chicken chickened, potatoes saladed, eggs deviled, soup souping, chili chiliing.

"Lunchtime for the cook: I sit down and eat a piece of chicken, a little potato salad, and a deviled egg.

"1:00 P.M.: I take 3 pounds of ground beef-pork-veal mixture and divide it into two portions for meat loaves. To each portion I add 1 egg, ¾ cup milk, ¼ cup chopped onion, ¼ cup ketchup, salt and pepper. I place them in two small casseroles and top each with three slices of bacon. I pop them into oven at 350 degrees for about 90 minutes.

"I take another 3 to 4 pounds of ground beef-pork-veal mixture and divide it into 3 portions for stuffed green peppers, Swedish meatballs, and cabbage rolls.

"Wait a minute, the chili is done; I set it aside to cool.

"Now, I slice the ends off of four large green peppers, clean the seeds out, and place the peppers in about a cup of boiling water to parboil for about 5 minutes. I take one portion of ground meat and add a little chopped onion, chopped green pepper, 1 egg, a little milk, ¼ cup minute rice, and salt and pepper. In a small saucepan I brown ¼ cup chopped onion, garlic powder, and salt and pepper; I add one can of tomato sauce and 1 teaspoon cinnamon. I simmer this mixture for 20 minutes. I arrange the four green peppers in a medium-sized baking dish, stuff them with the meat mixture, and pour sauce over all. Then I bake them in the oven at 350 degrees for 60 to 90 minutes.

"At about this point I add two packages of frozen mixed vegetables to the soup and taste for additional seasoning. I also check on the meat loaves. They will be done when the bacon is brown.

"Where are we? Oh, yes: chicken chickened, eggs deviled, potatoes saladed, soup still souping, chili cooling, meat loaves loafing along, and peppers bubbling. I think I've put on forty pounds just from the aromas. The cats are about to attack.

"Now we're getting close to the last round up.

"2:00 P.M.: I take eight thin slices of veal (veal scallopini) and dip them in egg and Italian bread crumbs and ½ cup Parmesan cheese. I brown them on both sides in 2 tablespoons of hot vegetable oil in an electric skillet, turning once. I place them in a large baking dish.

"I make sauce for the veal by browning ½ cup chopped onion and 1 teaspoon chopped garlic in 1 tablespoon vegetable oil. I add 2 cans tomato sauce, oregano, Italian seasoning, salt and pepper.

"I pour ½ cup sauce over browned veal slices, place slices of mozzarella cheese over the entire top, pour the remaining sauce over the mozzarella, and sprinkle with Parmesan cheese. Then I bake in the oven at 350 degrees for about 45 minutes.

"The meat loaves are done now, so I remove them from the oven, put in the veal, and check on the peppers.

"To one more portion of ground meat I add 1 egg, dash of nutmeg, ¼ cup rice, 1 cup sour cream, salt and pepper, 6 slices bacon browned and crumbled. This is for Swedish meatballs. I sit down (I'm getting tired) and make little meatballs, which I then brown in an electric skillet and remove to a small roasting pan. I make a gravy with juices from browning, add thickening, and water (a little beef bouillon makes it tastier); I add two cans of button mushrooms and a cup of red wine, and pour over meatballs. Into the oven they go, covered, for about 45 minutes.

"It's time to remove the peppers now.

"4:00 P.M.: The chicken is chickened, eggs deviled, potatoes saladed, chili cooling, meat loaves sitting, peppers peppered, veal Parmesan singing, Swedish meatballs intoxicating and . . . the soup's done.

"I get that head of cabbage out and put it in a big pot of water to parboil. I brown the remaining ground meat mixture, 1 onion, and 4 slices of bacon. I add salt, pepper, ¼ cup rice, 1 egg, and a little milk. I peel leaves off the cabbage and wrap about 1½ teaspoons of meat mixture in each leaf, and fasten them with toothpicks. (You may have to return the cabbage to boiling water periodically so that the leaves fall off easily.) Again, I make a tomato sauce mixture with two large cans of crushed tomatoes, a little onion, and seasonings. I arrange cabbage rolls in two large baking dishes and dab each roll with two or three dots of butter. I distribute 1 or 2 large cans of sauerkraut liberally over the cabbage rolls. I pour the tomato mixture over all, and add a little more water if necessary.

"I take the veal Parmesan and meatballs out of the oven and put the cabbage rolls in — for 2 hours at 350 degrees. I add more juice (water) if necessary, but I do not let them bake dry.

"Now I clean up the mess, take a shower, and get containers for the freezer together.

"6:30 P.M.: Okay, smorgasbord! Fried chicken, potato salad, deviled eggs, vegetable soup, meat loaf, stuffed peppers, Swedish meatballs, veal Parmesan, chili and cabbage rolls. (And everything can be frozen except the potato salad and deviled eggs.)"

3

The McMillen Method, *Part 2:* Support Activities

Q: What happens at the end of a cooking session when you've got three meat loaves, two baked chickens and a pot roast?
A: If you don't wrap the food and freeze it properly, it will spoil, and all your work will be wasted.
Moral: Learn to store food quickly and properly.

My Philosophy of Freezing

There are very few items I would not freeze. I even buy packaged cookies on sale and freeze them. Some foods won't keep as long as others, but most will freeze quite nicely for a reasonable period of time if packaged properly. I also freeze mashed potatoes, although in my experience they are the least susceptible to successful freezing. (When you thaw them, they become grainy, but if you heat and keep stirring them, they'll become smooth — I promise.) The one thing I never freeze is corn on the cob; the corn retains the flavor of the cob regardless of how I prepare it for the freezer.

The freezing of food is actually a serious technical subject on which opinions vary. A number of books have been written about it. For an authoritative discussion of freezing, you might read *Complete Book of Home Freezing* by Hazel Meyer, (New York: Lippincott, 1970). Here are some tips from my own experience and a chart of how long foods keep.

Tips on Freezing

1. Don't overcook food that you are going to freeze.

2. No matter what it is, I prefer to freeze it only once.

3. Frozen meat should not be refrozen. If your meat has thawed, I'd say cook it and use it as soon as possible. Food poisoning could be much more costly than throwing away a piece of spoiled meat. It just isn't worth taking a chance on eating bad meat, which can make you and your family very ill.

4. Most items with mayonnaise such as salad and sandwich spreads should not be frozen.

5. Cook in oven-to-freezer casseroles, lined with foil, if you wish. The casseroles will freeze quicker if, after you have let them cool for a bit, you cover them and chill them completely in the refrigerator before freezing them. When a casserole is frozen, if you have lined the casserole dish with foil, you can slip the food out and wrap, seal, tape, and label it. If you haven't lined the pan or dish, just invert it under hot running water, holding the frozen food in place with your fingers until it releases. Then either wrap it or place it in a plastic bag and return it immediately to the freezer. Now you can use your casserole dish for something else while the frozen food waits to be used. When you are ready to heat the food, remove wrapping, place the food in the correct casserole and reheat. You haven't tied up all your casserole dishes in the freezer.

6. Frozen sandwiches can save lots of time when you or the kids get up late. Also, if you're going to be late getting home and nothing else is ready, your child can thaw a sandwich to stave off hunger until you can get there and prepare dinner. And if you make sandwiches ahead to freeze, you'll make them by the assembly-line method, and that saves time in the long run.

7. Keep popcorn in the freezer. It keeps longer, pops better, and is always there for an emergency snack.

8. Freeze the highest quality foods you can afford to buy. You do not lose quality when freezing, but you also don't improve it either. You can afford to buy a slightly better cut of meat because you'll be saving by buying on sale most of the time.

9. Do not put more food in the freezer than will freeze in fifteen to twenty hours. Otherwise foods can freeze too slowly and spoil. Of course, if you chill the food completely before freezing it, the freezer won't have to work so hard.

Recommended Average Storage Time for Frozen Foods

Baked Goods	4–6 months
Unbaked Goods	1–2 months
Casseroles and Cooked Entrées	4–5 months
Meats:	
Beef	12 months
Lamb and pork	8 months
Sausage (unseasoned)	6 months
Ground meat, fish, poultry	3–6 months
Foul and veal	6 months
Shellfish	4 months
Lobster and crab	2–4 weeks
Ham and seasoned sausage	2–3 months
Sliced bacon	1–2 months
Dairy Products	
Eggs	6 months
Butter	4–6 months
Cheeses	4 months
Milk and cream	2–4 weeks
Ice cream	2–6 weeks
Fruits	8–10 months
Vegetables	8–10 months

Packaging Foods for the Freezer

Packaging is as important as preparation when you are going to freeze food for future use. Try to make food packaging as airtight as possible. When you are wrapping an item with freezer paper, tear off enough paper to make a double-fold seal. Turn the ends up, fold over and seal with freezer tape; then label and freeze. Always burp plastic containers holding foods to be frozen: lift corner and let excess air out, then replace corner tightly. I also tape around the lid of a plastic container unless I know I will be using it very quickly. I feel it gives it a tighter and more secure seal.

To save space in your freezer, buy containers that will stack easily; freeze food in them and put one on top of another. Who says spaghetti sauce has to be frozen in a stand-up container? It will freeze just as well and actually thaw faster if it is lying flat on a tray inside a sealed plastic bag.

I have some TV dinner trays (they can be purchased new), and I use some freezer tins that I've washed and saved. I also have plastic microwave TV dinner trays. These are a little more expensive, but an excellent idea if you can afford them. For large amounts I prefer to use plastic freezer containers, self-sealing freezer bags (two sizes — small and large), seal-a-meal bags, aluminum foil, and baking dishes (covered and sealed with masking or freezer tape).

Do not fill containers too full. Leave at least one-half to one inch at top of container to allow for expansion.

Freeze individual pieces of food (e.g., chicken) separately on a cookie sheet or other flat surface so that they won't stick together; then put them in a bag. You can take out only the amount needed for immediate use. (It took me forever to learn this. Only after I had to use a hammer to break frozen items apart did it sink into my brain. I've served some rather unrecognizable pieces of chicken using the hammer method of separation.) All items done this way should be quick-frozen and bagged immediately so they won't get freezer burn and taste bad.

If you buy your meat in large packages and do not plan to cook it before you freeze it, you should open and repackage it to suit your family's needs. I suggest making meatballs, hamburgers, and other shapes from ground meat before freezing. This also saves time if you forget to take this meat out to thaw; you can cook it while it is still frozen. I also place freezer or waxed paper between such items as hamburgers and chops. They will be easier to separate and will defrost faster.

You'll discover what works best for you as you go along. For instance, I find the large airtight snap-lock freezer bags good for storing large batches of homemade cookies. You can open the bag, take out the number of cookies you need, and reseal the bag. You don't have to thaw the whole batch. (If you keep three kinds of cookies in the freezer at a time, you can have chocolate chip today, oatmeal tomorrow, and peanut butter the next day. You won't get tired of one kind before they're all eaten.) Only a compulsive eater would eat cookies while they're frozen, but I hate to admit I've done so on occasion.

Keeping an Inventory List

I have already suggested that you label all food going into your freezer (Chapter 2). It is also a good idea to maintain an inventory list of what you have. Then you won't have to rummage through the freezer numbing your fingers and wasting BTUs. In a small notebook keep information like this:

Name of Item	Date Frozen	No. Servings
Creamed Turkey	1-18-83	5
Baked Steak	4-8-83	4
Spaghetti	8-10-82	6

List desserts, vegetables, entrées, and so forth on separate pages for easy reference. Keep your notebook, freezer pen, tape, labels, and a pencil in a drawer or cupboard near the freezer so it will be convenient to use.

Using Freezer Foods

I usually thaw my foods in the refrigerator while I am at work during the day. When I get home, they are ready to be cooked or heated and served. If you forget to defrost frozen meats, you can still cook them, but the cooking time will be about half again as long as for the thawed meat. If you are broiling frozen meat, do not put it too close to the heat; if you are frying, brown the meat first, then lower the heat and allow it to cook through.

If you have a microwave oven, just follow the defrosting instructions on your oven guide; then cook either conventionally or in the microwave.

Outsmarting Freezer Raiders

Until you're sitting pretty with a freezer full of meals, an inventory list, and the same feeling you have when your savings account is big and fat, you can't know the frustration a freezer raider can cause you. One day you'll go to the freezer expecting to pull out a package of Sloppy Joes for dinner and — what's this? — the Sloppy Joes aren't there. Congratulations, you will have just had your first experience with a freezer raider, a family member who eats away at your stockpile of frozen dinners.

To cope with freezer raiders, you can employ the tactic my friend Joyce uses. Her kids insisted on eating her frozen dinners as snacks, even though she always had luncheon meats, fruit, cookies, and other goodies on hand. One night after Joyce had gone to bed, her sixteen-year-old came home from a party with a friend. They thawed the sliced roast pork she had planned to serve later in the week, and the two of them went through over half of it in microwaved sandwiches. They also gobbled up the frozen brownies. That experience started Joyce thinking. Now she labels everything with the name of a food her kids hate. She puts the word "Raw" in front of it, and "to be used in" — for example, "raw eggs to be used in brownies" or "raw cauliflower to be used with pork slices." The key words in this code are "brownies" and "pork slices," the true contents of the packages. Joyce's secret is that she has never told anyone in the family her code. She okayed my using it here because her kids don't read cookbooks!

More Ways to Organize: Shopping Smart

So far we've talked about organizing your food preparation. But you can also organize the activities that precede a cooking session, such as meal planning and shopping. (Meal planning is such a big topic that it will have the next chapter to itself.)

As you learn to cook ahead, learn to buy ahead, too. You'll find that you save money as well as time. For instance, at the store where I shop, pork roast is usually on sale every four weeks. So that's when I buy, sometimes saving as much as thirty cents a pound. If I buy three roasts, I freeze one as is and cook the other two ahead (each with a different recipe or with the same recipe if I'm in a rush) and freeze them. If your freezer and your family are both big, you should buy as much of a sale item as you can afford. If you can't spare the cash during sale week, don't try to stock up with large quantities, but do take advantage of the sale to buy what you can. You'll still save.

During the following week rolled rump, round steak, or pot roast may be on sale. Save again by buying, cooking ahead, and freezing as your storage space allows. Use the recipes that suit the particular sale item and your family's appetite. The worst thing that can happen when you buy larger quantities on sale is that when cooking time comes, you'll be too busy or too tired to do it; if that happens, just put the meat in the freezer. You still have the satisfaction of extra savings. You won't need to shop again when you need that particular item, and you have some good meat on hand if you have guests. (And if in a pinch you just have to run in and buy the quickest, priciest thing on the shelf, you won't feel so bad about it; you've saved along the way, and your budget won't be ruined.)

In most towns and cities the best night to shop is Thursday. Markets are usually more crowded on Friday evenings and Saturdays. And Thursday is the day grocers seem to stock up with the best and freshest food for the weekend. There's a psychological advantage as well. When the weekend comes, you'll be all set.

It also pays to frequent the same store as much as possible. You save time because you know the store layout. And you can develop check-cashing privileges. Chasing around town to sales at different markets usually doesn't pay. If another market is on your way and offers more than one sale item you need, fine. But in general, stopping at different markets and going out of your way for a single sale item isn't worth the time and gasoline.

It's also a good idea to shop only once a week. Your shopping cart may be fuller than it is when you shop frequently, but you will save time. Repeated trips to the market during the week waste time. If you shop once a week, you save money, too, because you reduce the number of times you expose yourself to temptation to buy on impulse.

Be sure to make out a shopping list. It will save you time in the supermarket. And coupons can save you money. There can be enough valuable coupons in a magazine to return the price of it (or more). Working women don't have time to become heavy couponers, on the whole, but if you see a coupon you can use, save it. It may only be worth a quarter, but four quarters equal a dollar saved. Even if you only save two to five dollars a week on groceries, that comes to $104 to $260 a year.

Since my time is limited, I always read magazines and newspapers with a pair of scissors beside me. When I see a coupon, recipe, or article I want to clip, I do it immediately. Going back to look for it later takes too much time; besides, you'll probably never get back to it.

I keep my coupons in two large, heavy envelopes; jumbo-sized metal paper clips hold each category: meats, main dish items, drinks, snacks, desserts, paper products, toiletries, soaps, cereals, spreads, cheeses, and miscellaneous. Some women prefer coupon wallets they can carry to the store with them.

Making meal plans that incorporate coupon items on a large scale takes more time than most working women have. But if you set aside ten minutes a week to familiarize yourself with the coupons you've collected, you can match them with your meal plans and cooking sessions. For instance, if you have a coupon for a new sausage product, plan to have a sausage, sauerkraut, and boiled potato dinner. Then look for a coupon to assist you in the dessert area.

Manufacturers are always putting new products on the market to make food preparation easier. Coupons are offered for new products to get you to try them. New products can keep your menus from becoming predictable and boring.

4

The McMillen Method, *Part 3:* Meal Planning

So far we have established that the way to avoid The Syndrome is to cook ahead. But what about the weeks when for one reason or another you have no time for cooking sessions?

If dinner can't be cooked ahead, it can still be planned ahead. Then, when dinnertime approaches and you're tired, you won't have to think. Half the trouble with the What-to-Have-for-Dinner Syndrome is that it forces you to think at the wrong moment — when you're tired and in a hurry. Efficiency is partly just this: doing a task when you're most able to do it well.

By "planned" I mean more than the selection of a menu: you choose the menu and think out the steps necessary to get the meal on the table. You *think* in advance, since you can't *cook* in advance. You make a list of the food needed for that meal and sketch an efficient sequence of cooking and serving steps. Remember, the point is not to have to do any extra work or thinking when you're tired.

Meal plans give you the same kind of psychological lift that cooking ahead does. You *know* what you're going to have for dinner. You know how much work is involved, whether you have to shop or not, and how much time you'll spend in the kitchen.

In this chapter, I will give you several meal plans to try. Some are modest family menus; others are fancier. As you will see, they include a market order and a set of steps for preparation and serving. The approximate time it takes me to prepare each meal is also given, so that you can choose accordingly. Any of these dinners can be prepared on the day you plan to serve them, even those listed as "cooked ahead"; they will simply take longer to produce. You can cook one of these meals even if you don't have much on hand just by purchasing exactly what is on the shopping list. You can also serve these meals to guests. If you want to impress guests, just do the marketing a day ahead of time, and do a few of the cooking tasks in advance (for instance, clean the vegetables).

By all means, regard these plans as flexible. If a menu calls for cole-slaw and you hate it, substitute your favorite salad or another salad from the recipe secion of this book, making adjustments in the market list and preparation plan accordingly. You decide what would go well with that particular meal.

Sample Meal Plans

EASY TO FIX   Planned for 4

Pear and Cheese Salad   Ice Cream with Caramel-
Stuffed Pork Chops   Marshmallow Sauce
Baked Potatoes   Coffee, Tea, or Milk
Broiled Tomatoes

MARKET ORDER

Pear halves	*1 16-ounce can*
Cottage cheese	*1 small container*
* or grated Cheddar*	*1 small pkg. to grate (or grated)*
Parmesan cheese	*1 8-ounce can*
Pork chops	*4 double with pockets*
Stuffing mix	*2 large packages*
Bread	*2 or 3 slices*
Celery	*1 stalk or smallest bunch*
Baking potatoes	*1 per person*
Tomatoes	*1 medium to large per person*
Vanilla ice cream	*½ gallon*
Heavy cream	*½ pint*
Miniature marshmallows	*Small package*
Light brown sugar	*1 box*
Corn syrup	*1 bottle*
Bouillon	*Granules or cubes (chicken flavor)*
Eggs	*1*

Lettuce (leaves for salad)	*1 small head or leaf any type*
Parsley	*1 small bunch*
Butter	*if not on hand*
Onion	*if not on hand*
Coffee and/or tea	*if not on hand*

ORDER OF PREPARATION:

Prepare the Stuffed Pork Chops (page 176).

Put the foil-wrapped potatoes in the oven when you put the chops in to bake.

Assemble the Pear Salad on plates and refrigerate.

Prepare the Caramel-Marshmallow Sauce according to the recipe on page 239.

Prepare the tomatoes for broiling (page 205).

Prepare the coffee or tea.

Set the table and serve the meal.

QUICK TO FIX   Planned for 6

Jumbo Shrimp in the Shell
  (served over crushed ice)
Cocktail Sauce
Tossed Green Salad
Corn on the Cob

Butter-Baked French Bread and
  Butter
Floating Rainbow Sherbet
  with Rainbow Mints
Coffee, Tea, or Milk

MARKET ORDER

Spinach	*1 pound*
Bibb lettuce	*2 small heads or 1 large*
Iceberg lettuce	*1 head (use only ½)*
Cherry tomatoes	*1 carton*
Fresh jumbo shrimp (in shell)	*5 to 8 per person*
Corn on the cob	*1 ear per person*
Rainbow sherbet	*½ gallon*
Mints (round, flat, or	
* multicolored)*	*8 oz. box (3–6 per person)*
Lemons	*5*
French bread	*2 medium-sized loaves*
Butter	*1 pound*
Cocktail sauce	*1 8-ounce bottle*

Parsley	*1 small bunch*
Coffee and tea	*if not on hand*
Whipped topping	*8-ounce container*

If necessary you can pick up all of the above items on your way home from work. This meal can easily be adjusted for 1 to 10; just buy more or less of each item. If you use frozen corn, cook it with a little butter, salt, and a dash of sugar. Serve the iced shrimp in a large punch or fruit bowl. If you don't have a large supply of ice cubes to crush, you will need to add a small bag of crushed ice to your market order. Any items you have on hand can be eliminated from the market order.

Preparation time: 30 to 45 minutes

ORDER OF PREPARATION

Set the table.

Crush the ice and put it in a large glass bowl. Place it in the freezer.

Pour the shrimp sauce into a small bowl, quarter the lemons, and wash and mix the salad fixings. Place all these items in the refrigerator.

Set oven at 350 degrees. Melt a stick of butter in a saucepan over low heat. While the butter is melting, slice both loaves of bread partly through and place them on large piece of foil. Now, using pastry brush, baste the melted butter between cuts in the bread. Brush the remaining butter on the top of each loaf. Wrap the loaves and place them in the oven for 5 to 10 minutes.

Place 2 large pans of salted water on stove. Add the corn on cob plus 1 teaspoon sugar to one pan. Bring to a boil and cook for 5 to 7 minutes. Bring the second pan of water to a boil. Add the shrimp, boil it for 4 to 8 minutes, depending on the size of the shrimp. Just before the shrimp are done, remove the bowl of ice from the freezer. Place the bowl of shrimp sauce in the middle, and garnish the outer edge with lemon wedges and parsley. When the shrimp are done, remove them and place them in the ice. Return bowl to freezer until everything else is on the table and everyone is seated.

Put the coffee on to perk, take dinner to table, uncork the champagne, and enjoy.

For dessert place 1 or 2 dips of rainbow sherbet on bed of whipped topping. Stick mints into the sherbet or place them alongside it. Serve coffee or tea with dessert.

INSTANT DINNER
PRE-PACKAGED FOODS WITH
FAST FOOD ASSIST   Planned for 4

Cream of Spinach Soup (from
    frozen food counter)
Fast-Food Fried Chicken (pick
    up on the way home)
Au Gratin Potatoes (boxed or
    frozen)
Mixed Vegetables (canned or
    frozen)

Cherry Tarts (purchased
    Graham cracker tart crusts
    and prepared cherry pie
    filling)
Coffee, Tea, or Milk

> Oven-heat the soup, potatoes, and vegetables.
> Fill the tart shells with filling and refrigerate.
> Prepare the coffee.
> Heat the chicken for 5 to 10 minutes if necessary.
> Set the table.
> Preparation time: 15-30 minutes.

MARKET ORDER

Cream of spinach soup	*2 packages frozen*
Fried chicken	*2 or 3 pieces per person*
Au gratin potatoes	*1 box or 2 frozen packages*
Mixed vegetables	*1 or 2 packages*
Cherry pie filling	*1 20-ounce can*
Tart-sized Graham cracker crusts	*1 package*
Whipped topping	*1 small container*
Bread and butter	*if not on hand*
Coffee or other beverage	*if not on hand*

SPAGHETTI AND SPAGHETTI SAUCE MENU
IF YOU ARE STARTING
FROM SCRATCH   Planned for 4

Tossed Salad
Spaghetti with Meat Sauce
Hot Sliced Italian Bread with
    Butter

Ice Cream and Fresh Fruit
    Parfaits
Coffee, Tea, or Milk

MARKET ORDER

Ground beef	*2 pounds*
Green pepper	*1*
Mushrooms	*1 pound fresh or 2 4-ounce cans*
Onion	*1 medium-sized*
Spaghetti sauce	*1 32-ounce jar*
Spaghetti sauce mix with mushrooms	*2 packages*
(Thin) spaghetti	*1-pound package*
French bread	*1 large loaf*
Butter (garlic or chives optional)	*1 pound (if not on hand)*
Parmesan cheese	*1 8-ounce container (as you will use it in future cooking)*
Fresh fruits (or frozen)	*2 kinds of fruit (enough to layer with ice cream in parfait glass)*
Vanilla ice cream	*½ gallon*
Iceberg lettuce	*1 head*
Celery	*1 stalk or less if available*
Tomatoes	*2*
Carrots	*1 package*
Olives (green or ripe)	*1 small jar*
Cheese	*1 package individually wrapped cheese slices (your taste)*
Coffee and/or tea	*if not on hand*

10-15 MINUTES
FROM FRONT DOOR TO DINNER ON TABLE   Planned for 4

To do this meal plan in ten to fifteen minutes, you have to have made the spaghetti and spaghetti sauce ahead of time. Sliced and buttered the bread, wrapped it in foil, and frozen it. Unless you have a microwave oven, you must remember to put the spaghetti and spaghetti sauce in the refrigerator to thaw the night before or in the morning before you leave for work. Leave the buttered frozen bread in the freezer until you are ready to put it into the oven.

ADVANCE PREPARATION

Made-ahead and frozen spaghetti and spaghetti sauce thawed. Buttered, sliced bread should remain frozen until time to put it in the oven.

ORDER OF PREPARATION

Put the bread in a 350-degree oven to warm for 10 to 15 minutes.
Heat the spaghetti sauce.
Chop and mix the salad.
Heat the spaghetti in a lightly buttered nonstick sauce pan or in the oven with the bread.
Layer fruit and ice cream dessert in tall sherberts or parfait glasses, and place the glasses in freezer until dessert time.
Make the coffee.
Set the table.
Serve.

DINNER COOKED AHEAD   Serves 1 to 8

Elegant Spinach Salad
Pork Roast with Raisin Sauce
Baked Sweet Potatoes with
   Honey Butter

String Beans Amandine
Hot Rolls and Butter
Chocolate Cake
Coffee, Tea, or Milk

MARKET ORDER

Pork roast	*½ to ¾ pound per person*
Golden raisins (or dark if you prefer)	*1 8-ounce package*
Leaf lettuce	*1 large bunch*
Spinach	*1 small package*
Large onion	*1*
Mandarin orange slices	*1 16-ounce can*
Butterflake rolls	*enough to serve your group*
Sweet potatoes	*1 per person (2 extra for every 4 people if potatoes are small)*
Butter	*if not on hand*
Honey	*small amount*

String beans	*1 or 2 cans*
Almond slivers	*¼ cup*
Chocolate cake and icing mixes	*1 each*
Pecan halves	*½ to 1 cup*
Coffee and/or tea	*if not on hand*

You are doing this menu ahead, so you do it in your own time. Prepare it all at one time, or do an item here and there. Obviously, this menu can be done the day of serving. It will take approximately 2 hours.

Making Your Own Meal Plans

I hope that my sample meal plans will encourage you to create your own. Once you develop this habit, you will find that you can do it quickly. Start with the menu. It can be as extensive or as simple as you like. Some people insist that a meal isn't complete without dessert; others steadfastly ignore sweets. In my household, there is always a salad, but I know people who hate salad and never eat it. Some people want bread and butter on the table; many dieters don't.

Here are the standard categories of a dinner menu:

1. First course or appetizer
2. Salad or soup
3. Main course or entrée
4. Vegetables (potatoes or rice and/or green vegetable)
5. Bread and butter
6. Dessert
7. Beverage

If this seems like a lot of food, remember that during the Edwardian period, a fish course and a game course were also standard, as was a savory after dessert!

Tailor this general outline to your own situation, choosing how much or how little to prepare. Let me repeat: these are just the elements to work with. Personal choices rule the day. In some parts of the country, salad or soup is served as a first course; in others, salad is served with bread after the main course. And some people prefer to eat their salad with the main course. Many busy people (especially dieters) streamline their menus, during the week especially, serving only a main course, a vegetable, and a beverage. I often eliminate an item or two from the menu, such as the potato or a particularly heavy dessert. I have also begun to serve dinner without bread; bread usually means butter, too, and the two of them add unnecessary calories, particularly if you've already had bread at lunch or breakfast.

But don't yield to personal preference altogether and have potato chips, spaghetti, and cake for dinner. Balance your menus for nutrition and for color and texture. Everything shouldn't be sweet, soft, salty, or the same color. Strive for a variety of tastes and textures. A meal of meat, sweet potatoes, and pasta would not just be heavy, it would be too high in carbohydrates. If you do not remember the basic food groups that make up a nutritionally balanced diet, I urge you to refresh your memory.

Also try to balance the amounts of fresh and canned or frozen food in a dinner. The more fresh food, the better, particularly if you are using a frozen entrée from a cooking session. Fresh fruits make a good, nutritious dessert and needn't frighten off dieters. And fresh vegetables need not take long to prepare.

You can peel carrots, steam them, and add a little butter and dill in no time. It takes only five minutes to sauté sliced zucchini in butter with a few onion rings and bacon pieces (from your freezer, remember?). Or cut the top off a tomato, sprinkle it with bread crumbs, drizzle it with butter, add a shake or two of Parmesan cheese, and place it under the broiler for three or four minutes, and you have a delicious vegetable. Note, also, that it is much more nutritious not to overcook vegetables. If your family likes them cooked to mush, gradually start making them just a little crunchier each time you prepare them. Without realizing it, your family may start liking them better if they are cooked a little less.

I serve fresh vegetables on the first three or four days after they are purchased, and I use canned or frozen vegetables later in the week. Since I like to have a fresh salad at almost every dinner, the canned vegetables are balanced. (Lettuce and other items for a tossed salad, if stored properly, can usually be held in the refrigerator for about a week.) Salads do not have to be only lettuce, spinach, and other vegetables. You can add cheese, olives, nuts, fruit slices, meats, or an egg — sliced, diced, chopped, halved, or quartered.

When you've chosen your menu, write out the foods you will have to buy for it — your market list. Then write out a list of things to do, putting the first thing to be done at the head of the list. As my examples indicate, you needn't write out every move you'll have to make. The point is to do your thinking in advance so that when you come home tired you can just follow instructions mechanically. When a particular menu becomes a favorite and you make it often, you won't have to sketch out a sequence of preparation steps. As you know, once you've made a dish a few times, it becomes part of your repertoire, and you can make it without thinking.

If you're interested and have time to do so, you can start a notebook of meal plans that you like. As it grows, it will become a personal food journal or cookbook-plus. Using it, you won't have to recopy or rethink the market order or list of preparations each time you want to serve a particular menu. And if you're a good cook, and your children really enjoy your cuisine, a copy of it will make an especially thoughtful present for them when they grow up and start living away from home.

Putting It All Together

Meal plans have another benefit. Combined with the cooking session, they enable you to solve the question of what to have for dinner for a week or weeks at a time. As I've said, the meal plan can be used as an *alternative* to the cooking session. But if you use it *in conjunction* with the cooking session, you can get way ahead of the food game.

Let me illustrate. Let's say that you want to plan your family's meals for an upcoming week, Monday to Friday, when you know you'll be very busy at work and will want to do the minimum at home. On a Monday (or Tuesday or Wednesday — one evening early in the week), sit down and make a list of five menus. Separate the "to do" lists for each meal into preparation of the entrée and preparation of the rest of the meal. Then make a shopping list of all the food necessary. List in hand, shop on Thursday evening. Over the weekend, in one or two cooking sessions, prepare and freeze the five main courses. Come Sunday night, you will be ready. When your busy week arrives, all you will have to do each morning, Monday through Friday, is thaw the entrée; in the evening you can heat it and, using your "to do" list, mechanically put together the rest of the meal.

For instance, using the meal plans given in the next chapter, you could have these entrées for your busy week:

Monday: Baked Chicken in Chicken Sauce
Tuesday: Spaghetti with Meat Sauce
Wednesday: Baked Round Steak
Thursday: Barbecued Spareribs
Friday: Creamed Shrimp

If you're used to cooking sessions, you can prepare two quantities of some of your main courses to get a second meal's worth. Then, in the following month you can serve that main course again, with different accompaniments for variety, or, in a pinch, using the same accompaniments and "to do" list.

Here's a tip: when you do your meal planning, do it with your freezer inventory by your side. Make some menus around the food you already have.

Another Advantage

Meal plans give you another option for avoiding The Syndrome. If you're married, or if you have a family, get your husband and/or children involved in food preparation. Request a role reversal once a week or once a month — as often as you can negotiate — and let someone else cook dinner for *you*. This is particularly easy if you do the planning and shopping and let the others simply prepare the food when the time comes, following the "to do" list. Even if they use one of your frozen entrées to complete a meal plan, it's a night off for you. If they're more ambitious than that, let them plan, shop, cook, and serve the dinner (using the sample meal plans in this chapter, perhaps). If your children are too young, your husband can cook with or for them. Older children could even cook dinner one night and your husband another, setting you free for two nights.

If the kitchen is your domain and the thought of having it invaded by others (who might not clean up, for instance) seems more painful than liberating, this option probably isn't for you. But if you can let go of your territory, you may find there are indirect benefits as well as the obvious advantage of a night away from the stove. Should you ever have to be away from home, your family will be able to provide for themselves. They will also be able to appreciate what you do for them every night, and their competence in the kitchen may make them good helpers when you need them. Cooking together can also be fun. One couple I know "team cook," as the husband calls it. They meet in their kitchen in the evening after work. While they prepare dinner together, they chat, gossip, and "catch up" on each other's day. And I'm told a kiss in front of the stove is not uncommon.

5

What You Can Have for Dinner — and Lunch

If you haven't cooked ahead, haven't done a meal plan, and can feel The Syndrome setting in, don't panic. All is not lost. This chapter presents many complete dinner menus. You can leaf through them and choose something that appeals to you.

These menus should serve you well, not only in a crisis but also when you're planning meals at your leisure. They will stimulate your imagination and give you ideas. Or, if you don't want to think, you can just pick out as many menus as you need from the list. You could plan every dinner for a month or more.

If you're fresh out of ideas for tomorrow's dinner, look at these menus tonight or in the morning before you go to work. Make your choice. (Remember that you can substitute dishes to suit your preferences.) Make a shopping list for the meal if you don't have everything you need on hand. Then you can go off to work free of worry.

Menus

Pear and Cheese Salad
Baked Round Steak
Twice-Baked Potatoes
Creamed Peas and Onions
Hot Rolls and Butter
Angel Food Cake* with Partially
 Thawed Frozen Strawberries
Coffee, Tea, or Milk

Gazpacho
Creamed Shrimp
Rice Soufflé
String Beans Amandine
Onion Rolls and Butter
Chocolate Cake*
Coffee, Tea, or Milk

*Recipe not included; ingredients or product purchased or made from your own recipe.

Tossed Salad
Sliced Rolled Rump Roast in
   Gravy
Baked Potatoes
Buttered Green Peas*
Crescent Rolls and Butter
Stacked Blueberry Dessert with
   Vanilla Ice Cream
Coffee, Tea, or Milk

Melon Wedges
Shrimp and Vegetable Sauté
Steamed Rice
Vanilla Ice Cream with Hot
   Chocolate Sauce*
Coffee, Tea, or Milk

Lemon-Lime Gelatin Fruit Salad
All-Day Stew
French Bread and Butter
Plain White Cake* with
   Caramel Sauce
Coffee, Tea, or Milk

Tossed Spinach Salad
Lamb Kebabs* on Rice Pilaf
Warm Pita Bread and Butter
Pineapple Upside-Down Cake
Coffee, Tea, or Milk

Vegetable-Gelatin Salad
Potato Chip Chicken
Mashed Potatoes
Scalloped Corn
Hot Biscuits and Honey
Double Fudge Brownies with Ice
   Cream
Coffee, Tea, or Milk

Oriental Salad
Bernie's Chop Suey
Steamed Rice
Fortune Cookies*
Amaretto-Topped Vanilla Ice
   Cream Balls
Green Tea

Tomato Juice Cocktail
Pan-Broiled Ham Slice with
   Pineapple Slices*
Browned Potatoes
Steamed Spinach*
Crescent Rolls and Butter
Ice Cream Balls Rolled in
   Shredded Coconut
Coffee, Tea, or Milk

Coleslaw
Beef Roast with Vegetables
Bread and Butter
Lemon Cake* with Lemon
   Dessert Sauce
Coffee, Tea, or Milk

Cream of Asparagus Soup
Turkey Loaf
Baked Sweet Potatoes
String Beans or Mixed
   Vegetables with
   Cheese Sauce
Hot Rolls and Butter
Ice Cream with Hot Chocolate
   Pudding*
Coffee, Tea, or Milk

*Recipe not included; ingredients or product purchased or made from your own recipe.

Marinated Mushroom Salad on
Lettuce Leaves
Baked Fish Supreme
Broiled Tomatoes
Mixed Vegetables with Bacon
and Onion Sauce
Hard Rolls and Butter
Chocolate Charlotte Russe
Coffee, Tea, or Milk

Chicken Kiev
Brown Rice*
Brussels Sprouts with Nuts
Spiced Apple Rings*
Dinner Rolls and Butter
Pumpkin Pie with Whipped
Topping
Amaretto Coffee, Tea with
Cinnamon Sticks, or Milk

Honeydew Melon Wedges
Taco Salad with Tortilla Chips
Chocolate Cake with Ice
Cream*
Coffee, Tea, or Milk

Vegetable Medley Salad
Bologna, Kielbasa, Sausage
Ring, or Wieners
Sauerkraut
Mashed Potatoes
Raisin Pumpernickel Bread and
Butter
Hot Apple Pie with Sliced
Cheese
Coffee, Tea, or Milk

Tossed Salad
Fancy Meatballs in Gravy
Noodles or Rice
Buttered Broccoli*
Rolls and Butter
Praline Parfaits*
Coffee, Tea, or Milk

Vegetable-Gelatin Salad
Pork Roast with Gravy
Oven-Roasted Potatoes (roasted
with Pork Roast)
Cauliflower with Cheese Sauce
Rolls and Butter
Hot Cherry Pie
Coffee, Tea, or Milk
Caesar Salad
Cheese-Stuffed Pasta Shells with
Tomato Sauce
Italian Rolls and Butter
Angel Confetti Loaf
Coffee, Tea, or Milk

Tossed Spinach Salad
Chicken Veronique
Steamed Rice*
Dilled Carrots
Hot Rolls and Butter
Amaretto Pears
Coffee, Tea, or Milk

Elegant Spinach Salad
Broiled Lamb Chops* with Mint
Jelly
Molded Potato Bake
Buttered Corn*
Crescent Rolls and Butter
Cupcake–Ice Cream Surprise
Coffee, Tea, or Milk

*Recipe not included; ingredients or product purchased or made from your own recipe.

Coleslaw
Barbecued Pork Chops*
Scalloped Potatoes
Buttered Broccoli*
Corn Bread and Butter
Peach Fruit Fluff
Coffee, Tea, or Milk

Vegetable Medley Salad
Chicken Parmesan*
Buttered Thin Noodles
Tasty Fried Eggplant
Italian Rolls and Butter
Lemon Sherbet
Coffee, Tea, or Milk

Chilled Steamed Asparagus
   Spears with Basic Salad
   Dressing
Chicken Breast Sauté*
Cheese-Baked Rice
French Bread and Butter
Ambrosia Dessert Salad
Coffee, Tea, or Milk

Split Pea Soup
Cornmeal-Fried Haddock
Dilled Vegetable Medley
Rolls and Butter
Ice Cream and Sugar Cookies
Coffee, Tea, or Milk

Sliced Tomato Salad*
Ham Loaf–Spinach Roulade
Mashed Potato Flowerets or
   Baked Sweet Potatoes
Steamed String Beans*
Dark Brown Bread and Butter
Strawberry Shortcake*
Coffee, Tea, or Milk

Marinated Mushrooms and
   Sliced Tomatoes on
   Lettuce Leaves
Vegetable or Spinach Lasagne
Hot Italian Bread and Butter
Sherbet
Coffee, Tea, or Milk

Carrot Salad
Beef and Pot Pie Squares
Baked Sweet Potatoes
Buttered Green Peas*
Dark Brown Bread and Butter
Baked Apples
Coffee, Tea, or Milk

Coleslaw
Baked Ham with Cherry Sauce*
Scalloped Potatoes
Buttered String Beans*
Corn Fritters and Syrup
Lemon Tarts*
Coffee, Tea, or Milk

French Onion Soup
Beef Tenderloin Roast
Chantilly Potato Casserole
Dilled Carrots
Crescent Rolls and Butter
Double Strawberry Meringues
Coffee, Tea, or Milk

Gazpacho
Lemon-Cream Baked Sole
String Beans Amandine
Acorn Squash Rings
Dinner Rolls and Butter
Cherries Jubilee
Coffee, Tea, or Milk

*Recipe not included; ingredients or product purchased or made from your own recipe.

Three-Bean Salad*
Cabbage Rolls
Glazed Carrots
Rye Rolls and Butter
Double Fudge Brownies and
    Vanilla Ice Cream with
    Hot Chocolate Sauce
Coffee, Tea, or Milk

Vegetable-Gelatin Salad
Stuffed Pork Chops
Lemon-Buttered Broccoli
Whole or Jellied Cranberry
    Sauce*
Pineapple Sherbet
Coffee, Tea, or Milk

Other Options

All kinds of things can happen to cause a crisis in your kitchen. On the day you have guests coming to dinner, for example, the boss might call you in at 4:45 P.M. and tell you to revise the economic structure of the company before you go home. Or your carefully prepared dinner could burn or be eaten by a freezer raider. Or unexpected guests could suddenly descend on you.

Having meals cooked ahead and stockpiled in your freezer can save your nerves (and your neck) in situations like these. When you're stuck at the office, you can call home and tell your kids or your husband or the cleaning lady to take something out of the freezer and put it in the oven. But even the best-laid plans can go awry. There may be times when you're very busy and have no opportunity to do cooking sessions. So you get home one night and the freezer is bare. What then?

That's when you consult the following group of quick menus for emergencies. These meals can be made from supplies kept in the cupboard. (A supply list is included.) They can also be handy when guests drop in unexpectedly. (More about that in Chapter 6.)

QUICKIE MENUS FOR EMERGENCIES

Spaghetti with Sauce (sausage
    chunks, vegetables with
    mushrooms, or ground
    beef)
Lettuce Salad or Fruit Salad
Toast Triangles, Buttered and
    Sprinkled with Garlic Salt
Ice Cream or Canned Fruit

Heated Canned Meat with
    Buttered and Parsleyed
    Noodles
Canned Vegetable Platter
Boxed Potatoes
Ice Cream Balls Rolled in Nuts
    or Coconut

*Recipe not included; ingredients or product purchased or made from your own recipe.

Heated Canned Ham with
  Pineapple Rings and
  Brown Sugar Butter Glaze
Instant Mashed Potatoes
Green Peas
Coleslaw
Pudding

Canned Beef with Barbecue
  Sauce
Deep-Fried Thick Potato Rounds
Baked Beans
Large Raw Vegetable Platter
Hot Brownies with Ice Cream

Leftover Chicken or Turkey à la
  King over Packaged Biscuits
Canned Sweet Potatoes or
  Leftover Mashed Potatoes
  with Grated American
  Cheese, Onion, and
  Bacon Bits
Lettuce Wedges with Green
  Pepper Rings
Cake from a Mix Topped with
  Hot Pudding

Skewered Meat, Meatballs,
  Shrimp, Chicken, Sausages,
  Vegetables, and/or Fruits
  Served on Bed of Rice
Ice Cream or Fruit

FOOD LIST FOR GUEST EMERGENCIES

If you have unexpected guests at meal times, you should have some of the following on hand for emergencies:

Brown bread (canned)
Frozen canned rolls
Bread and roll mixes
Frozen scalloped potatoes
  and/or boxed mix
Boxed mashed potato mix
Canned vegetables: string
  beans, carrots, onions,
  peas, pork and beans or
  vegetarian beans, whole
  tomatoes, mushrooms
Packaged almond slivers
Chunk and sliced pineapple
Peaches and pears
Cherry and apple pie filling

Vanilla ice cream
Brownie mix
Cake mixes
Piecrust mix
Canned ham
Canned beef, tuna, chicken
Frozen frankfurters and
  sausages
Frozen hamburger patties
Canned or frozen soups
Packaged noodles, rice,
  spaghetti
Instant coffee and tea
Envelopes of dried sour cream
  and salad dressings

Note: Emergency frozen food supplies should be used and recycled about every 2 to 3 months. Canned goods can go longer; however, they can't be kept forever. Don't waste precious food dollars by letting your emergency store of food become too old to serve.

What about those occasional nights when you can't even face heating an entrée you've already cooked?

That's when you go out to dinner or bring home food already prepared by your local pizzeria or Chinese restaurant. I don't need to tell you how to go to fast food places. But I can offer some hints for "off" nights.

If the meal you are planning calls for fried chicken, and you are too tired to fry the chicken even if you have cleaned it ahead of time, stop on your way home and buy prepared chicken. Then toss a salad, cook a vegetable, and make a quick, simple, but elegant dessert, and in less than half an hour, you'll be eating a full-course dinner.

If even that seems like too much effort, then consult your list of stores and carry-out places. "My list?" you say. Yes. I recommend that you write down the names, addresses, phone numbers, and business hours of all stores where you shop: supermarkets, liquor stores, delicatessens, fast food places, and so on. Then make copies of this list for your purse, your briefcase, your car, your desk at work, and the kitchen at home. Note whether a place delivers and whether there's a delivery charge. Then, if guests are coming and you ruin the entrée or get home late, you can call the nearest restaurant, order dinner to be delivered, and relax. Or if you get home after a long, hard day and just want to go to bed, you can call out for dinner.

The list of stores and restaurants is also helpful in other circumstances. When you're in a rush, you can just look at the list, pick up the phone, and ask a store if it has what you need. If it doesn't, you won't have wasted time driving around. Also, if you tell a small store you are in a hurry, it may be willing to have your things ready for you when you get there.

Another solution for busy times — and also for entertaining, as you will see in Chapter 6 — is a "personal caterer." Look for a woman in your neighborhood who doesn't work outside her home and who is a good cook, and ask her if she'd like to prepare dishes for you to take home, heat, and serve. Many older women like to cook and are only too glad to have extra income.

Brown Bag Lunches

Making lunches to take to work or school in a brown bag or lunch box need not be a huge chore. You can use the planned leftovers approach: when you prepare dinner, deliberately make extra food, and save it for lunch. Two important tips here: (1) don't serve at dinner the extra amount intended for lunch; if it appears on the table, someone may eat it; (2) unless the leftover food is a favorite of the person taking the lunch, don't pack it for lunch the very next day. The cooking sessions to which you could quite easily add planned leftovers are those in which you cook ground beef, meat loaf, baked steak, roast beef, and pork. With microwave ovens in many work places now, you can take almost anything for lunch.

Meat need not always be *in* the sandwich. You could spread raisin bread with cream cheese and honey or peanut butter, and then pack cold slices of ham, chicken, turkey, or roast beef to be eaten *with* the bread.

Another approach is to make sandwiches ahead, label them, and freeze them. Ham, roast beef, turkey, and chicken are good for this. When you are in a hurry, just throw one in a bag with a piece of fruit and a couple of cookies, and you're all set. Frozen sandwiches are also a good idea if there is no cool place to store the food until it will be eaten; thus, they work well for kids who take their lunch to school. By lunchtime the sandwich is thawed, and the rest of the lunch has been kept at a somewhat cooler temperature because it is near the frozen sandwich. (Note that while you can freeze some packaged luncheon meats, not all of them freeze well. So experiment with your favorites to see which will freeze successfully.)

If you pack lunches regularly, it is a good idea to have fillers on hand, such as small individual containers of nuts, raisins, health food mixes, chips, cookies, and so forth.

Container of Frozen Yogurt
Carrot and Celery Sticks
Apple
Juice or Coffee

Tuna or Chicken Salad
Sliced Tomato
Hard-Boiled Egg
Crackers
1 or 2 Brownies
Milk

Ham, Cheese, Lettuce, and
  Tomato with Mayonnaise
  on Hard Roll
Banana
Oatmeal Cookies
Juice or Coffee

Leftover Fried Chicken
Cherry Tomatoes, Olives,
  Carrot Sticks, and
  Celery Sticks
Peanut Butter Cookies
Small Box of Raisins
Milk or Coffee

Cream Cheese and Jelly on
  Date-Nut Bread
Hard-Boiled Egg
Grapes and an Orange
Juice, Milk, or Coffee

Cold Roast Beef
Cold Cooked Vegetables (such
  as Carrots and String
  Beans) with Salad Dressing
Bread and Butter
Slice of Pound Cake
Milk or Coffee

Peanut Butter, Apple Slices,
  and Cheese on Whole
  Wheat Bread
Celery and Carrot Sticks
2 Chocolate Chip Cookies
Milk, Coffee, or Tea

Cold Boiled Shrimp with
  Cocktail Sauce
Lettuce Wedge
Hard-Boiled Egg
Blueberry Muffin and Butter
Juice or Coffee

Meat Loaf on Hard Roll
Coleslaw
Apple
Juice or Coffee

Ham Salad, Lettuce, and
  Tomato on Whole
  Wheat Bread
Potato Salad
Grapes
Juice or Coffee

Thermos of Chili with
  Frankfurter Slices
Small Bag of Taco Chips
Small Box of Raisins
Banana
Juice or Coffee

Thermos of Split Pea Soup
Crackers and Butter
Cheddar Cheese Wedge
Apple
Juice or Coffee

6

Guests: Expected
and Unexpected

The way to have a good time as a hostess is — surprise! — to be
organized. Plan ahead and cook ahead, using the techniques of efficient
everyday meal preparation discussed in Chapters 2 and 3: make lists,
shop once, cook in advance, freeze the food, and serve your meals efficiently as well as attractively. Planning and working ahead has paid off
for me. Once, for instance, I invited guests to a small dinner party for a
friend who is an anchorwoman on a news program. The evening before
the party, I was just finishing the roast and stuffing the potatoes when
the phone rang; the guest of honor was very embarrassed to say that she
couldn't come the next night; she had to fill in for someone. I was able to
tell her not to worry. We rescheduled the party for a week later. I just put
the food in the freezer and called the guests to tell them about the change
of plan. The dinner was saved, there was no waste, the food was just as
good the next week, and I was even more rested for the occasion.

I'm going to describe different kinds of entertaining in this chapter,
everything from how to handle weekend guests, theme parties, and that
special kind of guest, the one who isn't invited but just drops in. But first
let's cover some general topics.

Social Obligations

You may like people and want to be generous to them — but not if it
means spending all of your time and energy in the kitchen. If you *have* to
entertain — for business reasons or to return invitations — make it as
easy for yourself as possible.

One approach is to hire a caterer. This needn't be expensive: as I suggested in Chapter 5, find a woman in your neighborhood who might be happy to cook for you.

Another way to handle social obligations efficiently is to do a lot of entertaining — dinner parties, brunches, lunches, or other get-togethers — all in the same week. When your conscience begins to bother you because you've been to dinner at Jane's and at Sally's, and the Baxters have had you to brunch twice, but you haven't invited any of them over for ages, set aside a week and give a couple of dinners and a weekend luncheon or a large party. Ideally, you should pick a week when things will be slow at work to minimize the chance that a sudden work crisis will interrupt your plans. Be sure to give yourself plenty of time to plan and prepare all the food. Entertaining more than once or twice in a week can be tiring, and the more work you have out of the way before the week begins, the freer you will be to relax and enjoy yourself.

At the end of a year, one high-powered couple in politics in the East grew so embarrassed about their social obligations that they set aside a week and gave a dinner party for eight every night for four nights. They served the same menu every single night, and found that though they themselves got tired of eating the same food, the dinner party became easier to give each night, since they knew exactly what they had to do and when and how to do it. At the end of the week, they had that dinner down pat for the future. Their obligations were all honored, so they took themselves out to a restaurant to celebrate a job well done. They now plan to handle their entertaining this way every year.

To be sure, entertaining several times in one week may sound more like duty than pleasure or gracious hospitality. But for people whose lives *are* their work, it is one solution. It saves time, money, energy, shopping, housecleaning, and all the small jobs that go into having guests.

It is just as easy to cook three meals at once as it is to prepare one meal a day on three different days. You can buy a large amount of meat — turkey, ham, chicken, or beef — that can be fixed in three different ways; or you can fix it in one way, then in a different recipe the second time, and perhaps cold for brunch the third time. You can serve different food to different guests or some of the same food. You and your family may get bored by the same food, but your guests won't know the difference. (Be sure children understand that they should not blurt out in front of guests, "We had this two days ago when Aunt Ruth was here.") After all, you're just doing this for one week.

And don't feel you need to explain your secrets when guests admire your energy and wonder how you do it — unless you want to. The political couple unabashedly told all their guests what they were doing, because the guests all moved in the same circle and would have found out anyway. Because the guests were as busy as the host and hostess, they understood the problem and were not offended at all. On the contrary, the couple's solution became a great topic of conversation. The moral of this story is: how much you tell depends on who your guests are.

Another suggestion for those of you who are very busy is to do most of your entertaining in the summer. It is easier then because the foods available are fresh, tempting to the palate, and need less preparation. Corn on the cob, succulent tomatoes, melons, and green vegetables are plentiful. No one wants heavy meals because of the hot weather. Meats prepared on the grill can be done by the men, lightening the women's work. (For further information about outdoor cooking, see the Picnics and Backyard Cookouts section of this chapter, page 68.)

Entertaining with Style

If you enjoy entertaining and look forward to having guests, you'll approach it less as a duty to be performed than as an opportunity for fun and good feeling. You'll want to lavish more time and effort to make your occasion memorable. You can start by issuing an interesting invitation — more than just the routine phone call. For instance, you might want to tell your guests what you will be serving. They will get in the mood for that particular food. (Also, they won't have it for dinner the night before.) If you are going to serve turkey in February, tell them you are going to be serving a Thanksgiving menu. Your ideas and ingenuity will tempt their palates. They will enjoy your food more because they will have been looking forward to it.

It's also fun to follow up a telephone invitation with a confirmation in writing a day or two later. You might send it on the back of your favorite recipe card; or you could send the entire meal plan with the invitation at the bottom. You could also send just one of the recipes you are going to serve, noting that this is one of the dishes on the menu. You might save can labels and write the invitation on the back. If you are inviting people for lunch, you might write your invitation on a brown paper bag. An intriguing invitation heightens the party-going spirit, so be creative with invitations. Give your imagination free rein.

Formality and Informality

When you're thinking of inviting guests, remember that fancy dinner parties are not the only way to entertain. Sometimes it's more fun to be informal. We like to entertain after a ball game or our favorite sport, skiing. If the food is cooked ahead, it takes very little time to serve. Hungry people who have been outdoors exercising all day like to come into a comfortable house, have a little wine or beer and a meal that is ready in minutes. The three menus I use most often are:

1. Thick chili topped with cheese, tossed salad, hot buttered French bread, pumpkin and/or cherry pie, and hot chocolate.

2. Homemade chicken soup (large chicken chunks and chunky vegetables), 24-hour salad with hot buttered French bread, hot apple pie topped with melted cheese or ice cream, and hot buttered rum.

3. Hearty beef stew, a platter of raw vegetables with dip, hot rolls, and butter, sweet and cheese tray, chocolate cake, and coffee.

For the above dinners, the centerpiece is always a large bowl of fresh fruit, and the beverages are wine and beer. These menus are favorites of mine because they are easy. The dinners can be served around a table. After skiing, however, I like just sitting on the floor in front of the fireplace with foods served from the coffee table and kitchen stove.

Short-notice dinners — when you spontaneously decide it would be fun to have friends over in just a few days — are another way to enjoy having company. Give a do-it-yourself dinner; a wok meal or a fondue party; a cookout or picnic in summer; a chili supper in winter; or a Sunday night supper. For dessert you might want to offer homemade doughnuts fried fresh at the table. All you need is the dough, which you can make ahead of time, and two or three bowls of different kinds of sugar or icing for doughnut toppings. The emphasis here is on plenty of good food that isn't elaborate so that everyone can sit around and relax. If you want to do something a bit special, you can top the meal off with a fancy-easy dessert (see page 221).

Pointers on Party Planning

1. Remember not to fix too many hors d'oeuvres before a heavy meal: they will ruin your guests' appetites. If your dinner is going to be lighter fare, then the hors d'oeuvres can be more plentiful and substantial.

2. Don't begin a dinner party too early in the evening. You'll have to rush too much after work to do the last minute preparation, and your guests won't be hungry. Seven-thirty is a reasonable time to begin. Everything always tastes better when people are really hungry.

3. I prepare my breads ahead and reheat them before serving. (They always turn out better than if I do them at the last minute. Invariably, I forget them in the oven and thus have to serve very browned bread or rolls.) One of my favorites for a dinner party is hot, sliced, and buttered French bread. Melt plain or herbed butter and baste the outside of the entire loaf with it; also paint butter between each slice. Seal the loaf in aluminum foil ready to be heated. You can do this the night before, and it will work just as well. All you have to do before you serve is pop the loaf in the oven for ten to fifteen minutes.

4. The night before a dinner or party I take out all my serving dishes, utensils, pans, canned foods, and boxed products and line them up on the kitchen table or counter. I also set the table as much as possible. The less you have to do just before the guests arrive, the better. Also, having everything as nearly ready as possible can save your dinner party if you have to stay later at work than you had anticipated or if you are unexpectedly detained in traffic on your way home.

5. If you need members of the family to assist you with entertaining, assign their tasks well in advance of the guests' arrival — even a day or two before — to prevent last-minute bickering or foul-ups.

6. Always have two lists for entertaining: "To Buy" and "To Do." Check off the items as you buy them or do them. Then you don't have to keep rereading one long list. As your list dwindles to one or two things left to do, you'll feel relaxed, and you'll know you haven't forgotten anything.

7. I keep my used lists from parties, dating them, and listing the names of the guests. When I invite the same guests again, it saves me from unintentionally serving them the same food. If a particular plan was a hit with one set of guests, I can use it again for another group, thus saving time in menu planning and organizing. All I have to do is recopy or recheck the old list. If you suddenly decide to entertain on the spur of the moment, and you don't have time to do the usual planning, just grab one of your lists and head for the store. No thought required. You can feel assured of giving your guests a successful meal without making yourself crazy.

8. Remember that the way your food looks is as important as the way it tastes. Learn to decorate your food. I've heard it said that parsley

is a cook's best friend, and I think it is true. Other such friends are orange peels and twists; lemon, orange and lime slices; pickled crab apples; greens, flowers, leaves, and vegetable tops — anything (edible) to jazz up food that would otherwise look plain on the plate.

9. Present your food in interesting serving dishes. For example, serve salad in a long-stemmed bowl-type wineglass set on a small plate. A tequila glass or a balloon wineglass is best, but any smaller bowl type will do. Break lettuce into small pieces so that it can be eaten with only a fork; a knife would break the glass. The dressing can be on the salad or placed in a tiny container on the side. You can use old-fashioned salt dishes for this purpose. I have used saki cups for individual servings of salad dressing. Be creative. The balloon wineglass also offers a very elegant way to serve dessert. The dessert may simply be pudding, fruit, or ice cream; if it is served this way with a cookie or mint on the bottom plate, it suddenly becomes memorable.

10. When you are planning menus for guests, be sure to consider the color and texture of the foods you will serve, as well as calories or richness, nutritional groups, and the quantity of food. An entire meal shouldn't be a mixture of browns, yellows or whites; it would look bland and unappetizing. If everything is creamy, your guests will pray for a crunch. Too many rich foods, high in calories, will make guests uncomfortable. Good nutrition is a very important consideration: it is important not to serve all carbohydrates or all proteins. Serve generous portions to guests. Don't stuff them, but don't skimp, either. If you can't afford to serve twelve guests, then invite only six.

A Party Panorama

In this section you will find menus for the following kinds of gatherings:

- Weekend Dinner Parties
- Large Parties and Buffets
- Picnics and Backyard Cookouts
- Breakfasts and Brunches, Lunches, and Sunday Night Suppers

WEEKEND DINNER PARTIES

Formal dinner parties, with a lovely table and guests nicely dressed, can make you feel that you're leading a luxurious life. They perk up your spirits, especially in winter when you need a bit of festivity. Use your candles, crystal, silver, china, and lace. Think of food more elaborate than your everyday cuisine. Although these dinner parties are suggested for weekends, they can also be given during the week when you need to entertain, say, for business.

Make a few fancy things like potato nests in which to serve the vegetables or fill tomatoes or large onions with vegetables. Garnish elegantly. If you have a standing rib roast, surround it with parsley and spiced apple rings or whole apples. If you have roast duck, garnish it with parsley and orange twists. When you cook vegetables, add nuts, scallion slices, or bacon bits rather than just butter.

Sauces also make a meal seem more elegant. Pour cherry sauce over ham, apricot sauce over pork, hollandaise, or cheese sauce over vegetables.

Some of the more elegant looking entrées are standing rib or crown roast of pork, Cornish hens or squab, pheasant under glass, leg of lamb, chicken breasts tarragon, chicken Kiev, and lobster.

Mixed Lettuce Salad with Basic
  Salad Dressing
Roast Duck with
  Amaretto-Orange Sauce
Rice Pilaf
Brussels Sprouts with Nuts
Crescent Rolls and Butter
Chocolate Parfaits*
Coffee, Tea, or Milk

Melon Wedges
Stuffed Cornish Hens
Peas in Potato Baskets
Glazed Carrots
Hot Rolls and Butter
Filled Angel Food Cake
Coffee, Tea, or Milk

Wine
Salad of Cherry Tomatoes,
  Cauliflower Flowerets,
  Zucchini Slices, Onion Rings,
  and Broccoli Flowerets
  Marinated in Italian Dressing
Roast Leg of Lamb with
  Pan Gravy
Twice-Baked Potatoes
Mushrooms and Peas*
Mint Jelly
Hot Rolls and Butter
Individual Meringues
  Filled with Fresh Fruit
  and/or Ice Cream
Coffee, Tea, or Milk

*Recipe not included; ingredients or product purchased or made from your own recipe.

Red or White Wine
Shrimp Cocktail* in a Balloon
   Glass
Beef Wellington Garnished with
   Cherry Tomato–Stuffed
   Mushroom Caps*
Chantilly Potato Casserole
Dilled Carrots
Hot Bread and Butter
Chocolate Charlotte Russe
Coffee, Tea, or Milk

White Wine
Cold Pureed Vegetable Soup
   Garnished with Sour Cream
   and Parsley
Chicken Elyse
Fluffy White Rice
Brussels Sprouts with Nuts
Cloverleaf Rolls or Croissants
   and Butter
Stacked Blueberry Dessert
Coffee, Tea, or Milk

White Wine
Creamy Broccoli Soup
Elegant Spinach Salad
Crown Roast of Pork with
   Nutted Pineapple Rice
Mixed Vegetables with Onion
   and Bacon Sauce
Hot Rolls and Butter
Chocolate Cake with Hot
   Chocolate Sauce
Coffee, Tea, or Milk

Wine
Vegetable–Gelatin Salad
Pork Roast with Gravy or
   Stuffed Pork Chops
Mashed Potato Flowerets
String Beans Amandine
Hot French Bread and Butter
Pecan Pie
Coffee, Tea, or Milk

PARTY BUFFET

Champagne Punch
Shrimp and Pasta Salad
Marinated Mushrooms
Deviled Eggs
Cheese Log* with Crackers and
White Grapes
Warm Sliced Baked Ham with
   Horseradish Sauce*
Kaiser Rolls and Brown Rolls
Warm Beef Tenderloin Roast
Thin Sliced Party Rye and
   White Breads

Elegant Chicken Salad
Scalloped Corn
Baked String Beans
Platter of Date Nut Bread*
   Spread with Cream Cheese,
   Honey Butter, or Peanut
   Butter
Homemade Petit Fours, Fudge
   Cookies*, Brownies, and
   Sugar Cookies
Coffee, Tea, or Milk

*Recipe not included; ingredients or product purchased or made from your own recipe.

INTERNATIONAL DINNER

White Wine (French)
Minestrone (Italian)
Greek Salad
Chicken Kiev (Russian)
Wild and White Rice (American)
Steamed Snow Peas, Celery,
   and Carrots (Asian)

Assorted Breads and Butter
   (Scandinavian)
German Chocolate Cake*
Coffee (South American)
Whipped Cream and Irish
   Whisky for the Coffee

ROMANTIC DINNER FOR TWO

Champagne
Grapes and Cheese Wedges
Bibb Lettuce Salad Garnished
   with Cherry Tomatoes and
   Red and Green Pepper Rings
Broiled Rock Lobster Tails with
   Butter Sauce
Parsleyed Potatoes*

String Beans Amandine
Hot Buttered French Bread
Chocolate Dessert Cups with
   Tiny Ice Cream Balls,
   Marshmallow Topping,
   and Maraschino Cherries
Coffee, Tea, or Milk

Large Parties and Buffets

One way to entertain with flair is to give your dinner or party a theme. Themes make guests feel special, but don't require a lot of work. The following list of themes could be used for a dinner party, a small party, or an all-out big group blast:

Large Do-Ahead Buffet
Fondue Party
After-Ski or Snow Party
Soul Food Dinner
Christmas or Thanksgiving in
   July

Country Supper for a Crowd
Oktoberfest
Luau
Stir-Fry Dinner
Turkey for Twenty
Open Bar Company Buffet

Menus for these parties follow.

*Recipe not included; ingredients or product purchased or made from your own recipe.

LARGE DO-AHEAD BUFFET

Red and White Wine
Overnight Layered Salad
Spiral Macaroni–Seafood Salad
Peas and Carrots with Cheese
  and Celery*
Cold Sliced Roast Beef
Pineapple Upside-Down Ham
  Loaf
Sliced Turkey with Caper Sauce
Cherry Tomatoes Stuffed with
  Cheese*
Marinated Mushrooms

Hot Mixed Vegetables in Cheese
  Sauce
Mixed Breads and Rolls in Large
  Basket
Cutting Board, Knife, and
  Butter Bowl Served Alongside
Coffee and Tea
Pecan Pie
Fresh Mixed Fruit Bowl and
  Whipped Topping
Large Bowl of Vanilla Ice Cream
  Balls and Chocolate Sauce

FONDUE PARTY

White Wine
Cheese Fondue with French
  Bread Chunks
Beef and Chicken Fondue
Wiener Chunks (dipped in
  pancake batter) Fondue
Cheese Chunks (dipped in egg
  batter and seasoned bread
  crumbs) Fondue
Fruit and Cheese Tray
Peanut Butter Fondue
Chocolate Fondue

Marshmallows
Banana Slices
Apple Wedges
Strawberries
Quartered Pear Halves
Pitted Dates
Maraschino Cherries
Angle Food Cake Cubes
Chopped Peanuts
Flaked Coconut
Coffee and Hot Cider with
  Cinnamon Sticks

AFTER-SKI OR SNOW PARTY

Hot Mulled Wine
Chili with Grated Cheese
Meat Lasagne
Sandy's Overnight Salad

Apple Dumplings* and Brownies
  or Apple and Pumpkin Pies
Cheese and Fruit Tray
Hot Chocolate and Coffee

SOUL FOOD DINNER

Red or White Wine
Barbecued Spareribs
Fried Chicken
Bacon with Beans or Black-Eyed

Peas or Bacon or Salt Pork
  with Collard Greens
Corn Bread
Sweet Potato Pie
Coffee, Tea, or Milk

*Recipe not included; ingredients or product purchased or made from your own recipe.

CHRISTMAS OR THANKSGIVING IN JULY

Roast Turkey, Ham, Duck, or
  Goose
Baked Sweet Potatoes
Creamed Peas and Onions
Dilled Carrots
Stuffing
Mashed Potatoes
Hot Rolls and Butter
Chocolate Cake*

Pistachio Ice Cream Dips
  (heaped to look like
  Christmas trees) with
  Chocolate Sauce*
    or
Pumpkin Pie and Whipped
  Topping
Coffee and Liqueur

OKTOBERFEST

Different Beers
Brats
Sausages
Frankfurters
Fresh Green Salad and
  Vegetable–Gelatin
  Salad
Buns and Breads

Sauerkraut
Scalloped Potatoes
Hot Applesauce or Apple
  Strudel*
Carrot Cake* and Chocolate
  Cake*
Coffee or Tea

COUNTRY SUPPER FOR A CROWD

Red Wine
Sandy's Overnight Salad
Pork Chops and Sausage Links*
Boiled and Browned Potatoes
Sauerkraut or Hot Slaw with
  Apple Slices
Scalloped Corn
Navy Bean and Ham Casserole

Corn Bread
Large Loaves of Homemade or
  Bakery Bread (to be Cut
  on a Board at the Table)
Banana Pudding*
Chocolate Cake*
Coffee, Tea, or Milk

LUAU

Piña Coladas and Hawaiian
Rum Punch
Chicken Elyse
Barbecued Spareribs

Broiled or Grilled Skewered
  Seafood on Rice*
Ambrosia Dessert Salad
Coconut Cake*
Coffee, Tea, or Milk

*Recipe not included; ingredients or product purchased or made from your own recipe.

TURKEY FOR TWENTY

Roast Turkey with Stuffing and
 Gravy
Yam Rounds with
 Marshmallows*
Scalloped Potatoes or Au Gratin
Potatoes
Lemon-Buttered Broccoli

Mixed Vegetables with Bacon
 and Onion Sauce
Sandy's Overnight Salad
Hot Cranberry Sauce*
Pumpkin Pie with Whipped
 Cream
Pineapple Sherbet
Coffee, Tea, or Milk

OPEN BAR COMPANY BUFFET

Beef Tenderloin Roast
Scalloped Potatoes
Overnight Layered Salad
Relish Tray: Deviled Eggs,
 Celery Sticks, Carrot
 Sticks, Cherry Tomatoes,
 Green and Black Olives,

Cheese Wedges, and Seedless
 Grapes
Hot Rolls and Butter Balls
Cherry Pie
French Apple Pie*
 Banana Cream Pie*
Coffee, Tea, or Milk

Picnics and Backyard Cookouts

Picnics should be fun and relaxing for everyone, even the cook or
the hostess. This is a good time to get the men to help without a lot of
hassle. The fare need not be gourmet but just good solid food. The trick
here is not to fix too many items, just plenty of each. Everything should
be ready when guests arrive, so that you can go out and start the party
immediately.

The food should be good but doesn't have to be all homemade. If
you are fixing almost everything from scratch, you needn't have any
compunctions about buying pie at your favorite pie place or potato salad
at your favorite deli. You can spice them up with your personal touches.
(You don't have to tell anyone you've done this.) If you do purchase
some ready-made food, be sure you've tried and tested it before, so that
you will know it is almost as good as your own; then you will not have
to worry whether the item you bought will pass the test of your guests —
you'll know it will.

If you have a lot of picnics and backyard cookouts, it would be wise
to invest in an ice cream freezer. What could be better for your summer
picnic in hot weather than homemade ice cream? You'll be spared having
to think of different desserts. And as with the barbecue grill, the men will
usually take over.

*Recipe not included; ingredients or product purchased or made from your own recipe.

OLD-FASHIONED PICNIC

Lemonade
Fried Chicken and Baked Ham
Potato Salad
Deviled Eggs
Olives, Pickles, and Mustard
Potato Chips

Zesty Baked Beans
Variety of Breads and Butter
Watermelon
Chocolate Cake*
Chocolate Chip Cookies* and
    Oatmeal Cookies*

PICNIC IN THE SNOW

This is a good romance rekindler. You actually do go out in the snow and find a picnic table that's bolted down and left out all winter, brush off the snow, and lay out meal. This is really a lot of fun and can work wonders when winter boredom sets in about January or February.

Thermos of Hot Chocolate
Large Thermos of Chili and Hot
    Dogs
Boiled Eggs

Cheese
Potato Chips
Brownies

ELEGANT MADE-AHEAD PICNIC

Champagne
Cold Sliced Baked Ham and Eye
    of Round Beef*
Potato Salad Garnished with
    Cold Cut-Wrapped Pickles
    Pickles
Mozzarella or Swiss
    Cheese–Stuffed
    Cherry Tomatoes*
Pimiento Cheese–Stuffed Raw
    Zucchini

Watermelon, Cantaloupe, and
    Honeydew Melon Slices
Deviled Eggs, Black and Green
    Olives, and Celery and
    Carrot Sticks
Caramel-Banana-Butter Pecan
    Cake with Caramel Icing
Coffee, Tea, or Milk

*Recipe not included; ingredients or product purchased or made from your own recipe.

FISH ARE BITIN' COOKOUT

Chilled White Wine or Iced Tea
Fresh Strawberry–Melon–
  Pineapple–Peach Kebabs
Cheese and Crackers
White Fish (or Your Catch)
  Barbecued with Lemon
  Slices and/or Lemon Butter
  and Onion Rings, Grilled in

Foil
Potatoes Baked on Grill
Corn on the Cob (in Husks)
  Barbecued on Grill
Tossed Green Salad
German Chocolate Cake
  Squares*
Coffee, Tea, or Milk

KEBAB PICNIC

Beer and Punch with a Punch
Melon Chunks and Strawberries
  with Honey–Yogurt Dip or
  Powdered Sugar
Kebabs* of Bratwurst,
  Frankfurters, and/or
  Kielbasa, with Apple,
  Banana, and Pineapple
  Chunks
Corn on Cob, Green Pepper

Chunks, and Large Whole
  Mushrooms
Buns and Brown Rolls
Baked Beans
Sauerkraut
Cheese Chunk-Macaroni Salad
Potato Chips
Hot Apple Strudel* with Vanilla
  Ice Cream
Coffee, Tea, or Milk

BACKYARD COOKOUT

Lemonade or Wine Spritzers
Fresh Fruit Platter with
  Pineapple, Watermelon,
  and Grapes
Barbecued Spareribs and
  Barbecued Chicken
Corn on the Cob Roasted in

Herb-Lemon Butter
Tomato, Onion, and Green
  Pepper Slices Marinated
  in Italian Dressing
Coleslaw
Homemade Ice Cream and
  Cherry Pie

RANCH OR BARBECUE PARTY

Beer
Texas Chili and/or Barbecued
  Steaks, Spareribs and Chicken
Grilled Corn on the Cob
Zesty Baked Beans
Tossed Salad and Sliced

Tomatoes
Melon and Fresh Fruits
Chocolate-Nut Cake*
Corn Bread and Hot Rolls and
  Butter
Lemonade and Spiked Tea

*Recipe not included; ingredients or product purchased or made from your own recipe.

BREAKFAST, BRUNCHES, LUNCHES, AND SUNDAY NIGHT SUPPERS

These menus are meant for weekends, when you have the leisure to enjoy yourself in the kitchen and to do something a bit special for your family or guests. As a working woman you probably don't have time to prepare elaborate meals during the week, so it can be fun to cook when you have time. The Sunday night suppers, for either family or guests, are particularly appropriate when you've been out all day — visiting a museum, skiing, or swimming — or when you want to send weekend guests on their way home with a meal that is pleasant yet leaves you time to relax before the work week begins. All of these menus can be adapted to your mood. You can present them simply or elaborately, as you wish.

If you've invited guests to a weekend brunch, you may want to serve them one of the traditional alcoholic beverages — champagne, Bloody Marys, or screwdrivers — rather than other hard liquors. These drinks are appropriate and give your gathering an elegant touch. However, they are not necessary; the food will definitely carry the occasion. You may serve drinks or not as you and your guests prefer.

BREAKFAST MENUS

Mushroom Omelet*
Sliced Tomatoes
Raisin Bread
Cream Cheese, Butter, and
    Honey
Coffee, Tea, or Milk

Orange Juice
Hot Oatmeal* with Brown
    Sugar and Sliced Bananas
Boiled Eggs
Baked Sliced Bacon
Hot Toast and Butter
Coffee, Tea, or Milk

Fried Eggs
Broiled or Fried Sausage Links
Potato Pancakes with
    Applesauce
Hard Rolls and Butter
Coffee, Tea, or Milk

Orange Juice
Boiled Eggs
Broiled or Fried Sausage Patties
French Toast* with Butter and
    Powdered Sugar
Strawberries with Whipped
    Topping
Coffee, Tea, or Milk

*Recipe not included; ingredients or product purchased or made from your own recipe.

BRUNCH MENUS

Fresh Strawberries in
  Champagne
Sliced Avocado, Orange, and
  Banana Salad Platter
  with Lemon Wedges
Cold Sliced Ham
Broccoli Soufflé
Cherry Tomato–Stuffed
  Mushroom Caps*
Hot Rolls and Butter
Large Tray of Assorted Danish
  Pastries*
Coffee, Tea, or Milk

Blender-Made Frozen Orange
  Juice
Scrambled Eggs
Broiled Sliced Bacon and
  Sausage Links
Hot Toast and Butter
Hot Buttered Coffee Cake**
Whole Strawberries Dipped in
  Powdered Sugar
Coffee, Tea, or Milk

Bloody Marys
Grilled Ham, Sausage,
  Pineapple Chunks, and
  Cherry Tomato Kebabs
Steamed Rice
Bacon-Onion Quiche
Cheese Blintzes with Cherry
  Sauce*
Toasted English Muffins and
  Bran Muffins with Butter
  and Preserves
Ambrosia Dessert Salad
Chocolate Dessert Cups Filled
  with Sliced Kiwi Fruit
  and Whole Strawberries and
  Topped with Whipped Cream
Coffee, Tea, or Milk

Red Wine Spritzers
Pasta Spiral–Egg Bake
Cream Cheese, Lox, Onion
  Slices, and Bagels
Relish Tray with Three-Bean
  Salad*, Corn Relish*, Pickles,
  Carrots, Celery Stalks,
  Cottage Cheese, and
  Longhorn and Swiss Cheese
Hard Rolls and Blueberry
  Muffins with Butter
Lemon-Lime Gelatin Fruit Salad
  with Whipped Topping
Easy Coffee Cake
Coffee, Tea, or Milk

*Recipe not included; ingredients or product purchased or made from your own recipe.
**Dot store-bought coffee cake with butter and heat in the oven.

Breakfast OR Brunch Menus

Tomato Juice
Eggs in Hash Cups
Corn Fritters with Syrup
Hash Brown Potatoes with
  Onions*
White and Rye Toast and Butter
Fresh Fruit with Yogurt-Honey
  Dip
Coffee, Tea, or Milk

Tomato Juice
Scotch Eggs
Waffles* and Syrup
Fresh Fruits with Cheese Wedges
Easy Coffee Cake
Coffee, Tea, or Milk

Grapefruit Juice
Tunnel of Eggs
Broiled or Fried Sausage Links
Sliced Tomatoes
Vanilla Cake Squares* with Hot
  Fruit Sauce
Coffee, Tea, or Milk

Orange Juice
Molded Scrambled Eggs and
  Cheese
Fried Sausage Balls*
Hash Brown Potatoes*
Variety of Melon Slices, Grapes,
  and Cheeses
Jelly Rolls, Cream Puffs, and
  Doughnuts
Coffee, Tea, or Milk

Tomato Juice Cocktail
Spinach Omelet with Cheese
  Sauce*
Creamed Chicken and Egg Slices
  on Biscuits or Eggs à la
  King on Toast Points
Sliced Tomatoes, Onion Rings,
  and Green Pepper Rings
Cupcake–Ice Cream Surprise
Coffee, Tea, or Milk

Lunch Menus

Tossed Spinach Salad with
  Tomatoes and Mushrooms
Quiche Lorraine
Angel Food Cake* with
  Partially Thawed Frozen
  Strawberries
Coffee, Tea, or Milk

Sliced Tomatoes and Cucumbers
  with Oil and Vinegar Dressing
Chicken à la King–stuffed
  Crepes with Medium White
  Sauce
String Beans Amandine
Pound Cake* with Creamy
  Chocolate Icing
Coffee, Tea, or Milk

*Recipe not included; ingredients or product purchased or made from your own recipe.

Cheese Chunk-Macaroni Salad
Cold Roast Beef
Italian Bread and Butter
Fresh Fruit
Brownies
Coffee, Tea, or Milk

Tomato Stuffed with Chunky
  Chicken Salad
Hard-Boiled Egg Wedges
Cold Steamed Asparagus Spears
  and Lemon Wedges*
Sherbet
Soft Sugar Cookies
Coffee, Tea, or Milk

Mixed Fruit Cup*
Tuna Salad on Lettuce with
  Sliced Tomatoes, Olives,
  Pickles, Carrot Sticks,
  and Celery Sticks
Rolls and Butter
Vanilla Ice Cream with
  Butterscotch Sauce
Coffee, Tea, or Milk

Pineapple Upside-Down Ham
  Loaf
Coleslaw
Hot Biscuits and Butter
Brownies
Coffee, Tea, or Milk

Pureed Vegetable Soup
Pasta-Asparagus Salad
French Bread and Butter
Ice Cream and Cookies
Coffee, Tea, or Milk

Chicken-String Bean Salad
Sliced Tomatoes
Hard Rolls and Butter
Melon Wedges
Coffee, Tea, or Milk

Fruit Plates of Mixed Melon
  Wedges, Grapes, and
  Strawberries with Sherbet*
Raisin Bread and Cream Cheese
  and Jelly Sandwiches*
Coffee, Tea, or Milk

Omelet with Green Pepper,
  Mushroom, Onion, and
  Cheese
Sliced Tomatoes
French Bread and Butter
Coconut Cake*
Coffee, Tea, or Milk

Cream of Asparagus Soup
Broiled Ham, Cherry Tomato,
  and Green Pepper Kebabs*
Rice Pilaf or Steamed Rice*
Carrot Cake*
Coffee, Tea, or Milk

Ham and Cheese
  Sandwich Melts
Tossed Salad
Potato Chips
Assorted Cookies
Coffee, Tea, or Milk

*Recipe not included; ingredients or product purchased or made from your own recipe.

Fresh Fruit Cup*
Bacon, Lettuce, and Tomato
  Sandwiches*
Brownies with Vanilla Ice
  Cream and Hot Fudge Sauce*
Coffee, Tea, or Milk

Ham Salad Sandwiches*
Pasta-Asparagus Salad
Strawberries with Whipped
  Topping
Cookies
Coffee, Tea, or Milk

Hot Tomato Soup*
Pita Veggi-Melt Sandwiches
Cold Chicken Platter,* optional
Deviled Eggs
Olives and Pickles
Pineapple Sherbet on Pineapple
  Slices
Coffee, Tea, or Milk

Reuben Sandwiches
Potato Chips
Tomato Wedges, Olives, and
  Pickles
Ambrosia Dessert Salad
Coffee, Tea, or Milk

SUNDAY NIGHT SUPPERS

Pear and Cheese Salad
Quick Sloppy Joe Sandwiches
French Fried Potatoes*
Corn on the Cob
Chocolate and Vanilla Ice
  Cream Pie*
Coffee, Tea, or Milk

Mixed Fruit Salad*
Navy Bean and Ham Casserole
Spinach and Lettuce Tossed
  Salad*
Corn Bread and Butter
Cherry Pie à la Mode
Coffee, Tea, or Milk

Tossed Green Salad
All-Day Stew
Buttered Green Peas*
Hot Biscuits and Butter
Banana Pudding with Nuts*
Coffee, Tea, or Milk

Marinated Mushroom Salad on
  Lettuce Leaves
Chicken Pot Pie
Mashed Potatoes
Buttered Peas and Carrots*
Pineapple Upside-Down Cake
Coffee, Tea, or Milk

Tossed Salad
Stuffed Green Peppers
Buttered Corn*
Bread and Butter
Caramel-Banana-Butter Pecan
  Cake
Coffee, Tea, or Milk

Smoked Sausage*
Hot German Potato Salad
Lemon-Buttered Broccoli
Corn Bread and Butter
Apricot Upside-Down Cake*
Coffee, Tea, or Milk

*Recipe not included; ingredients or product purchased or made from your own recipe.

Coleslaw
Meat Loaf
Baked Potatoes, Carrots, and
    Onions (roasted with
    Meat Loaf)
Hot Rolls and Butter
German Chocolate Cake*
Coffee, Tea, or Milk

Creamy Broccoli Soup
Sliced Cold Roast Beef
Mixed Vegetables with Bacon
    and Onion Sauce
Baked Sweet Potatoes
Hot Rolls and Butter
Stacked Blueberry Dessert
Coffee, Tea, or Milk

Pear and Cheese Salad
Irish Spaghetti
Buttered Green Peas*
Rolls and Butter
Vanilla Pudding* with Sliced
    Bananas
Coffee, Tea, or Milk

Marinated Mushrooms and
    Sliced Tomatoes on
    Lettuce
Chicken and Noodles
Buttered Brussels Sprouts*
Hot Biscuits and Butter
Cherry Tarts* with Whipped
    Topping
Coffee, Tea, or Milk

Overnight Guests

Let's face it: Having house guests — even beloved ones — can put a strain on the most hospitable hostess and her family. You've got to keep your usual schedule — get to work on time, function smoothly — and also be concerned with feeding and housing extra people whose presence, no matter how considerate their behavior, does change your usual situation. I find that organizing in advance makes all the difference. My job takes me away from my family and friends. When I have guests, which is one of the ways I see my nearest and dearest, having meals prepared ahead allows me time to sit around the dinner table with them, catching up on their lives. The feeling of being in my home together in a relaxed and private setting is close and warm; we couldn't have the same experience in a noisy or formal restaurant.

Eating at home eliminates the sometimes embarrassing question of who will pay the restaurant check. Often the host or hostess plans to, but the guests feel they should. Having meals planned ahead also eliminates the problem of guests wanting to help. If they "help," you have to show them where things are and tell them what to do, and this usually takes more time and strains your nerves. If you prepare the food in advance, you can honestly tell your guests that everything is ready. At the last minute they can help you bring the meal to the table.

*Recipe not included; ingredients or product purchased or made from your own recipe.

When guests are out sight-seeing, occasionally I stay home and catch up with things I need to do or take a nap. After all, I've already seen the sights, and I can put the time to good use, if they don't mind going out without me. About an hour before the guests are scheduled to return, I start preparing dinner; I can have dinner ready for as many as eight when they return. They will enjoy this meal all the more because they're tired and hungry after their adventure, and they don't have to do any of the work. It's always nice to come home and smell a delicious meal as you walk in the door. By using my time to get caught up physically and mentally, I'm more relaxed for the rest of their visit.

In short, plan meals, shop, and do as much cooking as you can before your guests arrive. The less food preparation you have to do while they are with you, the better. On the other hand, if guests are to be with you for more than a couple of days, don't try to fix all the entrées ahead. Plan to go out or have food delivered now and then so that you won't exhaust yourself. On the day the guests arrive, give them a good dinner to welcome them. They will be tired after traveling and would probably like to get settled rather than go out. The next evening you can serve something more modest — spaghetti with a sauce you made ahead, salad, fresh bread, and either cheese and fruit or ice cream. Once your guests ahve settled into a routine with you, they may want to try one of your town's restaurants. Thoughtful guests may invite you out to dinner.

When you plan food for visitors, remember breakfasts and lunches. If guests are going to be with us during the week when I am working, I buy three or four kinds of hot or cold cereal, milk, eggs, fresh fruits, and bread and rolls. I show the guests where everything is and trust them to fend for themselves. For lunches I have on hand cold cuts, soups (made ahead), fruits, cheeses, breads, egg and potato salad, raw vegetables, and cookies. Again, the guests are on their own. I usually tell them what's for dinner that night so that they won't inadvertently eat dinner for lunch.

While guests are with us, I keep a copy of my master food plan in my purse. This stratagem has four advantages: (1) there is no chance that guests will run across it; my menus become public only when I choose to make them so; (2) I can do any extra shopping on my way home from work; (3) if I forget to take out my frozen entrée before I leave for the office, I can call home and tell someone what to thaw, or I can change my plans on the basis of the information I have.

One other thing I like to do for guests is have fruits and other snack foods on hand for all times of day or night. Guests — particularly those from out of state — may be on a different "body clock" from yours and may feel hungry at odd hours. Another touch my guests have enjoyed is a dish of little candies in their bedrooms. Again, if guests are hungry, something like this can tide them over until the next meal. After all, some guests don't feel comfortable telling their hostess they're starved and would she please hurry dinner? These little touches also make guests feel welcome.

Guests — Unexpected

There is one kind of guest to whom the preceding material on entertaining does not apply, and that is the guest you don't expect — otherwise known as a drop-in.

You know the situation: it's mealtime, and you're in the kitchen getting dinner. The phone rings, and your old friend Josephine Jovial announces she's in town for one night only; she'll be right over. Or your son suddenly tells you he's asked his friend to stay for dinner because they're studying for an exam. Or your bachelor cousin Fred stops by to leave off some important papers on his way home. The variations are endless, but the bottom line is the same: you've got to feed more mouths than you planned for. Noticing that dinner is in the offing, drop-ins who have good manners will swear they couldn't touch a thing, that dinner is waiting at home, or they've already eaten. They'll just sit with you, they say. But it's hard on the soul not to feed someone who's sitting with you. And it's awful to have guests feel they've stopped by at an inopportune time. I grew up in a family that always served something to anyone who dropped in — a farmhand, Aunt Mary, or the plumber. I still feel uncomfortable if people stop by and I don't offer them something, even if it's only a cup of coffee and a cookie.

So, what to do?

When unexpected guests arrive, give yourself time to say hello and collect your thoughts. Serve them some type of beverage — a glass of wine, a mixed drink, something cold in summer or hot in winter. Offer nuts or cheese-flavored crackers if you have them. This will give you time to think about how to stretch the meal you were planning or to order something additional from a restaurant that delivers.

First, let's talk about stretching meals. If you are cooking ahead, particularly if you regularly make more than one batch of a recipe at a time, you will always have something in the freezer that you can heat and serve (extra hamburgers, perhaps. or meat loaf, or spaghetti sauce).

If you don't have something prepared ahead in the freezer, or if you can't thaw it out quickly enough, you could fix any of the following meals if your cupboards and refrigerator are stocked according to the plan I set forth in Chapter 2, p. 7.

Before I started using the cooking-ahead method, an unexpected guest could upset my apple cart. Bob and I would end up having a whispered conference in another room, and either he'd sneak out to a store or all of us would go out to dinner. A few times I felt that the guests were embarrassed that they had stopped. Now that I use the cooking-ahead system, I'm prepared for extra mouths to feed, and I'm relaxed. My guests no longer feel that they've come at an awkward moment.

Clearly, if guests arrive just as you're sitting down to the table, they can't expect you to give up your own food. Give them whatever extra there is; if there isn't any, offer them fruit, cookies, or a beverage. They should understand, and you should not feel inhospitable.

Here are some other meal-stretching tricks:

1. If company arrives when you're baking potatoes, just cut the ones you have in half; mash and stuff them with bacon, sour cream, onion, or cheese; and serve half a potato to each person. If you have more mouths to feed than this trick will handle, slice the potatoes and make cottage fries.

2. If guests appear when you're almost ready to sit down to dinner, add another vegetable to the menu and quickly heat some soup. Serve the soup as a first course in an elegant manner, and use the extra vegetable to stretch the rest of the food.

3. If guests arrive when you have nothing for salad, fill canned pears with cottage cheese or grated Cheddar, or serve peach halves on lettuce leaves sprinkled with raisins and served with a dollop of mayonnaise. If you're short of fresh salad vegetables, you can serve grated carrot salad with or without raisins and stretched with pineapple, nuts, or marshmallows.

Boxes of instant mashed or scalloped potatoes can be a blessing when company drops in at the last minute, as can the various boxed rice and macaroni dinners. These things certainly do not make a meal in themselves, but they make a very tasty addition to a meal.

Canned fish and meat can save you time also. You can choose from many varieties: salmon, tuna, chicken, beef, turkey, ham, and Vienna sausages, just to mention a few.

Canned entrées are a good idea too. Try to keep one or two of them on hand. Canned ravioli, for instance, does quite nicely in a pinch and will help fill and nourish hungry people.

I also keep one canned bread and one canned cake on the cupboard shelf so that if my stock of everything else is depleted, I have these to fall back on in an emergency.

The boxed, canned, or frozen foods you store for emergency occasions will not keep forever, of course, so be sure to use them in your menu planning for the family occasionally. You wouldn't want your emergency store of food to become too old to serve and thus waste precious food dollars.

If the cupboard and freezer are bare and you really can't stretch your meal, you can quietly call the nearest deli, chicken, rib, or Chinese take-out place and order food that will complement your meal. Have them deliver, if possible; if you have to pick the food up, choose a place that is close.

7

Some High-Powered Working Women and How They Cope with Cooking

When I began to think about the problems women face when they're on a busy schedule, I found myself becoming more and more curious about how other women managed. I knew what I did, but I also knew that others would have interesting answers. So I chose sixteen women in different parts of the country and in different walks of life and sent each of them a copy of the same questionnaire.

My questionnaire asked for basic information: job description, location, working hours, and travel time; spouse, number of children, other relatives living at home. Then it asked, "Do you entertain regularly? Do relatives or friends come to dinner unannounced? How do you cope with daily cooking? How do you manage a dinner of ten to twenty people?" Finally, I asked for favorite menus or recipes or cooking hints that might help other working women.

As you will see in the profiles that follow, I chose a range of working women, from those with visible, glamorous careers to equally high-powered women who are not so visible. Since I regard full-time wives and mothers as working women, I have included some of them here. Women in high-pressure jobs do cook, of course, and they have the same culinary problems that other women face. Contrary to popular belief, not all glamorous career women have cooks and maids. More often than not they do their own cooking. Even though their work may be exciting, they still have to eat when they go home at night, and many have families who depend on them to prepare dinner.

I found some common threads running through the answers to my questions. Although the respondents were not all as organized as they would like to be, they all recognized the importance of organization. Many of the women prepare two entrees when they feed a large group of people; they believe buffet style works best, with meats cooked and sometimes sliced ahead of time. Casseroles cooked in advance were also a favorite for larger groups or parties. Many of these women use easy extras to make a meal look elegant. They add chopped egg and nuts to a salad, for example, or arrange a few fancy decorations on the table.

Above all, I was interested to see that most of these women plan ahead and cook ahead, usually on weekends, and freeze food for later use.

Kathie Berlin
Public Relations Executive
Rogers & Cowan Public Relations
New York, New York

As senior vice-president, Kathie Berlin heads the New York office of Rogers & Cowan, one of the largest public relations firms in the field of entertainment; its divisions include motion pictures, television, music, personalities, books, corporate and product accounts. Among her personal clients are Paul Newman, Marlo Thomas, Sylvester Stallone, Phyllis George Brown, and Norman Lear. Her corporate accounts include the Ford Motor Company.

Kathie's husband is Richard Valeriani, NBC News correspondent in Washington. Since Kathie and Richard work in different cities, they maintain an apartment in New York and a house in Washington and commute between them on weekends according to occasion, weather, and need. Richard is the weekend cook, specializing in *la cucina Italiana;* food for the rest of the week is up to Kathie.

Kathie says, "I have discovered what I consider to be a life-saver for the working woman — certainly a work-saver. It is a clay pot (not to be confused with a pressure cooker or a crock pot). The clay pot has to be soaked for fifteen minutes in cold water before use, but you do not have to preheat the oven when you use this pot. It's good for beef, veal, or pork roasts, but I like it especially for chicken. My favorite recipe calls for a whole roasting chicken with two medium-sized onions, peeled; six whole, fresh, scraped carrots; and four to six unpeeled 'new' potatoes. After soaking the clay pot in cold water, I drain out the water, pour one cup of white wine or chicken broth into the bottom of pot, add the vegetables, then the chicken with the onions stuffed in the cavity; I sprinkle the food with salt and pepper to taste, and tarragon, sage, rosemary, and thyme (with credit to Simon and Garfunkel), plus a sprig or two of fresh parsley. I cover the pot and place it in a cold — that's right, cold — oven. Then I turn the oven on to 500 degrees and cook the food for 45 to 75 minutes, depending on the size of the chicken. The top of the pot comes off for the last ten minutes to allow the chicken to brown.

"While the chicken is cooking, I set the table, take a bath, and watch the news. Then I make a salad to go with the main course."

An added attraction for Kathie is the fact that the pot requires very little cleaning — "No soap, just water."

When Kathie wants to make an impressive meal, her favorite is Cornish game hens served with wild rice and spiced apples. (If she really wants to impress the guests, she lights candles on the table.) For a large party, she calls in a good caterer.

Neither of Kathie's favorite meals is expensive or time-consuming, yet each makes an impressive dinner. When time is not a factor, she fixes her favorite lasagne recipe, which is also a good dish to fix ahead and re-heat.

Erma Bombeck
Author and Syndicated Columnist
Self-Employed
Arizona

Everyone knows Erma Bombeck. She is the author of a syndicated column that appears three times a week in nine hundred newspapers. She has been a regular on *Good Morning, America* for the last eight years and has written many books. Her seventh, *Motherhood: The Second Oldest Profession,* appeared in 1983. She lives with her husband and their one son who is still at home. She works eight hours a day six days a week, except when she travels, which is often. Friends and relatives do not drop by unannounced, and her husband rarely brings business associates home to dinner.

Erma says, "When my children were all at home, guilt played a big part in my meals. In the early years when I was flying to Cleveland to give a luncheon speech and flying home again in time for dinner, I felt guilty that I was wearing pantyhose and eating smoked almonds on the airplane, so I used to plan very special casseroles, hot rolls, and fancy desserts. My family ate better when I became a 'professional' than when I used to stay at home and fill up the trough with spaghetti.

"Generally, it's a myth to think you can give children chores to do while you work and that they will be done when you come home. This only happens on *The Brady Bunch*, when it is scripted and kids are getting $1,500 to do the segment for TV. (They'll say and do anything.)

"I leaned heavily on casseroles because they were cheap; they could be made ahead and even frozen; and I like one-dish meals. Everything is there.

"I have the best of all worlds because I have always worked from home. I can put in a load of laundry and don't have to leave the type-writer until it belches. Same deal with cooking. I have the luxury of putting on a roast in a slow oven that women who work outside the home don't have."

Grace Brewer
Wife and Mother
New Milford, Connecticut

Grace Brewer and her husband, Tad, have five children — four boys and one girl. Her household has grown on two occasions, when her father and Tad's father, after being widowed, made their home with the Brewers for a time. As a busy wife and mother, Grace knows what it is to be on call twenty-four hours a day seven days a week.

Yet Grace entertains regularly. Relatives live too far away to drop by for meals, but they are invited for dinner or for the day or a holiday. Although her husband has rarely brought the boss home for dinner, plenty of friends stop in unannounced. Grace says, "The children have always brought friends home — for a day, a week, or even a month or two. (Honest!) Many of these friends feel comfortable enough to visit even when their immediate link to our family is absent, because they know they're always welcome." About her entertaining, she explains, "I *plan ahead*, check recipes, and make lists. For drop-ins, I raid the freezer and figure that beggars can't be choosers! When I make casseroles, I always prepare one to eat and one to freeze. I do this especially with Beef Bourguignon or Chicken with Sherry. Then all I have to do is cook the noodles and make a salad.

"When I am planning dinner for ten to twenty, and doing the cooking myself, I make cheese sticks to go with drinks. My recipe makes ten to eleven dozen and freezes well, so I make them ahead; now that I have a food processor, the preparation is easier than ever. I like to serve a seafood casserole as an entrée. The shrimp, lobster, and crabmeat can all be prepared the day before. Then it can be assembled during the day of the party and put in the oven before dinner. Amounts can be varied as necessary, and it takes no attention from the hostess. Popovers are always impressive to serve with it. You can mix the batter an hour ahead of time and let it stand till baking time. Grated zucchini can be sautéed just before dinner. Grate the zucchini early in the day and press all the water out. Set it in the refrigerator until you're ready to cook. Sautéing it in butter takes only two or three minutes. Add dill. Delicious! Spinach salad is nice, too, with Bermuda onion rings and salted peanuts and a dressing of lemon juice and oil. For dessert, I serve chocolate chip pie made the day before. It's easy, and everybody likes it.

"I employ the following methods to make meal planning and cooking simpler and easier, and they work! I make lists for *everything*. I plan dinner menus for at least a week at a time, make a grocery list, and shop once. (As a hobby, I spend several hours a week refunding and I love it. However, it means I have to sneak into my menus certain foods that have labels I need. So I have a file of recipes that use sausages, frozen potatoes, corned beef hash, packaged cookies, and whipped toppings.) I double all casseroles, soups, stews, and sauces, and freeze, freeze, freeze. Four loaves of quick bread instead of two, three dozen cookies instead of one. Frozen food is like money in the bank.

"My husband knows how to boil water — but just barely. However, he takes over the outdoor barbecue, which helps me. We especially like beef or lamb kebabs.

"I recommend introducing kids to the kitchen early. Their free help has countless rewards. (However, you have to find a 100% failproof hiding place for prepared party goodies or the kids will inhale them for an afternoon snack.)

"I'd like to share one additional thing that has been fun for our family. For many years we had a weekly tradition called 'restaurant night.' For this dinner, I prepared a complete meal from an ethnic cuisine. I printed out a menu to put on the table; took out the best linens, china, and silver; and made the occasion as special as I could. We all looked forward to it, and as an extra bonus, my kids learned to eat anything.

"At the present time my life is not so hectic as it once was, though it's still open house around here. Two of my children work, two are in college, and one is in high school. A few years ago it was a very different picture and a very different daily schedule. Our children were involved in every activity imaginable, and once the school bell rang, I had to be in five places at once. I sometimes felt like a juggler. With so much practice, I rarely dropped the ball."

Shirley Drexler
Vice-President, All American Bank of Chicago
Chicago, Illinois

Shirley Drexler is responsible for the operation of a $40 million bank in neighborhood Chicago. Her husband Bob shares much of the cooking responsibility. He is the vice-president of the Lake Shore Bank in downtown Chicago.

Shirley drives to work and works ten or more hours a day. There is also some outside travel involved with her position.

Shirley and Bob entertain regularly, and their relatives do stop by for dinner unannounced. When this happens, Shirley dips into the large supply of commercial frozen foods which are life-savers that she keeps for just such occasions.

Her husband never brings (or you might say he always brings) the boss home to dinner. He is the boss.

The kitchen in Shirley's house is the property of her husband. All cupboards and drawers are arranged for his convenience. No changes are allowed without his permission. He takes great pride in the efficiency of his system. Shirley prepares the regular meals, but all holiday meals and dinner parties are the responsibility of the King of the House. She says, "Dinner parties are always held on Saturday night so that he has all day to slave over a hot stove. However, he does no cleaning up as he goes along, so by the time the meal is ready, the dirty pots and pans are piled high. Guess who does the cleanup?"

Their favorite dinner party recipe actually came from Robert's ex-wife. It is lasagne, which can either be fixed and served immediately or frozen for serving later. There is a great story behind this recipe.

Shirley says, "Bob's ex-wife is an excellent cook. Imagine how I felt, hardly being able to cook at all, always hearing from Bob's friends as well as Bob what a great cook his ex-wife, Alene, is. One night, after a few failures, we decided to try to make lasagne together the way Alene did. As you might have guessed, it was a disaster. So right then and there, I grabbed the phone, dialed her number and when she answered I said, 'Alene, I am sick to death of hearing what a fantastic cook you are. I would like your recipe for lasagne because Bob says you make the greatest lasagne in the whole world.' She said, 'Who is this?' and I said, 'This is Shirley, and I need your help if you don't mind.' She was so surprised that she gave me part of the recipe on the phone and agreed to write the rest down and send it. Now, family and friends enjoy lasagne made from Alene's recipe with a few of our added touches. Also, this un-expected sharing and my asking Alene for her help assisted in breaking the ice between us."

As advice to help working women cope with cooking, Shirley has this to say, "Get your husbands involved. They are reluctant at first. However, once they start to master this thing called cooking, they are looked upon as *gods* by their male friends."

Barbara Kauffman
Hairdresser; Owner-Operator, Hairdressing Salon
Oak Ridge, Tennessee

Barbara Kauffman is married and has one daughter, Angela. She owns and operates a beauty salon, employing three operators. Her schedule varies from day to day and season to season, but she usually works thirty-four to forty hours a week.

Since her relatives all live in other states, they don't drop in on Barbara at mealtime, but friends do. Barbara copes with drop-ins by fixing her "fast favorite," a sausage-rice casserole; a food processor helps her do the required chopping in seconds. During the winter, she serves coleslaw with it, and in the summer she offers sliced tomatoes and cucumbers. For a fast, delicious dessert, she makes a special topping for vanilla ice cream while the casserole bakes. The entire meal, including setting the table, can be done in fifty minutes flat. If company cannot wait that long, then everyone drives to Oak Ridge for fast food.

Barbara doesn't entertain regularly, but when she gives a party for a large group and does the cooking herself, she again chooses a casserole and makes it with either chicken or turkey. The poultry can be cooked ahead and cut into small pieces. The vegetables — mushrooms, noodles, and green pepper — can also be chopped, ready to put into the casserole, which is prepared in layers. She doubles or triples the recipe as necessary and bakes it in two or three deep dishes. She serves a cauliflower salad with it, which she can make ahead. She also favors a tray of deviled eggs with sprigs of parsley and sweet pickles. Dessert is a Frozen Strawberry Delight, which she can prepare several days in advance.

To make cooking simpler and easier Barbara offers the following: "I try to find recipes that can be prepared ahead and frozen. It also works out well for me to make large amounts of chili, stew, spaghetti, and so forth, and serve them two or three times, alternating them with carry-out fast foods. My crock pot and microwave oven are a big help. Another trick that works for me is to cook the entire supper ahead on my day off.

I make round steak, mashed potatoes, gravy, and green peas; put the food in sectioned paper plates; and refrigerate or freeze it. When my twelve-year-old comes home from school and expects supper by five o'clock, and when my husband works the third shift, it helps to have food they can eat at any time. We put the made-ahead dinners in the microwave for two to three minutes, and we eat when we're ready."

Barbara recommends that working women who have to cook stay on the lookout for recipes that are low in calories yet delicious, pretty, and easy. If they lend themselves to the use of time-saving devices, such as a food processor, so much the faster.

Carol Kleiman
Journalist and Author
Columnist, "Women at Work," *Chicago Tribune*
Chicago, Illinois

Carol Kleiman is a writer. In addition to writing her nationally syndicated column, which deals with the issues of women in paid employment, she is a contributing editor to *MS.* magazine; she writes another column called "Tennis Everyone"; she is the author of two books, *You Can Teach Your Child Tennis* and *Women's Networks*; and she is on the national speaker's circuit. She has three children in college — a sophomore, a junior, and a senior — and all are in and out of the house, keeping Carol up on her homemaking skills.

Journalists are journalists seven days a week twenty-four hours a day; they work as much as the job requires. Carol lives in the suburbs and drives to and from her job in downtown Chicago. Besides commuting, she also has to travel on the job occasionally.

Although relatives do not come by for dinner unannounced, friends do stop without notice for meals at Carol's. She usually takes them out to one of her favorite pizza places, or else orders pizza, picks it up, and serves it at home. Otherwise she prepares some variation of chicken, which she always has on hand.

When she wants to fix an impressive dinner for just two, she broils strip steaks, bakes and stuffs potatoes, and makes a marvelous salad "with love and care." If her guest is a vegetarian, she fixes meatless lasagne and salad. For a dinner for six, she has a great baked steak recipe, though she says she needs "a loan from the bank these days for the 3½-inch-thick sirloin roast the recipe requires." Because of her demanding schedule, Carol says she doesn't cook for ten or more. Instead she hires a caterer, so that she can relax and enjoy her guests.

Carol says, "When all my kids were home and hungry, dinner each night was a challenge — it still is when they arrive for the holidays — because we all were on different schedules and had different appetites and tastes. For instance, Rob hates chicken, Cathy's lips will not touch meat, and Ray doesn't like fish. On holidays this means I have to make a turkey *and* a roast *and* a salad *and* vegetables. But one simple dish seems to satisfy them all, even Cathy who usually disdains meat: a London broil that's very tasty. I marinate flank steak in Italian (or low-calorie) salad dressing overnight, seasoning it with salt (optional), pepper and garlic. When I get home from work, I broil it and slice it diagonally. It's cheap, simple, and delicious."

Carol adds, "For woking women, organization in advance is essential for survival. Also, I'm willing to spend my very limited funds on anything that permits me to enjoy an occasion and relax. For example, this past Thanksgiving, with my three kids coming in on different planes, my having to work late and long hours, I hired a young woman to do my shopping and stuff the turkey and deliver it to me on Thursday morning ready to roast. The smell of food cooking is essential to holiday enjoyment, and to the house! The young woman also prepared sweet potato casserole, washed all the salad fixings, made a dip, baked a pecan pie, prepared the cranberries, and brought bread and rolls. I still had a ton of work to do — the gravy, the details, the turkey, organization — but I sat down and enjoyed Thanksgiving as a sane person. I enjoyed the occasion this time so tremendously that I did the same thing at Christmas!"

Jude Lujack
Photographic Model
Chicago, Illinois

Jude Lujack has been a photographic model for the last eighteen years and claims she is no more organized than she was the day she started. Her career includes just about every aspect of modeling: head to toe, commercial work, bit parts in movies, runaway modeling, conventions. Some assignments require location shots in other cities and states, so Jude occasionally has to travel. The work hours for a model are very erratic, and time at home cannot be planned well in advance. Sometimes Jude works on a daily basis, anywhere from one to eight hours a day; but occasionally she works only one hour a week.

Jude lives with her husband Larry and her son Taber, and drives to and from her modeling assignments. When she's working, the job must come first. Because of her crazy work schedule and her husband's even crazier schedule (he's the early-morning WLS-Chicago drive-time disc jockey), she's forced to prepare simple meals such as roasts, chicken, casseroles, and other things that can be saved and eaten the next day. She sometimes combines basic dishes with a couple of frozen side dishes so that the result looks as if she's slaved all day.

"I never make time-consuming gourmet meals," says Jude. "My idea of gourmet is a quiche and salad. Many nights when I race in at six-thirty or seven o'clock and my family looks at me as if to say, 'We're starving,' I make omelets, or soup and sandwiches, and they love it. I guess when you get that hungry, anything tastes great. Cooking isn't on my list of favorite things to do." But her family does enjoy her chicken salad and a special chicken casserole she calls Crunchy Chicken-and-Rice Bake.

Jude has a unique way of coping with unannounced dinner guests. She says, "As a rule, it's only one additional person, and I usually make up some excuse as to why I'm not eating. Then the guest eats my portion." Since Jude is a model, guests are likely to believe her.

Large parties are not the Lujacks' style of entertaining, but Jude favors a catered buffet for big parties, with a table decorated to look very pretty.

Jude has several tips for women coping with working and cooking: "My husband is interested in quantity not quality, so I can get away with just about anything. But if I couldn't, I would always make sure to defrost the meat portion before I left; then I'd wing it when I got home. Also, I'd make and freeze lasagne, spaghetti sauces, or something fancy or tasty like a frozen fruit and gelatin salad to add to a basically boring meal so that it would look as though I'd fussed. The easiest and simplest little extras can make you look like a hero — like making hot rolls, or blueberry muffins or putting chopped eggs in a salad, or serving deviled eggs (which are a real biggie at my house). Also, I could probably serve bird seed as long as I had a socko dessert. So zero in on your family's weakness. Make the meal interesting for them but easy on yourself."

Mary McFadden
Designer
President, Mary McFadden, Inc.
New York City

Mary McFadden is a nationally known designer of women's wear, fabrics, jewelry, and home furnishings. A very busy and creative woman, she lives in New York City with her child, and takes a taxi to and from work. She works seven days a week, and it is not unusual for her to work from nine in the morning until midnight. She also has to travel a lot.

Although friends and relatives do not come to dinner unannounced, Mary does entertain regularly. Cuisine for guests is distinctive, and it is the same, whether there are two guests or twenty-two. She always serves an elegant meal of cold foods, such as cold soup (always a green soup: asparagus, spinach, or lettuce); a selection of caviar (red, yellow, black, gray); smoked quail, cold poached salmon with green sauce; cucumber salad; raspberries with sour cream; and coffee. Mary uses design artistry in her meals as well as in her work.

When she fixes dinner for two for someone she really wants to impress, her menu consists of pâté, cold salmon, salad, fruit, champagne, white wine, and several cheeses.

Mary has specially selected the best places to buy the foods she serves. She orders caviar, cheese, fruit, and cold soups from Fraser-Morris on Madison Avenue. She thinks Macy's has the best pâtés. She orders her smoked meats from Broadbent's B & B Food Products, Route No. 1, Cadiz, Kentucky 42211. She can entertain quite easily even though she works many and long hours because she has an organized plan that works.

Suzanne S. McFarlane
Executive Assistant to Henry A. Kissinger
Washington, D.C.

Suzanne McFarlane says, "It's easier to describe what I don't do. I don't get involved in substantive issues of foreign policy. I don't write his books and articles, or handle Henry Kissinger's appointment schedule. I do just about everything else: arrange his speeches, public appearances, and travel; handle his personal and professional finances; oversee his investments, payroll, taxes, and Christmas card list; brief his lawyers and accountants; negotiate his fees and honoraria; walk his dog on occasion; handle his correspondence; coordinate security; talk endlessly to the captains and the kings; worry about everything and catch hell when something goes wrong." I've worked with Suzanne on occasion, and not only does she do all of these things, but she follows through to make sure that all is going right.

She lives alone and works an average of twelve hours a day five days a week. Suzanne has no husband. "I'm never home at mealtimes, which is probably why!"

She notes, "When cooking for myself, I am not averse to preparing a large amount of something really good and eating it all week. When I get home for dinner at ten o'clock, I'd much rather reheat a casserole or part of a chicken than eat a TV dinner. Chicken is the working woman's best friend. I can get four or five meals out of one, and when I finally grow tired of it, I can cut up what's left and freeze it for future use."

When Suzanne fixes an important dinner for two, she doesn't try to impress her guest. She just serves a perfect steak from the grill, broccoli or artichokes with hollandaise sauce, arrugala salad, and ice cream. She says, "It works!"

She adds, "In summer, when tomatoes, zucchini, and eggplant are fresh and plentiful, I fix a kind of ratatouille with hamburger and grated cheese on top, bake it in small casseroles, freeze it, and pull out servings for two whenever I need them."

For a large dinner for ten to twenty, she prepares a good, rather hot chicken curry (she makes her own curry powder) with at least twelve condiments, so that people can mix and match. She likes this meal because it's easy, she can make it days ahead of time, and people find it fun.

Suzanne says, "Even though I work long hours during the week, on as many summer Friday nights as possible, I fly up to my country house in East Hampton, Long Island. Friends and family usually make six to eight for dinner on Saturday. What we like best is a meal of very fresh bluefish fillets, local corn, and salad from the garden. To cook bluefish fillets, oil a broiling pan and put in two 12- to 18-inch fillets, skin side down. Coat the fillets lightly with mayonnaise. Add a little soy sauce, about ½ cup of white wine, and a light sprinkling of chopped fresh chives. Broil for about ten minutes — do not turn — until the fillets are lightly browned. Serve with sauce verte — green mayonnaise: to blender mayo recipe add green scallion tops, parsley, and fresh basil and blend."

Kathy Ann Mitchell
Assistant to Ann Landers
Chicago, Illinois

Kathy Ann Mitchell's job as assistant to Ann Landers includes handling the columnist's personal and business correspondence; setting up lectures, television appearances, and radio dates; and making all travel arrangements. Kathy also does research for the column and works on reader questions and booklet material. Some travel is involved but not mandatory. Kathy says she travels whenever she can conquer her fear of flying.

She usually works from 9:00 A.M. to 6:00 P.M. Monday through Friday. There are extra workdays — sometimes Saturdays and Sundays — depending on Ann's schedule. Kathy is fortunate that she lives close enough to her office so that she can walk to work.

Kathy, who is single, does not entertain regularly and does not have friends or relatives who stop by for dinner. However, when she does give a dinner for as many as ten to twenty people, she wants to spend as much time as possible with her guests, not running back and forth to the kitchen. So a dinner for a large crowd is usually spaghetti and meatballs with garlic bread, a large salad, and relish trays, and she prepares most of it ahead of time.

Kathy says, "When I want to fix a romantic dinner for two, the safest choice for me, since I do not cook frequently, is to have Cornish hens with dressing, cranberry salad, candied yams, ice cream torte, and Alka-Seltzer." She believes that the easiest and most interesting way for working women to cope with cooking is to "find a gem of a man, as I did, who is a gourmet cook."

Judith Ann Nielsen
Evening Supervisor, LifeLine
Rochester, New York

Judith Nielsen is an evening supervisor for the counseling staff of LifeLine, a twenty-four-hour telephone service in upstate New York, which handles suicides, medical emergencies, information and referrals, general counseling, and crisis intervention. It also provides backup phone service for other social service agenices in the evenings and on weekends. Judie's position is a job-sharing one, and she works from 5:00 P.M. to 1:00 A.M. The drives to her office at Strong Memorial Hospital in Rochester three evenings a week. Since Judie works outside her home only three evenings a week, it may seem that her life is not as pressured as that of many other working women. Not so.

She explains: "We now have sixteen children in our family. Our oldest daughter is twenty-two and our baby is three and a half. One daughter is married and living nearby. She works and attends college. Her husband also holds a full-time job and goes to school. We have two boys in college. All of our children attend school. Our little one, Joshua, goes to a half-day program for children who are developmentally behind.

"We have two sixteen-year-old girls in high school; three girls age thirteen and one boy age fourteen in junior high; one girl age thirteen in Rochester Christian School; two eleven-year-old boys; two ten-year-olds, a boy and a girl; one eight-year-old boy; and little Josh.

"Three of our children were born to us, the remaining have either been adopted by us or are in the process of being adopted. We are also foster parents for the State of New York Division for Youth.

"We live in a big old house that has almost six thousand square feet of floor space, so we are not cramped by any means. We are surrounded by three acres of land, which enables our kids to enjoy the outdoors. In the summer we plant a large garden and swim. In the winter we skate on our own pond and enjoy snowmobiling.

"My situation is probably different from that of other women in that I leave for work as my family is just beginning to settle down after a long day at work or school. My responsibility is to have a nice warm meal ready for them to eat while I am at my job. This takes planning!

"I usually begin the preparation for dinner around 3:00 P.M. while the children are coming home from school. This gives me a chance to be in the kitchen with them so they can tell me about their school day, and it also offers me an opportunity to involve them in the meal preparation. This is very important to me because I want them all — both boys and girls — to know how to cook and plan adequate meals.

"Because of the size of our family and the present price of meat, I try to plan two weeks in advance and gear my shopping to a specific list. I manage to organize my meals two weeks ahead of time and thus have to shop only every other week. I make use of coupons sent to me by people in other states who either read about us or saw us on television. In our area the supermarkets offer triple value for coupons, so I take advantage of this and shop accordingly. We buy our milk from the neighborhood dairy just down the road. I buy fifty loaves of bread at a time from a discount store, and we purchase a side of beef when we can save enough money to do so. Some staples I order by the carton from a friendly local store manager. These items can include things we use a lot such as applesauce, dog and cat food for our pets, tissues, and laundry products.

"When I cook, I plan on cooking for twenty. This way, if my daughter and her husband drop by, I have enough food. I also have my parents for dinner several times a week from May to October when they are living in the area.

"We also have what we call Anything Night, and that means you may cook anything (provided you check with Mom or Dad), that is easily available, such as eggs, French toast, pancakes, or frozen pizza. It is terrific. In fact, the kids ask to do this more than once a week. For our family it is good because it means all leftovers are used up and not thrown out or given to the animals. It also teaches the kids about cooking, about being on their own and depending on themselves for a meal instead of on Mom, and it teaches them about the basics of cooking. Because some of our kids have handicaps, this Anything Night is a valuable tool in teaching them about meals and the kitchen.

"We also have each one of the kids bake something during the week so that they all learn how to bake and know what goes into doing things from scratch instead of using a prepared mix. In the fall we pick apples from a friend's orchard, and we usually have kids experimenting with apple recipes for the next two months.

"I rely on my crock pot quite a bit, and use it weekly. I can start a meal at 8:00 A.M., and it is ready for my family at 6:00 P.M. If it is a night when I have to go to work and the older kids who have jobs are coming home at different hours, I plan to use the crock pot. This means there is a good, warm meal waiting for late-comers.

"I also cook ahead and have extra meals in the freezer, and cook for more than my family members, so I always have extra portions. When I cook lasagne, meat loaf, chili, and homemade soups, I double what I am making and freeze an extra dish. In this way I am prepared if unexpected company arrives. I am also ready for that evening when I just don't feel like spending any time in the kitchen.

"My favorite recipe is Pork Chops Supreme. For this recipe, I can use my crock pot or a large casserole dish. I wait until pork chops are on sale and then buy around twenty chops. Pork steaks can also be used in this recipe. With this meal, I like to make a green bean vegetable dish. Then I add rice covered with gravy from the pork chops, and I make a green salad to round out the meal.

"We have discovered tofu, and our kids are crazy about it. Dishes using it can be made in advance, frozen, and heated when needed. Tofu can be found in the natural health food section of the grocery store. Some favorites are Tofu Lasagne, Tofu Meatballs, Zucchini and Tofu, Tofu and Broccoli, Tofu with Vegetables and Rice, and Tofu and Eggs. Another trick works well for us: sometimes when all the children are in school, I will take an entire morning to prepare three or four main dishes and freeze them. Then if I have a week where the kids are sick and I am extra tired, I can still serve good, nourishing meals from the freezer."

Susan O'Connell
Travel Agent
Hubbard Woods Travel
Winnetka, Illinois

Susan O'Connell is married, has two daughters, and works as a travel agent in Winnetka, Illinois. She plans and arranges business and vacation trips. Her job also requires her to do some traveling. She works at the office on Monday, Wednesday, and Friday. Because she lives close to the office, however, she often runs in on her days off to change arrangements for someone who has a last-minute emergency. Since she also takes calls at home, it is misleading to say she works only part-time. Being a travel agent means making not only airline arrangements but reservations for car rentals, hotel accommodations, limousines, restaurants, and entertainment. Susan can arrange every moment of your trip, from the time you leave your office or home until you return. One of her biggest worries is that while a tour group of twenty-two people is visiting a foreign country, the airline on which they are scheduled to return will suddenly go on strike. That's the kind of event that sends her to the office on her day off.

Susan entertains regularly, and friends frequently stop by for meals unannounced. Susan says, "When friends stop by, I have no standard emergency method of cooking. Depending on the entrée, I will attempt to stretch a meal with additional side dishes or a dessert. Then I hope the unexpected guest isn't terribly hungry."

"When I'm planning a dinner or a party for fifteen or twenty people, experience and neurosis have taught me to prepare and serve two entrées such as poultry and beef, or ham and turkey." The variety is valuable if a guest doesn't like one or the other, and it's insurance in case one entrée doesn't turn out right.

When company is coming and Susan is busy, her favorite menu is Company Chicken, Broccoli Casserole, Waldorf Salad, and a dessert.

This meal has everything — color, texture, nutrition, and great taste — and it is easy to prepare.

Susan offers the following suggestion for dinner guest emergencies: "One night my husband brought someone home for dinner when all I was planning was a very simple pork chop dinner. I always love the large cold relish trays that restaurants serve before and with the meal. So when Dennis walked in with a guest, I thought of that. I have a very large lazy susan that works nicely for a colorful array of cold vegetables. It's like a small salad bar; placed in the center of the table it gives a festive look. I actually use this in place of a salad. If you don't have a large lazy susan, a long tray or two or three smaller ones will do. Serve anything cold you have in the cupboard or refrigerator. I always have a few canned items on the shelf. For instance, my lazy susan might include an assortment of the following: green and black olives, three-bean salad, smoked oysters, sardines, corn relish, cottage cheese with chives, marinated artichokes, pickled beets, celery sticks stuffed with sour cream and chopped onions and olives, cauliflower flowerets, and liver pâté. There is something for everyone on a tray like this. It fancies up any plain meal and also goes well with a simple backyard barbecue of hot dogs and hamburgers on a hot evening.

Patricia A. Straus
Assistant to the Director, Radio/TV Publicity
Time, Inc.
New York City

Patricia Straus does radio and television publicity for *Time, People, Life, Money, Fortune,* and *Discover* magazines. She keeps radio and television producers and show hosts supplied with materials and apprised of information that might be of interest on their upcoming programs. If a person featured in an upcoming issue is available for an interview, Patti can work as a liaison between that person and a particular television or radio show. She is interested in talking to anyone who can publicize Time, Inc.'s magazines in person or in a movie, on a television or radio show, in the print media, and so forth. Patti may also be called on to work with Time, Inc. reporters and the people featured in their articles. Her job can be glamorous or tedious, depending on the day of the week or the article she is publicizing. She works forty-plus hours a week, Monday through Friday, but travels very little. However, she does occasionally have to work at public relations parties given by Time, Inc., in New York and in other major cities around the country.

Patti is single, lives in Manhattan, and walks to work. She does not entertain regularly, but friends (not relatives) do drop in unannounced. Patti says that her refrigerator is half-size, so she never keeps much food on hand. Unexpected guests can be assured of plenty of drinks (always on hand in large quantities) and hors d'oeuvres, both hot and cold, until she can have the next course delivered from a local Chinese restaurant or pizza parlor.

When she serves elegant dinners for two, she chooses one of her favorite dishes: scampi, veal marsala, lamb chops, or a small roast. She tops off her meal with a dessert such as cherry cheese cake, which is simple to prepare but impressive to look at. With a terrific entrée and gorgeous dessert, anything in between is secondary anyway.

Patti says, "I have a couple of favorite casserole dishes, and when I cook for ten to twenty people, I make one of them. They can be prepared in advance, and all you need to serve with them is garlic bread and a hearty salad. When the day of the party arrives, if I've had a particularly hectic day at the office, I don't have to worry about food. It's basically ready, and I can enjoy the party and my guests."

She adds, "When I know guests are coming, I try to do as much as possible the night before: I set the table, fix hors d'oeuvres, clean and cut up the vegetables. I also try to serve a favorite recipe of mine, such as Chicken Paprika, Scampi, or Chicken Baked in Sour Cream. I don't think you should try to fix an exotic new dish for guests and feel pressured, worrying about how it's going to come out. Something can always go wrong in cooking. That happens to the best of cooks. So I often use sherry, port, or another wine in my cooking; it can disguise any mistakes."

Angie Urbano
Promotions Coordinator, *Rebate Ramble*
Wilmette, Illinois

Angie Urbano explains, "It's my job to alert people to the service provided by *Rebate Ramble*, a monthly refunding newsletter, through television, radio, and print media. I act as liaison between *Rebate Ramble* and grocery and personal products manufacturers insofar as the various refund offers are concerned. Refunds or rebates are not limited to foods. They are now being offered on clothing, furniture, large and small appliances, car maintenance, and even cars in some cases. Almost every aspect of your life may have a refund involved.

"I usually work around five hours per day, seven days per week. Although I work from my home primarily, I also travel, either by car or plane. My other job is being a homemaker for my husband and two children, a boy and a girl.

"I do not entertain regularly, and friends and relatives do not stop by unannounced. If they did, they would have to take pot luck on whatever I could defrost from the freezer in the microwave. My husband rarely brings business associates home to dinner, so I am fortunate not to have to worry about that, either.

"If I were planning dinner for ten to twenty guests, I would make two easy-to-slice meats, such as a beef roast and a boneless turkey roll, which could be prepared ahead, sliced, and then nicely arranged for serving at the proper time. Such a large crowd would definitely have to be served buffet style at our house, so the meats would be accompanied by made-ahead salads and relishes. Then I might add my old family favorite recipe for dessert, an easy cheese cake that came from one of the Chicago newspapers around twenty years ago; it's been a favorite and a big hit with all our guests since we first found it.

"Anyone who works knows time is at a premium. This includes those who work away from home as well as those who work from home. The most helpful thing I have learned through my work with refunds and coupons is that organization is absolutely necessary.

"I plan my menus for the week to come by checking each Thursday's food guide. My grocery list is planned accordingly; I pull out my coupons, which correspond to those items on sale. The advance menu planning means that I'm never out of some important ingredient when I cook. It also helps cut down on needless runs to the store for 'just a few things.'

"I apply the same plan-ahead principle to company entertaining. When we decide to throw our big July 4 or New Year's party, I begin way ahead of time to watch the papers like a hawk for sales on soda, buns, chips, and other extras that can cost a lot if you don't look for special prices and coupons. I've found that the grocery industry has its cyclical sales just as department stores do with 'white sales' in January and July, and that's when I shop."

Cindy Lee Walker
Television Career Woman
Program Manager, WBBM-TV (CBS)
Chicago, Illinois

Cindy Lee Walker is a single mother with two children — Tracey and Mark. She lives in Chicago and commutes to work (about 30 minutes each way) by cab or subway. She is responsible for the total on-air look of the TV station and for the selection and placement of all syndicated and locally produced programs. The local producers and the entire production staff along with the members of the film department report to her. Her hours can go from 8:00 A.M. to 9:00 P.M. Monday through Friday; she has to cover any program emergency, whenever it may occur, any day or evening of the week.

Although relatives do not stop by for meals unannounced, friends do; and Cindy enjoys entertaining regularly. She says, "I love to have people in because I'm from a large family. So when I cook I tend to over-cook. I always have enough food for an extra person or two, so drop-in guests are no problem. In general, I entertain at Sunday brunch or any-time on weekends.

"Weekdays are a different story. On Sundays I plan the menu for the week based on my schedule and the kids' activities. I chart out days we'll be in and evenings I work late. On the evenings I work late, I plan TV dinners or something precooked that my kids can pop in the oven. For evenings when I have time to prepare dinner, I plan quiche or warm up casseroles or meals I cooked on Sunday.

"I cook casseroles or the like on Sunday for use as needed during the week. This means less time in the kitchen after work and more time for relaxing with the kids.

"The key is planning. It only takes me one-half hour at most to schedule my meals for the week; once I've done that, grocery shopping is simpler and my weekday schedule less hectic."

When Cindy wants to impress a guest with an intimate dinner for two, her three favorites entrées are Cornish hens (with sausage, wild rice stuffing, and asparagus with hollandaise sauce), seafood quiche, and stuffed pork chops. She rarely cooks for groups as large as ten to twenty, but when she does, she lays out a buffet with a large ham, roast turkey for slicing, salad, breads, cheeses, wines, and a fruit salad. A shepherd's pie from an old family recipe is her favorite dish when she needs some-thing easy.

8

Stocking Up

Everything you need to implement the McMillen Method is described in the following section:

1. Appliances
2. Cooking Utensils
3. How to Stock Your Kitchen Shelves
4. How to Stock a Bar

Appliances

You need only two appliances to start cooking ahead: your refrigerator and your stove — the one for cooking, the other for freezing. After that, the question of appliances is up to you.

Although it may seem at first that you need to buy a freezer to make this plan work, actually you don't. The trick is to use your freezer space efficiently, as I noted in Chapter 3. Just throwing things in any old way wastes space. But if you store foods in flat trays and keep them in organized groups, you'll find that your capacity is adequate.

Once you get used to cooking ahead and learn to adapt it to your life, you can always consider investing in an extra freezer. I can imagine that if you cook ahead in large quantities, if you have a large family or buy meat in quantity, you may eventually want to supplement your freezer room. Two years ago, I finally bought a very small freezer. I find it helpful, but it is not necessary. I followed the plan for three years without it.

The same is true of a microwave oven: it is helpful, but not necessary to make the plan work. Again, I cooked ahead for a long time before I bought one. (I thought speed of cooking would ruin quality, that a good cook wouldn't be caught dead using such a fast method. I was wrong!) The primary advantage of a microwave oven to this plan is the speed with which you can heat a frozen meal that you prepared ahead of time. If in the morning you forget to thaw food for dinner, a microwave will enable you to serve dinner in a short time. Again, that's helpful, but not necessary.

Crock pots, blenders, and food processors are great time-savers. If you already own one or all of these appliances, you'll find that using them speeds things up. A crock pot will enable you to cook a roast or a stew while you are using your oven and the top of your stove. It provides an extra source of cooking heat. A blender or a food processor will speed up preparation time. (If you decide to buy a blender or a food processor, research carefully what each can do; their functions overlap.)

Finally, if you live in the country or anywhere that permits you to cook outdoors, remember that a barbecue grill is another source of cooking heat to supplement your stove; it can become a valuable part of a cooking session. You needn't buy an expensive one to get the benefit, either.

SMALL APPLIANCES

Toaster	Seal-a-Meal
Electric hand mixer	Spatter-free rotisserie*
Heavy-duty electric mixer	Toaster oven*
Coffeemaker	French fryer
Blender	Wok
Food processor	Ice crusher*
Electric can opener	Crepe pan
Electric knife*	Microwave oven*
Crock pot	Convection oven*
Fondue pot	Waffle iron
Electric skillet	Hot-air corn popper*

Cooking Utensils

Almost every woman already owns some of the items needed to start cooking ahead. If you accumulate too many gadgets, appliances,

*Luxury Items

tools, and cooking utensils, you will find that they just get in your way. At the end of this section, I'll give you a list of the most helpful items to get you started, whether you are setting up a kitchen from scratch or just adding to your equipment.

Some extremely helpful cooking utensils are inexpensive. Others are very expensive. If you can't afford all the equipment you'd like to have, make a list, putting the items in order of need — what you need most first, and so forth. Carry it in your purse. If you see a kitchenware sale, the list will help you decide what to buy; it will also deter you from the impulse purchases we all are tempted to make, thus helping you avoid clutter in the kitchen. When your mother asks you what you want for a gift, you will be ready to tell her exactly what you need. Kitchen items are easier for someone else to buy for you than personal things like clothes are.

One way to save money is to buy things like large, expensive roasting pans or very large cooking pots at house sales or auctions. The larger the pot, the less it has probably been used, because most people don't cook regularly in large quantities. Used iron skillets and pots are especially desirable because they are already seasoned, so food won't stick in them. It can be very frustrating to try to cook in a new iron skillet. Used items may not be as shiny as brand-new ones, but remember that the shine you pay for dulls with time.

I also recommend owning a granite pot. At a bargain store, for $11.98, I bought a new twelve-quart porcelainware pot and lid to use when I make chili. I've since used it for stew, chicken, vegetable soup, punch, potato salad, corn on the cob, and other things. It is also an all-in-one item: you can cook, refrigerate, heat, and serve in it without fear of contaminating the food. You save time and energy when you don't have to transfer food from one utensil to another. For a country supper, you can just tie a red workman's hanky on each handle of a large granite pot and serve directly from it. It will look decorative and be in key with the food. (One warning: if you beat a granite pot too hard with a spoon, the pot will chip. However, you really shouldn't pound the edges of any pot.)

Cooking and Baking Utensils

Pressure cooker	Large roasting pan
Egg poacher	Dutch oven
Double boiler	Cast-iron kettle

Cast-iron skillet
Large cooking pot (10 to 12 quart)
Large frying pan (12 to 14 inches in diameter)
Baking sheet (nonstick saves time)
Cupcake pan
Jelly roll pan (doubles as baking sheet)

Pizza pans (2 sizes)
Oblong cake pan
Square cake pans (2)
Round cake pans (2)
Pie pans (2 glass, 2 metal)
Griddle pan
Bundt cake pan
Loaf pan

SERVING PIECES

Chafing dish (1 or more)
Hot tray
Wine carafe
Wine caddy
Oblong platters (2 large, 1 small)
Large salad bowl and individual salad dishes (12)
Salad serving tongs (glass or wood)
Small glass fruit bowls (12)
Parfait glasses (12)
Large balloon-style wineglasses (12), for wine, dessert, or salads
Egg cups (12)
Wineglasses (fancy, for champagne or other special beverages)
Ice bucket and ice tongs
Corn-on-the-cob dishes and holders

Trivets (3 or more)
Baskets for bread, rolls, snacks, and fruit
Lazy Susan (for appetizers or hors d'oeuvres)
Steak knives
Grapefruit spoons
Clear glass pitcher
Coffee carafe
Cake saver
Serving trays (1 large plain, 1 small fancy)
Large flat glass platter (for parties or entertaining dinner guests)
Meat platters (2 or 3. Larger sizes are better. Use also to present two or three vegetables to dinner guests. Meat and vegetables can be served on the same platter if it's big enough.)

Small Kitchen Utensils

Double-prong long-handled forks (2)
Wire whisks (various sizes)
Wooden long-handled spoons (3)
Pastry blender
Measuring spoons
Measuring cups (1 nesting set, 2 two-cup, 2 one-cup)
Kitchen shears
Strainers (1 large, and 1 small)
Colander
Vegetable brush
Vegetable peeler (all metal)
Rubber scraper (1 wide, 1 narrow)
Cutting board
Paring knives (2)
Butcher knives (2)
Cake knife
Tongs
Baster (suction type)
Rolling pin
Meat mallet (wood or metal)
Ice cream dipper
Melon baller
Butter baller
Spatulas (2)
Tomato slicer
Slotted spoon
Long-handled dippers or soup ladles (2)
Pizza cutter
Egg slicer

Egg quarterer
Meat thermometer
Candy thermometer
Pastry brushes (2)
Pastry decorating set
Cheese slicer
Garlic press
Rotary hand beater (the type that fits in a bowl if possible)
Strawberry stemmer
Corkscrew
Nutcracker
Hand food or nut grinder/chopper (if you do not have a blender or food processor
Powdered sugar shaker
Cinnamon and sugar shaker
Kitchen scale
Flour sifter
Cookie and doughnut cutters
Hand juicer
Mixing bowls (graduated sizes)
Funnels (large and small neck)
Timer
Hand grater or slaw maker
Plastic pitchers (2)
Plastic bowl covers
Egg separator (optional)
Pasta measure (optional)
1-cup saucepan (optional)
Potato nest maker (optional)

How to Stock Your Shelves, or Where's the Pantry?

Years ago kitchens were usually adjoined by pantries in which food and kitchen items were stored. With the advent of modern, smaller homes and streamlined apartments, the pantry disappeared, probably because most architects and builders were men who didn't realize what a wonderful asset a pantry was. If you aren't fortunate enough to have a pantry, set aside space somewhere in or near your kitchen in which to store extra canned and boxed grocery items. A small closet or one or two sections of your cupboard will do nicely.

A single person can usually get by without stocking the cupboard very much. However, if you feed two or more people, it is wise to keep a good supply of basics on hand. When you get organized enough to start using meal plans regularly, you'll find that you can eliminate such items as flour, salt, vinegar, chocolate, coffee, and butter from your market order for a particular meal, because you'll already have them on hand.

If you haven't stocked your shelves before, start now. Buy three to five extra items a week, or more if you can afford them. Don't try to buy everything in one week or you'll drain the food budget. When you stock up on staples, do not overstock on such things as flour or flour-based items, becuase they will get stale if not used quickly enough. Check the usage date on all products. Cake mixes or other boxed foods, if not used within a year, are usually not good.

Put foods on your shelves in an organized manner. I keep like items together: all cans of corn stacked on top of and beside each other; all cans of peas, beans, tomatoes, and carrots grouped similarly. On another shelf, I do the same with fruits. All the boxed products are together on my shelves, but sorted according to type — like items together. I use one shelf for miscellaneous items. This enables me to see at a glance which items are getting low.

Be sure to rotate your stock. When you add new stock, put it at the back of the group it belongs to, not in the front. That way, old items will be used first. If you don't do this, you'll find that you tend to grab for the closest box or can in a group, while the older one you should be using escapes your hand, only to sit on the shelf till it spoils. Be sure to use both canned and boxed goods by the suggested date.

CUPBOARD SHELF ITEMS

Cereals (dry, cooked)

Crackers (saltines, round, graham, mixed fancy)

Bouillon granules (chicken, beef)

Extracts (vanilla, almond, coconut)

Lemon juice

Lime juice

Vinegar

Soy sauce

Steak sauce

Worcestershire sauce

Tabasco sauce

Corn syrup (light)

Cornstarch

Baking powder

Baking soda

Baking chocolate

Cocoa

Spaghetti (dry)

Macaroni (dry)

Pasta shells

Pasta noodles (various widths)

Sugar (light brown, granulated, confectioner's)

Rice (instant, converted, long-grain, brown, mixed)

Raisins (white, dark)

Maraschino cherries

Cupcake liners

Toothpicks

Stuffing mix

Cinnamon sugar

Powdered orange drink mix

Hot chocolate mix

Instant coffee

Regular coffee

Tea (regular, herbal)

Artificial sweetener

Powdered milk

Honey

Cultured buttermilk powder

Peanut butter

Coconut (flaked or shredded)

Chocolate chips

Peanut butter chips (optional)

Instant tea

Oven-fry coating mix

Cornmeal

Pancake mix

Pancake syrup

Dry mashed potatoes

Olive oil

Cooking oil

Solid shortening

Snacks (chips, canned peanuts, pretzels, corn chips, popcorn, etc.)

Bread

Marshmallows

Tart shells

Dry chow mein noodles

Canned hard candy

Prepared piecrusts

Zip-lock freezer bags (large, small)

Waxed paper

Plastic wrap

Aluminum Foil

Paper plates

Napkins

SEASONINGS PACKETS

Spaghetti sauce with mushrooms	Omelet
Taco	Sour cream
Cheese	Chip dips
Hollandaise	Gravies
Meat loaf	Meat marinade
Chili	Dry soups
French toast	Plain gelatin (unflavored)
Sloppy Joes	Salad dressing mixes

SPICES

Allspice	Ground nutmeg
Basil	Italian seasoning
Bay leaves	Onion salt
Black pepper	Oregano
Cayenne (red) pepper	Paprika
Celery flakes	Parsley flakes
Celery seed	Pumpkin pie spice
Chili powder	Rosemary leaves
Chopped chives	Sage
Cinnamon	Salt
Cinnamon sticks	Seasoned salt
Cream of tartar	Sesame seeds
Dillweed	Tarragon leaves
Dry mustard	Thyme
Garlic powder	White pepper

CANNED OR BOXED GOODS

If you're starting from scratch, buy a few of the following items to establish your stock.

When there is more than one type or flavor, buy your favorite first; then add to your stock with other favorites.

Canned pie filling	Canned mushrooms
Canned fruit (2 or 3 cans)	Canned meat (1 or 2 kinds)
Canned vegetables plus pork	Soups (2 or 3 cans)
and beans, sauerkraut,	Cake mixes
whole tomatoes, tomato juice,	Prepared icing
tomato sauce	

Piecrust mix (if you don't make
   your own crusts)
Brownie mix
Cookie mix

Puddings
Flavored gelatin
Macaroni and cheese (boxed)
Scalloped potatoes

REFRIGATOR STAPLES

Yellow mustard
Ketchup
Pickles (sweet, dill, relish)
Chocolate syrup
Cheeses
Link salami
Milk
Eggs
Soft drinks
Beer
Butter and/or margarine
Dijon-style mustard
Salad dressing
Tartar sauce

Shrimp sauce
Steak sauce
Jams, jellies, preserves
Canned biscuits
Parmesan cheese, grated
Canned ham
Mayonnaise
Slaw dressing
Lemons and/or limes (optional)
Head lettuce
Tomatoes
Celery
Carrots
Canned coffee

FREEZER STAPLES

Coffee cakes
Frozen cakes
Frozen meats
Made-ahead entrées
Cookies
Homemade biscuits
Rice
Piecrusts
Blueberries
Strawberries
Orange juice
Lemonade

Limeade
Popcorn (unpopped)
Raspberries
Yogurt (plain, fruit)
Bread, buns, rolls
Sweet rolls
Purchased entrées
Purchased vegetables and side
   dishes
Butter or margarine
Homemade egg noodles

PANTRY SHELF ITEMS

Milk (evaporated, condensed)
Pickles (dill, sweet)
Barbecue sauce
Dijon-style mustard
Salad dressings (French,
  Thousand Island, Italian)
Pizza mix

Taco shells
Canned nuts
Fruit drinks
Soft drinks
Tonic and soda water
Ketchup

Canned pie fillings (blueberry, cherry, apple, pineapple)
Canned fruits (peach slices and halves, mixed fruit, fruit cocktail, plums, cherries [red, white, and dark], apricots, pineapple [crushed, rings, and chunks], mandarin oranges)
Canned vegetables (artichoke hearts, 3-bean salad, string beans, pork and beans, green peas, spinach, sauerkraut, corn [whole kernel and creamed], beets [whole, sliced, and Harvard], tomatoes [whole, stewed, crushed, sauce, puree, paste, and juice], vegetable juice, carrots [small whole, sliced, and diced], white potatoes [whole and sliced], sweet potatoes, asparagus, small whole onions)
Miscellaneous (mushrooms [whole, sliced, and pieces], pizza sauces, barbecue sauce, tuna, chicken [white meat], Vienna sausages, jelly [strawberry, cherry, grape, orange marmalade], chicken broth, beef broth, soups [vegetable, cream of chicken, cream of mushroom, cream of celery, tomato, chicken noodle, Cheddar cheese, split pea, bean with bacon, and your favorites], cake mixes, icing [mixes and canned], puddings [instant and regular], canned breads [Boston brown, nut, etc.], canned cake, scalloped potatoes [boxed], piecrust mix, corn bread mix, bran muffin mix, blueberry muffin mix, macaroni and cheese mix, brownie mix, pound cake mix)

How to Stock Your Bar

A well-stocked bar depends entirely on your individual needs and desires. Some people don't care to keep a bar. However, if you like to have drinks on hand for your guests, let me suggest some supplies.

Vodka
Scotch
Bourbon
Gin
Tequila

Brandy
Liqueurs
White wines
Red wines
Champagne

Beer (in refrigerator)
Orange juice
Tomato juice
Club soda
Tonic water

Soft drinks
Limes
Lemons
Maraschino cherries

You can add to your bar stock as you desire, but what I've listed will get you by nicely.

You also should take into consideration where your bar will be. If it is on one of your cupboard shelves, you'll need to keep it rather small. If you have a built-in bar, obviously you'll be able to carry a much larger supply and variety. I was stuck for a while as to where to put my bar supplies. I didn't want to take up valuable cupboard shelf space, and I finally came up with the idea to put it on a three-shelf serving cart on rollers. It works quite nicely and can be moved from room to room. I've seen bars in antique cupboards, on bookshelves, in dry sinks, and in credenzas. Be creative. Nothing says you have to have a bar to have a bar.

BAR TOOLS

Jiggers
Ice bucket
Ice tongs
Corkscrew
Bottle opener
Stirrers

Cocktail napkins
Coasters
Ice crusher
Strainer
Cocktail shaker

BAR GLASSES

White wine
Champagne or tulip
Bowl-style red wine
Cordial
Brandy

Old-fashioned
Highball
Beer mugs
Irish coffee cups

9

Recipes

Soups

CREAM OF ASPARAGUS SOUP

4 to 6 Servings

1   16-ounce can asparagus
    spears, drained
2   tablespoons butter
2   tablespoons all-purpose
    flour
½   teaspoon salt

Pinch of ground nutmeg
Pinch of black pepper
4   cups hot milk
    Toasted bread cubes for
    garnish

1. Cut the tips from the asparagus spears and set them aside. Rub the asparagus spears through a sieve or pass them through a food mill and set the puree aside.

2. Melt the butter in a heavy saucepan. When the butter is bubbling, blend in the flour, salt, pepper, and nutmeg. Add the reserved asparagus puree and hot milk and cook, stirring constantly, for 2 or 3 minutes, or until the mixture comes to a boil. Add the reserved asparagus tips. Serve hot or cold garnished with the bread cubes.

CREAMY BROCCOLI SOUP

8 Servings
Freezes Well

2   13¾-ounce cans chicken
    broth
2   pounds fresh broccoli,
    stalks trimmed and
    scraped
3   cups milk
1   cup finely diced ham
1   teaspoon salt

    Pinch of onion salt
¼   teaspoon black pepper
¼   teaspoon dried thyme
1   cup half-and-half
½   pound Swiss cheese,
    shredded
¼   cup butter or margarine,
    softened

1. Put the chicken broth and broccoli into a large saucepan. Bring to a boil and cook for 7 to 8 minutes, or until the broccoli is tender.

2. Strain the broth into another saucepan. Puree the broccoli in a blender or food processor and set aside.

3. Add the milk, ham, salt, onion salt, and pepper to the broth. Bring to a boil, lower the heat, and simmer for 5 minutes. Stir in the remaining ingredients and the reserved broccoli puree. Cook until just heated through, but do not boil. Serve hot or cold.

CREAM OF CAULIFLOWER SOUP   6 to 8 Servings

1	head cauliflower, broken into flowerets	2	cups milk
4	tablespoons butter or margarine		Pinch of white pepper
¼	cup chopped onion	1	teaspoon salt (if chicken broth is unsalted)
4	tablespoons all-purpose flour	4	ounces processed American cheese, shredded
3	cups chicken broth		Snipped chives or minced parsley for garnish

1. Put the cauliflower in a saucepan. Add 1 cup of water and bring to a boil. Cover and cook for 10 to 15 minutes, or until the cauliflower is tender. Drain well and chop the cauliflower. Set aside.

2. Melt the butter in a saucepan. When it is bubbling, add the onion and sauté until tender. Sprinkle the flour over the onion and mix well. Stir in the broth, milk, pepper, and salt, if needed. Cook, stirring constantly, until the mixture is slightly thickened. Add the cauliflower. Bring to a boil and fold in the cheese. Cook over low heat, stirring constantly, until the cheese has melted. Serve garnished with the chives or parsley.

CREAM OF SPINACH SOUP   6 Servings
                                                    Freezes Well

1	cup cooked spinach, squeezed dry	3	tablespoons butter or margarine
2	cups milk	3	tablespoons all-purpose flour
1	teaspoon parsley flakes		
1	teaspoon minced onion	1	teaspoon salt
1	bay leaf, optional		Pinch of black pepper
		½	cup half-and-half

1. Chop the spinach by hand or in a blender. Set aside until needed.

2. Combine the milk, parsley flakes, onion, and bay leaf in a saucepan and bring to a boil.

3. Melt the butter in another saucepan and add the flour, salt, and pepper. Stir to combine well. Remove the bay leaf from the milk mixture and stir the milk mixture gradually into the butter-flour mixture. Bring to a boil and then simmer, stirring constantly, for 3 to 5 minutes.

4. Add the spinach and half-and-half and heat just to the boiling point.

GAZPACHO   6 to 8 Servings

1 large zucchini, scrubbed, trimmed, and coarsely chopped	½ teaspoon minced garlic
	4½ cups tomato juice, or 2 cups tomato juice and 2½ cups chicken broth
1 medium-sized cucumber, scrubbed, trimmed, and coarsely chopped	4 tablespoons red wine vinegar
1 green pepper, washed, seeded, and coarsely chopped	2 teaspoons garlic salt
	4 tablespoons olive oil
	¼ teaspoon Tabasco sauce
1 medium-sized onion, peeled and coarsely chopped	4 slices crustless French bread, cut into small pieces
4 medium-sized tomatoes, peeled, seeded, and coarsely chopped	Thin cucumber slices for garnish

1. Combine all the ingredients, except the bread and thin cucumber slices, in a large bowl. Cover and refrigerate for 1 to 2 hours.

2. Pour 2 cups of the chilled soup mixture into the container of a blender. Add the bread pieces and blend until smooth. Stir the puree into the chunky soup mixture, cover, and refrigerate for at least 1 hour longer. Serve cold garnished with the thin cucumber slices.

Note: If you have any leftover cooked fresh corn, you can cut it off the cob and add it to the soup in step 1.

FRENCH ONION SOUP 8 Servings

8	onions, peeled and sliced	⅛	teaspoon black pepper
3	tablespoons butter or margarine	8	slices French bread, cut ¾ inch thick
3	10½-ounce cans condensed beef broth	8	ounces Swiss cheese, shredded
2	cups dry sherry	½	cup grated Parmesan cheese
1	bay leaf		

1. Put the onions and butter into a large saucepan. Cover and cook, stirring occasionally, for 20 to 25 minutes, or until the onions are tender but not browned. Add the broth, sherry, bay leaf, and pepper. Bring to a boil, cover, and simmer for 20 minutes.

2. Toast the bread slices under the broiler and put 1 slice in each of 8 ovenproof bowls. Put the bowls on a baking sheet.

3. Pour equal amounts of the soup into each bowl. Sprinkle an equal amount of Swiss cheese over each portion. Then sprinkle on the Parmesan. Place the bowls of soup under the broiler for 1 or 2 minutes, or until the cheese has melted. This will not take very long, so watch carefully.

SPLIT PEA SOUP 6 Servings
Freezes Well

2	cups split peas	1	cup milk
6	cups water or broth	1	teaspoon salt
2	carrots, finely shredded	⅛	teaspoon black pepper
½	cup chopped onion		Butter-toasted croutons for garnish
1½	cups chopped smoked ham		

1. Pick over the peas to remove any stones. Wash the peas well and put them in a 3-quart saucepan. Add the water, carrots, onion, and ham. Bring to a boil, then simmer over low heat for 1 to 1½ hours, stirring occasionally with a wooden spoon to prevent sticking.

2. Remove the chopped ham from the cooked peas and set it aside. Pour the soup into a blender or food processor and puree. Return to the saucepan and add the reserved ham. Add the milk and salt and pepper to taste. Simmer for 20 to 30 minutes longer. Serve the soup garnished with the croutons.

MINESTRONE

6 to 8 Servings
Freezes Well

1 28-ounce can tomatoes with liquid
1 6-ounce can tomato juice
1 13¾-ounce can chicken broth
1 6-ounce package minestrone soup mix
2 to 3 tablespoons chopped onion
1 8-ounce can white beans, drained
1 cup frozen peas and carrots
1 cup frozen string beans
1 celery stalk, chopped
1 cup finely chopped washed spinach, optional
1 or 2 medium-sized potatoes, peeled and diced
1 tablespoon dried chopped parsley
   Salt and black pepper to taste
1 teaspoon sugar
1 tablespoon grated Parmesan cheese
1 to 2 cups water
1 cup thin spaghetti broken into short lengths

1. Chop the tomatoes and put them with their liquid into a large soup pot. Bring to a boil and add all the remaining ingredients except the water and spaghetti. Add enough water to give the soup the consistency you like. Bring to a boil again, reduce the heat, and simmer, stirring occasionally for about 20 minutes. (You can add more water during this time if you think it is necessary.)

2. Slowly add the spaghetti to the boiling soup and cook for about 10 minutes, or until the spaghetti is tender. Stir the soup occasionally so that the spaghetti doesn't stick to the bottom of the pot or lump together.

Note: You can vary the ingredients to suit your own taste. For example, you can add chopped zucchini or omit the minestrone soup mix.

CHICKEN SOUP

6 to 8 Servings
Freezes Well

2 whole chickens, or 8 chicken quarters, washed
6 cups cold water
1 teaspoon salt
   Black pepper to taste
4 celery stalks, sliced diagonally
4 carrots, sliced diagonally
1 small onion, peeled and chopped
1 cup barley or rice
   (or 6 to 8 small matzo balls)
3 to 4 dashes of Tabasco sauce

1. Put the chickens, water, salt, and pepper in a large pot. Bring to a boil slowly, skimming off any scum that rises to the surface. Cover, lower the heat, and cook for 20 to 30 minutes, or until the chicken is tender. Remove the chickens and set them aside until cool enough to handle.

2. Add the celery, carrots, onion, and barley to the chicken stock. Cook over low heat until the barley is tender.

3. Meanwhile, skin and bone the chicken. Discard the skin and bones and cut the chicken into rather large chunks.

4. Return the chicken to the soup and add the Tabasco. Cook over low heat for 20 to 30 minutes longer.

FAVORITE VEGETABLE SOUP   6 to 8 Servings

2	*cups water*	1	*large carrot, trimmed,*
	Salt		*scraped, and sliced*
2	*pounds boneless beef, in*	1	*celery stalk, sliced*
	one piece	1	*medium-sized onion,*
2	*28-ounce cans whole*		*chopped*
	tomatoes, chopped if	1	*10-ounce package frozen*
	desired		*mixed vegetables, or 1*
1	*12-ounce can tomato juice*		*1-pound can*
1	*large potato, peeled and*	⅛	*teaspoon black pepper*
	diced	1	*to 2 teaspoons sugar,*
			optional

1. Combine the water, 1 teaspoon salt, and the beef in a saucepan. Cook over medium heat (or in a pressure cooker) until the beef is very tender and beginning to fall apart. Remove from the heat and set the beef aside to cool. Chill the cooking liquid and discard any grease that rises to the top of the broth.

2. Shred the cooled beef and discard fat and gristle. Return the beef to the skimmed broth and add the vegetables and pepper. Bring to a boil, lower the heat, and simmer just until the vegetables are tender. Taste the mixture as it cooks and add salt and sugar to taste.

PUREED VEGETABLE SOUP   4 Servings

Puree 3 cups of Favorite Vegetable Soup in a blender. Stir in a pinch of ground allspice. Serve hot garnished with slices of raw zucchini and parsley sprigs or serve cold in balloon wineglasses garnished with a dollop of sour cream and chopped parsley and crackers.

Salads and Salad Dressings

CHICKEN–STRING BEAN SALAD

8	small boneless and skinless chicken breast halves	3	tablespoons red wine vinegar
2½	cups water	½	teaspoon dried oregano
1	pound string beans, tips removed	1	clove garlic
			Salt and black pepper to taste
4	large carrots, scraped and sliced diagonally	2	large heads Bibb lettuce
3	tablespoons olive oil	4	tablespoons sliced almonds
3	tablespoons vegetable oil		Raw onion rings for garnish

1. Put the chicken breasts in a saucepan and add the water. Bring to a boil, lower the heat, cover, and cook until the chicken is tender, 15 to 20 minutes. Remove the chicken breasts from the liquid and put them on a plate to cool. Do not discard the cooking liquid in the pan.

2. Put the string beans and carrots in a steamer basket. Put the basket in the saucepan over the cooking liquid and bring to a boil. Cover and steam the vegetables until they are just tender. Remove from the pan immediately and let cool.

3. Put the oils, vinegar, oregano, garlic, and salt and pepper in a jar with a tight-fitting lid. Cover tightly and shake well. Let sit, covered, for 15 minutes.

4. Cut each chicken breast half into 3 long slices. Shake the dressing again and pour it over the chicken slices. Turn the chicken in the dressing until it is completely coated. Let sit for 30 to 45 minutes before serving.

5. To serve the salad, put a bed of lettuce on each serving plate. Add an equal amount of chicken, string beans, and carrot slices to each plate in a decorative pattern. Sprinkle 1 tablespoon of sliced almonds over each serving. Then lay 3 or 4 onion rings over the top of each serving. Serve the salads with any remaining dressing left from marinating the chicken.

CHUNKY CHICKEN SALAD   4 Servings

2½ *cups coarsely chopped*   ½ *cup finely chopped celery*
    cooked chicken   *Scant ½ cup mayonnaise*
                                    ¼ *teaspoon salt*

Combine all the ingredients in a mixing bowl. Cover tightly and chill briefly. Serve on lettuce leaves; in cantaloupe, papaya, or avocado halves; or in hollowed-out tomatoes.

Variations

Elegant Chicken Salad: To the above recipe, add halved red and/or green seedless grapes, cheese chunks, or nuts, or any combination of these ingredients.

Chicken Salad Sandwich Spread: Chop the chicken finely and add a tablespoon of minced onion, if desired. Combine the ingredients and chill briefly.

HAM SALAD   6 to 8 Servings

2   *cups finely chopped cooked*   ¼ *cup pickle relish, including*
    ham   *juice*
½   *cup finely chopped celery*   ½ *to 1 cup mayonnaise*
¼   *cup finely chopped onion*   *Worcestershire sauce to*
4   *hard-boiled eggs, peeled*   *taste*
    and chopped

Put the ham, celery, onion, chopped eggs, and pickle relish in a mixing bowl. Add the mayonnaise a little at a time, until the salad is the consistency you like. Mix in the Worcestershire sauce. Chill before serving.

Note: If you want a little more zip in your salad, you can add more pickle relish and/or Worcestershire sauce.

TACO SALAD   4 Servings

1½ *to 2 pounds ground beef*   4 *medium-sized or large*
1   *package taco seasoning*   *tomatoes, chopped*
1   *7-ounce bag taco-flavored*   1 *small head lettuce, sliced*
    tortilla chips   *thin*
8   *ounces mild Cheddar*   *Bottled taco sauce,*
    cheese, shredded   *optional*

1. Put the ground beef in a frying pan and brown it over medium heat. Drain well and stir in the taco seasoning. Let the beef cool to room temperature.

2. In a large bowl, make layers of tortilla chips. ground beef, cheese, tomatoes, and lettuce. Repeat the layers until you have filled the bowl. Save a few tomato chunks and tortilla chips to garnish the top of the salad. Serve the taco sauce on the side, if desired.

TUNA SALAD   4 Servings

1 *7-ounce can tuna*	1 *teaspoon minced onion*
1½ *hard-boiled eggs, peeled*	2 *tablespoons mayonnaise*
and chopped	*Salt to taste*
2 *teaspoons pickle relish*	

Drain the tuna and put it in a mixing bowl. Add the remaining ingredients and mix well. If the mixture is too dry, add mayonnaise or pickle relish to taste.

SPIRAL MACARONI-SEAFOOD SALAD   4 to 6 Servings

2 *cups spiral macaroni*	1 *pound fresh broccoli,*
1 *8-ounce bag frozen peeled*	*steamed to tender-crisp*
shrimp	½ *cup Herb–Lemon Butter*
1 *8-ounce bag frozen*	*(page 207), melted*
scallops, optional	

1. Cook the macaroni, following the package directions. Drain it well and put it in a large salad bowl.

2. Cook the shrimp and scallops, following the package directions. Drain well and add to the macaroni.

3. Cut the steamed broccoli into flowerets and small pieces and add to the salad bowl.

4. Drizzle the Herb–Lemon Butter over the salad and toss to mix well. Serve immediately.

SHRIMP AND PASTA SALAD   4 to 6 Servings

2   *pounds fresh jumbo shrimp*

2   *cups spiral macaroni*

1   *pound fresh asparagus or 1 10-ounce package frozen asparagus spears*

1   *pint cherry tomatoes, stemmed, washed, and drained*

½   *cup Italian salad dressing Grated Parmesan cheese to taste*

1. Cook the shrimp in boiling salted water until they turn pink. Drain immediately and let cool. When the shrimp are cool enough to handle, peel and devein them. Set the the shrimp aside.

2. Cook the macaroni, following the package directions. Drain it well and put it in a large salad bowl.

3. Cut the asparagus spears into 1-inch lengths. Put them in a steamer basket and cook over boiling salted water in a covered pot until they are tender-crisp. Remove from the pot and let cool.

4. Combine the asparagus, shrimp, and cherry tomatoes with the cooked macaroni. Toss well and chill for at least 30 minutes. Toss with the salad dressing and Parmesan cheese just before serving.

CHEESE CHUNK-MACARONI SALAD   6 to 8 Servings

2   *cups elbow macaroni, cooked, drained, and cooled*

1   *cup very small cheese chunks*

1   *cup frozen green peas, cooked, drained, and cooled*

¼   *cup grated onion*

½   *cup chopped sweet red pepper, optional*

1   *cup mayonniase*

½   *teaspoon salt*

1   *teaspoon sugar*

½   *teaspoon vinegar*

¼   *cup milk*

1. Combine the macaroni, cheese chunks, green peas, grated onion, and red pepper in a salad bowl.

2. Mix the mayonnaise, salt, sugar, vinegar, and milk together until well combined. Pour over the mixture in the salad bowl and toss well. Chill before serving.

PASTA-ASPARAGUS SALAD   4 to 6 Servings

2 cups spiral macaroni	1 pint cherry tomatoes, stemmed and washed
2 cups cold cooked asparagus pieces	½ cup bottled zesty Italian salad dressing

Cook the macaroni, following the package directions. Drain it well and put it in a large salad bowl along with the asparagus pieces and cherry tomatoes. Pour the dressing over all and toss well. Cover and refrigerate for about 30 minutes. Toss again before serving. If the salad seems dry, add more salad dressing.

Variation

Pasta-Asparagus Luncheon Salad: To the recipe above, add ½ pound each thick-sliced salami, sliced boiled ham, and sliced Swiss cheese, all of which may be cut into strips and mixed into the salad or rolled and arranged in an attractive pattern on top of the salad.

GREEK SALAD   4 Servings

¼ teaspoon dried oregano, crumbled	2 large tomatoes, cut into chunks
2 tablespoons olive oil	1 medium-sized onion, sliced and separated into rings
2 tablespoons lemon juice	1 small zucchini, thinly sliced
Salt and black pepper to taste	1 small can ripe pitted olives, drained
Pinch of sugar	Crumbled feta cheese to taste
Half a head of lettuce, broken into bite-sized pieces	

1. Combine the oregano, olive oil, lemon juice, salt, pepper, and sugar in a small jar with a tight-fitting lid.

2. Combine the lettuce, tomatoes, onion rings, zucchini, and olives in a large salad bowl. Shake the salad dressing to combine it and then pour the dressing over the vegetables in the salad bowl. Toss and refrigerate. Serve with crumbled feta cheese sprinkled over the top of each serving.

CAESAR SALAD   6 to 8 Servings

3   *to 4 heads romaine lettuce,*
     washed, drained, and
     chilled
½   *cup garlic olive oil (see*
     Note)
2½   *tablespoons red wine*
     vinegar
1   *lemon, cut in half*
2   *1-minute coddled eggs*

Salt and black pepper to
taste
Dash of Worcestershire
sauce
⅓   *cup grated Parmesan*
     cheese
1   *cup packaged Caesar*
     croutons
Drained anchovy fillets for
garnish, optional

Tear the romaine lettuce into large pieces and put them in a chilled salad bowl. Slowly pour the garlic olive oil and vinegar over the lettuce pieces. Squeeze the juice from the lemon halves over the lettuce. Break the eggs into the salad bowl. Add the salt, pepper, Worcestershire sauce, and Parmesan cheese. Toss until the lettuce is coated with the dressing. Add the croutons and toss a few more times. Serve immediately on cold salad plates, garnishing each serving with anchovies, if desired.

Note: To make garlic olive oil, add 4 to 6 cloves of peeled garlic, cut in half, to 1 cup olive oil in a jar with a tight-fitting lid. Cover tightly and let stand at room temperature for 1 to 3 days before using.

WALDORF SALAD   4 to 6 Servings

2   *large eating apples,*
     unpeeled
⅔   *cup chopped celery*
½   *cup raisins*
½   *cup miniature*
     marshmallows

½   *cup walnut halves*
¼   *to ¾ cup All-Purpose*
     Salad Dressing (page 130)
Lettuce leaves

Core the apples and cut them into small chunks. Put the apple chunks in a mixing bowl along with the celery, raisins, marshmallows, and walnut halves. Pour the salad dressing over all and mix well. To serve, line a serving plate with lettuce leaves and top with the salad mixture.

Note: You can cut the celery into thin slices on the diagonal, if you wish.

COLESLAW

6 Servings

Dressing 1
½ cup mayonnaise
¼ cup milk, cream, or half-
    and-half
1   tablespoon sugar
1   teaspoon white vinegar
    Pinch of salt

Dressing 2
¾ cup bottled slaw dressing
3   tablespoons milk, cream,
    or half-and-half
1   teaspoon sugar
½ teaspoon white vinegar
    Pinch of Salt

Dressing 3
¼ cup water
2   tablespoons sugar
2   tablespoons white vinegar
    Salt and black pepper to
    taste
1   teaspoon celery seeds,
    optional

Combine the ingredients for your choice of dressing in a jar. Cover tightly and shake until well combined. Shred half a head of cabbage and pour the dressing over it. Toss well and chill briefly before serving.

CARROT SALAD

4 to 6 Servings

2   cups grated carrots
½ cup raisins
1   8-ounce can pineapple
    tidbits or crushed pine-
    apple, drained

¼ to ½ cup All-Purpose
    Salad Dressing (page 130)

Put the grated carrots in a mixing bowl. Cover tightly and chill for at least 30 minutes. Just before serving, add the remaining ingredients to the carrots. Toss to combine well. Serve on lettuce leaves or in stemmed balloon glasses.

VEGETABLE-GELATIN SALAD

6 to 8 Servings

1   6-ounce package lemon or
    lime gelatin
1   cup grated carrots

1   cup grated cabbage
    Lettuce leaves
    Mayonnaise to taste

Prepare the gelatin, following the package directions. Pour it into an 8-inch-square baking dish and refrigerate until syrupy but not set. Stir in the grated carrots and cabbage and refrigerate for 4 to 6 hours, or until set. To serve, cut the gelatin into squares. Put a lettuce leaf on a salad plate and top with a gelatin square. Drop a dollop of mayonnaise on each gelatin square and serve.

Note: If you want a layered effect in this salad, add the carrots first and push them down into the gelatin. Then add the cabbage, pushing it down into the gelatin. Chill as above.

To vary the taste, you can add 1 well-drained 16- to 20-ounce can of crushed pineapple to the syrupy gelatin before you stir in the grated vegetables. If you use the pineapple, decrease the water in the gelatin by ¼ cup.

ORIENTAL SALAD   4 Servings

½	head lettuce, sliced	4	heaping tablespoons bean sprouts
6	radishes, sliced		
2	celery stalks, sliced diagonally		Canned Japanese mushrooms, drained
	Soy Dressing (page 130)		

Combine the lettuce, radishes, and celery stalks in a salad bowl. Toss with the dressing. Serve in individual salad bowls garnished with bean sprouts and mushrooms.

MARINATED MUSHROOM SALAD   4 to 6 Servings

1	pound small, very fresh raw mushrooms		Pinch of black pepper
⅓	cup olive oil	1	teaspoon Italian seasoning
⅓	cup vegetable oil	1	teaspoon minced parsley or parsley flakes
½	teaspoon salt	1	tablespoon minced onion
3	tablespoons tarragon vinegar		

1. Wash the mushrooms thoroughly in cold water. Dry them completely with paper towels. Set aside.

2. Put the oils, salt, vinegar, pepper, Italian seasoning, minced parsley, and minced onion in a deep bowl. Stir to combine. Add the mushrooms and toss. Marinate for 5 to 6 hours at room temperature, stirring occasionally.

POTATO SALAD   8 Servings

4	large potatoes
1	small onion, peeled and chopped
1	cup chopped celery
1	cup mayonnaise
¼	teaspoon prepared mustard
¼	to ½ teaspoon white vinegar
1½	tablespoons sugar
½	teaspoon salt or to taste
½	cup milk
7	hard-boiled eggs

1. Wash the potatoes and cook them in boiling water until they are fork tender. Cool, peel, ar.d dice. Put the potatoes in a large mixing bowl, and add the onion and celery.

2. Mix the mayonnaise, mustard, white vinegar, sugar, salt, and milk together. Pour the dressing over the vegetables and toss to combine.

3. Peel and chop 5 hard-boiled eggs and add them to the mixing bowl. Toss to mix.

4. Transfer the salad to a serving dish. Peel and slice the remaining eggs and lay them over the salad as a garnish. Cover and chill for about 1 hour.

HOT GERMAN POTATO SALAD   4 Servings

4	medium-sized potatoes
8	slices bacon
2	tablespoons minced onion
1	teaspoon sugar
4	teaspoons white vinegar
1	cup water
1	egg
½	teaspoon parsley flakes, optional
¼	cup thinly sliced scallions, optional

1. Wash the potatoes and cook them in boiling water until they are fork tender. Cool, peel, and slice them into a mixing bowl.

2. Fry the bacon until it is crisp. Drain on paper towels. When the bacon is cool, break it into small pieces.

3. Put the onion, sugar, vinegar, water, and egg in a small saucepan. Beat with a fork until the egg is combined with the other ingredients. Cook over medium heat, stirring constantly, until the mixture comes to a boil. Remove from the heat and add three-quarters of the bacon bits. Pour the dressing over the potatoes and toss with a wooden spoon.

4. Transfer the potatoes and dressing to a large saucepan or frying pan and cook over very low heat until heated through. Stir occasionally. Serve garnished with the remaining bacon bits, parsley flakes, and sliced scallions.

TOSSED SPINACH SALAD   4 to 6 Servings

6   slices bacon, cut into   2   tablespoons sugar
     1-inch pieces   1½ pounds fresh spinach,
¼   cup chopped onion   picked over, washed well,
4   tablespoons white vinegar   and drained
     Salt and black pepper to   2   hard-boiled eggs, peeled
     taste   and chopped

1. Fry the bacon and onion together in a small frying pan until the bacon is crisp and the onion is tender. Stir occasionally. Add the vinegar, salt, pepper, and sugar to the frying pan and bring to a boil.

2. Put the spinach leaves in a large salad bowl and pour the hot dressing over them. Toss to coat the spinach with the dressing. Garnish the salad with the chopped eggs and serve immediately.

Note: Cherry tomatoes and thinly sliced raw mushrooms can be added to this salad for variation.

This salad can also be served with the salad dressing of your choice.

ELEGANT SPINACH SALAD   4 to 6 Servings

1½ pounds fresh spinach,   ¾   cup pecan halves
     picked over, washed well,   4   tablespoons oil
     and drained well   1   teaspoon white vinegar
1   Bermuda onion, peeled,   ¼   cup water
     sliced, and separated into   2   tablespoons sugar
     rings   1   teaspoon celery seeds
1   small can mandarin
     oranges, drained

1. Put the spinach, onion rings, oranges, and pecan halves in a large salad bowl.

2. Combine the oil, vinegar, water, sugar, and celery seeds in a jar with a tight-fitting lid. Shake to combine well and pour over the salad. Toss and serve immediately.

VEGETABLE MEDLEY SALAD   4 to 6 Servings

1   *small head cauliflower*
2   *large stalks broccoli*
2½ *cups fresh spinach leaves*
    torn into pieces and
    washed well

1   *pint cherry tomatoes,*
    stemmed and cut in half
½   *to ⅔ cup All-Purpose*
    Salad Dressing (page 130)
4   *to 6 ounces blue cheese,*
    crumbled

1. Remove the green leaves from the cauliflower. Cut the cauliflower into small flowerets. Wash the flowerets in cool running water and drain them well. Put the drained flowerets in a large salad bowl.

2. Wash the broccoli and drain it well. Cut the top into small flowerets and the stalks into small chunks. Add to the cauliflower flowerets in the salad bowl, along with the spinach and cherry tomatoes. Cover and refrigerate the salad until chilled.

3. Just before serving, toss the salad with the dressing and sprinkle the blue cheese over the top.

Note: You can also put the blue cheese in a bowl and pass it separately.

SANDY'S OVERNIGHT SALAD   8 Servings

1   *head lettuce, sliced*
1   *head cauliflower, broken*
    into small flowerets
1   *pound bacon, diced, fried*
    crisp, and drained
⅓   *cup grated Parmesan*
    cheese

4   *hard-boiled eggs, peeled*
    and chopped
1   *pint cherry tomatoes,*
    stemmed and washed
2¼ *cups mayonnaise*
¼   *cup sugar*
¼   *teaspoon salt*
¼   *teaspoon white vinegar*

1. In a large glass bowl, make layers of the lettuce, cauliflower flowerets, bacon, Parmesan cheese, chopped eggs, and cherry tomatoes.

2. Mix the mayonnaise, sugar, salt, and vinegar together in a small bowl. Pour this mixture over the ingredients in the salad bowl, but do not stir. Cover the salad bowl tightly and refrigerate overnight.

3. Toss the salad just before serving.

Note: You can use some of the cherry tomatoes to garnish the salad, if you wish.

OVERNIGHT LAYERED SALAD   8 Servings

1	head lettuce, cut in half and sliced	½	teaspoon salt
2	cups well-washed torn spinach leaves	½	cup sugar
		½	cup mayonnaise
2	cups celery sliced on the diagonal	3	tablespoons cider vinegar
1	medium-sized red or white onion, peeled, sliced, and separated into rings	4	slices bacon, diced, fried crisp, and drained
		2	to 3 tablespoons grated Parmesan cheese
1	medium-sized cucumber, sliced	1	cup cherry tomatoes, stemmed and washed, optional
1	cup sour cream		

1. In a large glass salad bowl, make layers of the lettuce, spinach, celery, onion rings, and cucumber slices. Repeat the layers until there are only about 1½ inches left free at the top of the bowl.

2. Mix the sour cream, salt, and sugar together and pour over the top of the salad. Do not stir the mixture.

3. Mix the mayonnaise and cider vinegar and pour it over the salad. Do not stir the mixture.

4. Sprinkle the bacon over the salad. Then sprinkle the grated cheese over the salad. Cover the salad bowl tightly and refrigerate overnight to allow the flavors to blend. To serve, garnish the top of the salad with the cherry tomatoes, if you wish. Do not stir even when serving; just scoop up individual servings with salad servers.

PEAR AND CHEESE SALAD   4 Servings

8	lettuce leaves	4	tablespoons finely grated mild Cheddar cheese
4	large cans pear halves, drained	4	teaspoons mayonnaise
		12	carrot curls

Arrange lettuce leaves on 4 salad plates. Put 1 pear half on each plate, hollow side up. Fill each hollow with 1 tablespoon of grated Cheddar cheese. Put 1 teaspoon of mayonnaise on the lettuce next to each pear half. Garnish each plate with 3 carrot curls.

Note: You can use four tablespoons of cottage cheese instead of the Cheddar cheese. Garnish the salad with a dollop of mint jelly instead of mayonnaise and carrot curls.

BASIC SALAD DRESSING   Makes about 1½ Cups

1   *cup mayonnaise*
½   *cup sugar*

¼   *cup white vinegar*
Salt and black pepper to taste, optional

Combine all the ingredients in a jar with a tight-fitting lid. Mix well and cover tightly. Refrigerate for about 1 hour before using; the dressing thickens as it sits. It will keep for 3 or 4 days tightly covered in the refrigerator.

ALL-PURPOSE SALAD DRESSING   Makes about ⅔ Cup

½   *cup mayonnaise*
1   *teaspoon white vinegar*

2   *tablespoons milk*
1   *teaspoon sugar*
¼   *teaspoon salt*

Combine all the ingredients in a jar with a tight-fitting lid. Mix well and cover tightly. Refrigerate before using. This dressing will keep for 2 to 3 days in the refrigerator.

SWEET-AND-SOUR SALAD DRESSING   Makes about ⅓ Cup

2   *tablespoons vegetable oil*
2   *teaspoons white vinegar*
2   *tablespoons water*

1   *tablespoon honey*
Pinch of salt
1   *teaspoon sugar*
½   *teaspoon celery seeds*

Combine the oil, vinegar, and water in a jar with a tight-fitting lid. Add the honey and stir it in. Add the salt and sugar and stir again. Stir in the celery seeds and cover tightly. Refrigerate before using. This dressing will keep for about 1 week in the refrigerator.

SOY DRESSING   Makes about ⅓ Cup

½   *teaspoon soy sauce*
¼   *teaspoon sesame oil*
½   *teaspoon sesame paste (tahini)*

½   *teaspoon white vinegar*
6   *tablespoons water*
½   *teaspoon sugar*
Pinch of salt

Put all the ingredients in a small saucepan. Bring just to a boil and remove from the heat immediately. Cool the dressing and pour it into a jar with a tight-fitting lid. Cover tightly and refrigerate. Shake well before using.

SWEET MAYONNAISE SALAD DRESSING

Combine 1 cup mayonnaise with 2 tablespoons granulated sugar or 3 tablespoons confectioner's sugar, ¼ teaspoon vanilla extract, and a pinch of salt. Mix together well. Serve over shredded cabbage or lettuce.

Eggs

BASIC OMELET

2 Servings

4 tablespoons butter or
   margarine

4 eggs
4 tablespoons milk
¼ teaspoon salt

One or more of the following:

¼ cup chopped green pepper
¼ cup cooked sliced
   mushrooms
⅛ cup cooked diced onion
1 small cooked zucchini,
   chopped or sliced

1 tomato, sliced or chopped
¼ cup shredded mozzarella
   cheese
¼ cup grated mild Cheddar
   cheese

1. Melt the butter in a large frying pan or omelet pan.

2. Mix the eggs, milk, and salt together in a small bowl and beat vigorously. When the butter is sizzling, pour the eggs into the pan and cook the omelet until it is done to your taste. Remove the pan from the heat and add the vegetables of your preference to one side of the omelet. Fold the other half of the omelet over the filling and sprinkle the shredded or grated cheese over the top of the omelet. Serve immediately.

Note: You can garnish the omelet with cherry tomatoes and pickles and sprinkle on a dash or two of Tabasco sauce for a taste change.

EGGS IN HASH CUPS

6 Servings

2 12-ounce cans corned beef
   hash

6 eggs

1. Preheat the oven to 325 degrees.

2. Line the bottom and sides of 6 muffin tins with a ¼-inch-thick layer of hash. Break an egg into each hash cup and bake for 10 to 15 minutes, or until the eggs are set.

Note: This recipe can easily be doubled.

TUNNEL OF EGGS
8 to 10 Servings

1   *long loaf (about 12 inches)*
hard-crusted Italian or
French bread

4   *tablespoons butter or*
margarine plus melted
butter or margarine for the
bread

8   *to 10 eggs*

1   *cup large-curd creamed*
cottage cheese

1   *teaspoon salt*
Pinch of onion salt

1. Preheat the oven to 400 degrees.

2. Cut off one end of the loaf of bread and set the end aside. Hollow out the loaf, leaving about 1 inch of bread and crust all around. Brush the inside of the bread tunnel with melted butter. Set aside with the end of the loaf.

3. Put the eggs in the container of a blender and blend until thick, or beat the eggs with an electric mixer until they are thick. Add the cottage cheese and salts to the eggs and blend until smooth.

4. Melt the 4 tablespoons butter in a large frying pan. When the butter is sizzling, add the egg mixture and cook, stirring constantly, until the eggs are set. Spoon the eggs into the bread tunnel and close the loaf with the bread end. Place the filled loaf on a baking sheet and bake for about 15 minutes. Cut into 1-inch slices to serve.

MOLDED SCRAMBLED EGGS AND CHEESE
6 to 8 Servings

2   *recipes Scrambled Eggs*
(page 135)

1   *cup shredded Cheddar*
cheese

1   *cup shredded mozzarella*
cheese

2   *tablespoons butter or*
margarine

½   *cup chopped green pepper*

½   *cup chopped onion*
Crisp-fried small sausage
balls
Warm hash brown
potatoes

1. Preheat the oven to 325 degrees.

2. Prepare the scrambled eggs, but be careful not to overcook them. As each batch is done, put it in a large mixing bowl. Add the shredded cheeses and toss with wooden spoons.

3. Melt the butter in a small frying pan. When the butter is sizzling add the green pepper and onion and sauté, stirring occasionally, for about 5 minutes. Add the pepper and onions to the egg mixture.

4. Pour the egg mixture into a greased bundt pan and bake for 15 to 20 minutes. Unmold on a serving platter. Fill the center with small sausage balls and surround the edge of the egg mold with hash brown potatoes. Serve immediately.

PASTA SPIRAL-EGG BAKE

6 to 10 Servings

2 *cups spiral macaroni*	4 *tablespoons melted butter*
1 *can cream of chicken soup*	2 *to 3 cups diced cooked ham*
1¼ *cups milk*	¾ *cup packaged seasoned*
½ *teaspoon salt*	*stuffing mix (the crushed*
6 *eggs, beaten*	*type)*

1. Preheat the oven to 325 degrees.

2. Cook the macaroni in boiling salted water, following the package directions.

3. While the macaroni is cooking, combine the soup, milk, and salt in a large mixing bowl. Add the beaten eggs and 2 tablespoons of the melted butter. Mix well.

4. When the macaroni is cooked, drain it well and add it to the bowl with the cubed ham. Mix well. Pour the mixture into a buttered 9- by 13-inch baking dish.

5. Combine the stuffing mix with the remaining 2 tablespoons of melted butter, and sprinkle the bread mixture along the edges of the baking dish. Bake for 35 to 45 minutes. Stir the center once or twice about halfway through the cooking time, and then again about 3 minutes before you are ready to take the dish from the oven.

Note: For variety, you can add a sliced scallion to the egg mixture or ½ cup grated mild Cheddar cheese. (Add 2 additional tablespoons of milk if you add the cheese.) You can also substitute chopped cooked bacon or sausage for the ham.

EGGS À LA KING

4 Servings

1¾ cups *Medium White Sauce*
    (page 209)
¼   *teaspoon salt*
4   *to 5 hard-boiled eggs,*
    peeled and sliced
1   *4½-ounce can sliced*
    mushrooms, drained

1½ *tablespoons chopped*
    pimiento
⅓   *cup cooked green peas*
    Hot toast points, biscuits,
    or toasted English muffins
    Pinch of paprika

Mix the white sauce and salt together in a saucepan. Add the eggs, mushrooms, pimiento, and peas. Heat just to the boiling point and remove from the heat. Sprinkle each serving with a little paprika and serve over hot toast points, biscuits, or English muffins.

SCOTCH EGGS

3 to 4 Servings

6   *to 8 hard-boiled eggs*
¼   *cup all-purpose flour*
1   *pound bulk pork sausage*
    meat
½   *to ¾ cup fine seasoned or*
    unseasoned bread crumbs

Pinch of dried sage,
optional
¼   *teaspoon salt*
2   *eggs, beaten*
    Cooking oil for deep frying

1. Peel the eggs and roll them in the flour to coat them. Divide the sausage meat into equal portions to match the number of eggs. Cover each egg with sausage meat so that no egg white shows through.

2. Combine the bread crumbs and seasonings on a piece of waxed paper.

3. Dip the sausage-coated eggs into the beaten eggs and then coat them completely with the bread crumb mixture. Set aside on a plate to dry.

4. Heat 2 inches of oil in a deep frying pan. When the oil is very hot, add the eggs and fry for 5 or 6 minutes, turning occasionally, until they are golden all over. Serve hot or cold.

DEVILED EGGS
3 to 6 Servings

6 hard-boiled eggs	⅛ to ¼ teaspoon salt
2 tablespoons mayonnaise	Black pepper to taste,
1 tablespoon milk	optional
1½ tablespoons sweet pickle juice	¼ teaspoon prepared yellow mustard
	Paprika

1. Cut the eggs in half lengthwise. Carefully separate the whites from the yolks.

2. Put the yolks in a small mixing bowl and mash them with a fork. Add the mayonnaise, milk, pickle juice, salt, pepper, and mustard. Use the fork to mix to a smooth consistency.

3. Fill the egg white halves with the egg yolk mixture and sprinkle the paprika over the top for added color.

EGG BATTER

1 tablespoon all-purpose flour	¼ teaspoon salt
¼ cup cold milk	2 eggs

Put the flour in a small mixing bowl. Gradually add the cold milk to the flour, beating well with a wire whisk. Beat in the salt and eggs until all the ingredients are well combined. Use the mixture to coat fish, shellfish, or chicken before coating with flour or crumbs and frying.

SCRAMBLED EGGS
4 Servings

6   eggs
2   tablespoons milk
½   teaspoon salt
     Pinch of black pepper
4   tablespoons butter or margarine

1. Break the eggs into a small bowl or a 2-cup glass measuring cup. Add the milk, salt, and pepper and beat with a fork until well mixed.

2. Put the butter into a medium-sized frying pan and turn the heat to medium. As soon as the butter melts and begins to sizzle, pour in the eggs. Cook the eggs until the bottom begins to set. Then stir them with a wooden spoon, moving the cooked part to the center of the pan, so that the uncooked eggs run out to the edges of the pan to cook. Stir and cook the eggs until they are cooked as you like them. Serve immediately.

Fish and Shellfish

SOLE WITH SHRIMP SAUCE
4 Servings

2	tablespoons all-purpose flour	2	tablespoons lemon juice
1	cup cold milk	½	to 1 tablespoon dry sherry
½	teaspoon salt	1	6-ounce package frozen baby shrimp
2	tablespoons butter or margarine	4	sole fillets
			Dry white wine
			Lemon wedges

1. Put the flour in the top of a double boiler and add the milk gradually, stirring constantly with a wire whisk. Stir in the salt, butter, and lemon juice. Bring to a boil over medium heat, stirring occasionally with the whisk. Add the sherry and stir to mix well. Add the shrimp and return just to the boiling point. Remove from the heat and keep warm, covered, over barely simmering water while you prepare the fish.

2. Poach the fillets in a frying pan in dry white wine to cover until they are just fork tender. Use large spatulas to transfer the fillets to warm dinner plates. Spoon equal amounts of the sauce over each fillet and garnish with lemon wedges.

BAKED FISH SUPREME
8 Servings

2	pounds halibut, haddock, sole, or other whitefish fillets	1	10½-ounce can cut asparagus spears, drained
¼	cup melted butter or margarine	1	10¾-ounce can undiluted cream of celery soup
¼	teaspoon salt	2	or 3 scallions, thinly sliced
	Pinch of black pepper	1	to 2 cups grated Swiss cheese
			Paprika

136

1. Preheat the oven to 450 degrees.

2. Arrange the fish in 8 equal portions in a 9- by 13-inch baking dish. Drizzle the melted butter over both sides of the fish. Sprinkle the fish pieces with salt and pepper. Bake for 8 to 10 minutes.

3. Combine the soup and scallions. When the fish has baked for 8 to 10 minutes, distribute the asparagus pieces equally over the fish portions. Top each portion with an equal amount of the soup mixture. Return the baking dish to the oven for 10 to 12 minutes longer, or until the asparagus and sauce are hot. Sprinkle the cheese and paprika over the top of the dish and run under the broiler for 3 or 4 minutes before serving.

Note: This dish can be prepared with either fresh or defrosted frozen fish fillets. If you plan to freeze the dish, you will want to use fresh fish fillets.

CORNMEAL-FRIED HADDOCK   6 to 8 Servings

2 *pounds fresh or thawed frozen haddock fillets*	3 *cups cornmeal*
Milk	2 *teaspoons salt*
2 *cups all-purpose flour*	*Cooking oil for frying*
4 *eggs*	*Tartar sauce*
	Lemon wedges for garnish

1. Put the fillets in a bowl and add milk to cover them. Soak the fish for 30 minutes.

2. Spread the flour out on a sheet of waxed paper. Put the eggs in a small bowl and beat them thoroughly. Mix the cornmeal and salt together on a sheet of waxed paper.

3. Remove the fillets from the milk one at a time. Dredge each fillet in the flour and then dip it into the beaten eggs, coating it completely with egg. Then roll the fillet in the cornmeal, coating it as thickly as possible. Press the cornmeal onto the fillet with the palm of your hand. As each fillet is coated, lay it on a baking sheet. Continue until all the fillets have been coated.

4. Heat ⅛ to ¼ inch of cooking oil in a large frying pan. Fry the fillets a few at a time, turning only once, until they are crusty and brown on both sides. Drain on paper towels on an ovenproof platter. Keep the fillets warm in a 200-degree oven until all are cooked. Serve with tartar sauce and lemon wedges.

Note: Almost any whitefish fillets can be coated and fried in this manner.

RED SNAPPER AMANDINE

4 to 6 Servings

8	to 10 red snapper fillets		Paprika
	Milk	½	cup sliced almonds
1	cup all-purpose flour		Dash of Tabasco sauce
1	teaspoon salt	2	tablespoons lemon juice
	Pinch of white pepper	1	teaspoon seasoned salt
2	tablespoons cooking oil		Dash of dry sherry
½	pound (2 sticks) butter or margarine		

1. Put the fillets in a bowl and add milk to cover them. Soak the fish for 30 to 45 minutes.

2. Combine the flour, salt, and white pepper on a sheet of waxed paper.

3. Remove the fillets from the milk one at a time. Pat each one dry and then dredge it in the seasoned flour, shaking off any excess flour. As each fillet is coated, lay it on a baking sheet. Continue until all the fillets have been coated.

4. Heat the oil and 1 stick of the butter in a large frying pan. When the butter sizzles, sauté the fillets a few at a time, turning only once, until they are golden and cooked through. Drain on paper towels on an oven-proof platter. When all the fillets have been sautéed, brush them with a little melted butter from the frying pan and sprinkle them with paprika. Keep the fillets warm in a 200-degree oven while you prepare the sauce.

5. Wipe out the frying pan with paper towels. Melt the remaining stick of butter in the skillet over medium heat. When it is sizzling, add the almonds and cook and stir until they are lightly browned. Add the Tabasco sauce, lemon juice, seasoned salt, and sherry and mix well. Spoon the sauce over the fillets when serving.

LEMON-CREAM BAKED SOLE

4 Servings

2 **pounds sole fillets**	⅛ **teaspoon seasoned salt**
Milk	2 **tablespoons freshly**
4 **tablespoons butter or**	**squeezed lemon juice**
margarine	**Paprika**
¼ **cup heavy cream**	1 **lemon, sliced**

1. Put the fillets in a bowl and add milk to cover them. Soak the fish for 1 hour.

2. Preheat the oven to 325 degrees.

3. Melt the butter in a small saucepan over medium heat. Add the cream a little at a time to the melted butter, stirring constantly. Then stir in the salt and lemon juice. Cook for 1 to 2 minutes.

4. Pour the sauce over the bottom of a 9- by 13-inch baking dish. Remove the fillets from the milk and lay them over the sauce. Cover the baking dish tightly with foil and bake for 10 minutes. Uncover the dish and spoon some sauce over each fillet. Sprinkle the fillets with paprika and lay the lemon slices over the fish around the edge of the dish. Bake, uncovered, for 5 to 10 minutes longer, or until the fillets are tender. Serve immediately.

Note: This dish will freeze well without the lemon slices if you use fresh fish.

BAKED FISH ROLLS

4 Servings

4 **sole or flounder fillets**	½ **cup dry sherry**
Salt and black pepper to	½ **cup grated Swiss cheese**
taste	**Lemon wedges**
1½ **cups Cheese Sauce (page**	
210)	

1. Preheat the oven to 350 degrees.

2. Roll the fillets and fasten them closed with toothpicks. Put the rolls in a small baking dish and sprinkle them with salt and pepper.

3. Combine the Cheese Sauce with the sherry and mix well. Pour the sauce over the fillets and bake for 15 to 20 minutes.

4. Sprinkle the grated Swiss cheese over the top of each fish roll and run the dish under the broiler until nicely browned. Serve each portion with lemon wedges.

POACHED SALMON STEAKS WITH LEMON SAUCE 8 Servings

4 *cups water*	⅛ *cup heavy cream*
1 *teaspoon salt*	½ *teaspoon seasoned salt*
4 *to 6 tablespoons dry sherry*	2 *tablespoons freshly*
4 *large salmon steaks, cut ¾*	*squeezed lemon juice*
inch thick	2 *lemons, cut into wedges*
4 *tablespoons butter or*	
margarine	

1. Put the water, salt, and sherry into a large frying pan. Bring to a boil and add the salmon steaks. When the water is boiling again, reduce the heat to low, cover the frying pan, and simmer the steaks for 6 to 8 minutes, or until the fish flakes easily with a fork.

2. While the fish is poaching, make the sauce. Melt the butter in a small saucepan over medium heat. Add the cream a little at a time to the melted butter, stirring constantly. Then stir in the salt and lemon juice. Cook for 1 to 2 minutes.

3. When the fish is cooked, use a broad spatula to transfer the steaks from the frying pan to a large warmed platter. Cut each steak in half and remove the bone. Spoon some sauce over each portion and serve with lemon wedges.

SHRIMP AND VEGETABLE SAUTÉ 4 Servings

1 *tablespoon olive oil*	¼ *teaspoon Italian seasoning*
2 *tablespoons butter or*	¼ *teaspoon dried oregano*
margarine	1 *6-ounce package frozen*
1 *to 1½ pounds jumbo*	*snow pea pods, thawed*
shrimp, peeled and	4 *large tomatoes, cored and*
deveined	*quartered*
1 *tablespoon lemon juice*	2 *cups cooked rice*

Heat the olive oil and butter in a large frying pan. When the butter is completely melted and beginning to sizzle, add the shrimp and sauté for 1 minute, stirring occasionally. Add the lemon juice, Italian seasoning, and oregano and continue to stir the shrimp until they just begin to turn pink. Add the snow peas and toss and stir the mixture with wooden spoons for 1 minute. Add the tomatoes and sauté, stirring occasionally, for 2 to 3 minutes longer. Serve the shrimp and vegetables over the rice.

CREAMED SHRIMP
2 Servings

2 tablespoons all-purpose
   flour
1 cup cold milk or half-and-
   half
½ teaspoon salt

2 tablespoons butter or
   margarine
¼ cup dry sherry
1 6-ounce package frozen
   baby shrimp

Put the flour in a saucepan and add the cold milk gradually, stirring constantly with a wire whisk. Stir in the salt and butter and bring to a boil over medium heat, stirring occasionally with the whisk. Add the sherry and stir to mix well. Add the shrimp and return just to the boiling point. Remove from the heat immediately. If the mixture is too thick, add milk a tablespoon at a time until the desired consistency is reached.

FRIED COCONUT SHRIMP
4 Servings

16 to 32 fresh jumbo shrimp
2 eggs
2 tablespoons milk
1 tablespoon all-purpose
   flour

2 to 3 cups flaked
   unsweetened coconut
   Cooking oil for deep frying
   Warm jam or jelly
   (apricot, peach, pineapple),
   or orange marmalade

1. Shell and devein the shrimp.
2. Combine the eggs, milk, and flour in a small bowl and beat together well. Spread the coconut out on a sheet of waxed paper. Heat the oil for deep frying.
3. While the oil is heating, dip each shrimp in the egg mixture and then coat it with the flaked coconut, pressing the coconut on with the palm of your hand. As each shrimp is coated, lay it on a baking sheet.
4. When the oil is hot, drop the coated shrimp into the oil and fry until golden brown, turning once. Drain on paper towels. Serve with a bowl of warmed jelly or jam for dipping.

Variation

Fried Almond Shrimp: Follow the recipe above, but substitute thinly sliced almonds for the coconut.

BROILED ROCK LOBSTER TAILS   4 Servings

8   *4-ounce rock lobster tails*   *Tabasco sauce or*
    Melted butter   *Worcestershire sauce*

1. If the lobster tails are frozen, allow them to thaw for about 30 minutes. Snip through the center of the undershell of each tail with kitchen shears. Run a knife down the center of the lobster flesh, cutting it open slightly. (Do not cut through the lobster meat completely.) Put the prepared lobster tails on a broiler pan cut side up.

2. Preheat the broiler to hot.

3. Combine the melted butter with the Tabasco or Worcestershire sauce to taste. Brush the butter mixture over the exposed lobster meat. Broil 4 to 5 inches from the heat for 5 to 7 minutes, brushing occasionally with the melted butter mixture. Serve with additional plain melted butter on the side.

Poultry

FRIED CHICKEN

4 Servings

1   *2½- to 3½-pound chicken,*
    cut into serving pieces
    Salt and black pepper
    Mayonnaise
    Crushed corn flakes,
    crushed potato chips, or
    all-purpose flour for
    coating

½   *cup cooking oil*
2   *tablespoons butter or*
    margarine

1. Sprinkle the chicken pieces with salt and pepper. Then coat them with the mayonnaise.

2. Spread the crushed corn flakes on a sheet of waxed paper and coat the chicken pieces with them, pressing them on with the palm of your hand. Lay the coated pieces on a plate as you finish them.

3. Heat the oil and butter in a frying pan. When the butter is sizzling, add the chicken pieces and cook over medium heat, turning occasionally, for about 20 minutes, or until they are brown all over. Cover the pan, lower the heat, and cook for 5 minutes longer.

Note: The chicken can also be dipped in milk or beaten egg before coating with the crushed corn flakes, crushed potato chips, or flour.

Variation

Chicken Parmesan: Coat the chicken as directed above and fry over medium heat for about 10 minutes only, or just until the pieces are golden brown. Put the browned chicken pieces in a buttered baking dish. Mix together a 16-ounce can crushed tomatoes with 1 teaspoon sugar and ¼ cup water. Pour the mixture over the chicken in the baking dish. Sprinkle the chicken generously with dried oregano and 1 cup of grated Parmesan cheese. Bake in a 350-degree oven for 25 minutes. Sprinkle an additional cup of grated Parmesan cheese over the chicken and bake for 5 minutes longer.

POTATO CHIP CHICKEN

4 Servings
Freezes Well

2   *sticks (8 ounces) butter or*
     margarine
1   *2½- to 3½-pound chicken,*
     cut into serving pieces

1   *large bag potato chips,*
     rolled and crushed in the
     bag

1. Preheat the oven to 350 degrees. Put the butter into a 9- by 13-inch baking pan. Put the baking pan in the oven until the butter has melted.

2. Remove the baking pan from the oven and roll the chicken pieces in the melted butter until they are well coated. Then put the coated chicken pieces in the bag with the crushed potato chips.

3. Pour any remaining butter in the baking pan into a measuring cup. Shake the chicken in the potato chip bag to coat the pieces and return the coated pieces to the baking pan. Drizzle 2 or 3 tablespoons of the butter from the measuring cup over the chicken and sprinkle the chicken with any remaining potato chips.

4. Return the baking pan with the chicken to the oven and bake for 1 hour, or until the chicken is fork tender.

Note: You can also coat the chicken with crushed corn flakes, cracker crumbs, or finely crushed seasoned bread crumbs instead of potato chips.

CHICKEN CACCIATORE

4 Servings
Freezes Well

1   *2½- to 3½-pound frying*
     chicken, cut into serving
     pieces
     All-purpose flour for
     dredging
     Salt and black pepper to
     taste
1   *heaping tablespoon solid*
     shortening
2   *tablespoons butter or*
     margarine

1   *28-ounce can whole peeled*
     tomatoes
1   *tablespoon all-purpose flour*
1   *teaspoon sugar*
1   *teaspoon Italian seasoning*
½   *teaspoon dried oregano*
2   *medium-sized onions,*
     peeled, sliced, and
     separated into rings
1   *large green pepper, seeded*
     and cut into rings

1. Dredge the chicken in the flour, salt, and pepper.

2. Preheat the oven to 350 degrees.

3. Heat the solid shortening and butter until the mixture is sizzling. Add the chicken pieces and brown quickly on all sides. As the pieces brown, transfer them to a baking dish.

4. Drain the liquid from the tomatoes into a saucepan. Set it aside. Cut the tomatoes in half and put the pieces on top of the chicken in the baking dish.

5. Add the flour, sugar, Italian seasoning, and oregano to the tomato liquid in the saucepan. Cook over low heat, stirring constantly, until the sugar is dissolved, about 3 minutes.

6. Distribute the onion and pepper rings over the chicken pieces in the baking dish. Pour the sauce over all and bake for about 45 minutes, or until the chicken is fork tender.

Note: To make this dish on top of the stove, brown the chicken and remove it from the frying pan. Add the onion and pepper rings to the frying pan and sauté them until they are tender. Drain off the cooking fat and return the chicken to the frying pan. Add the remaining ingredients, omitting the flour, mix well, and bring to a boil. Cover the pan, lower the heat, and simmer for 45 to 50 minutes, or until the chicken is fork tender.

BAKED CHICKEN IN CHICKEN SAUCE

4 Servings
Freezes Well

1	2½- to 3½-pound chicken, cut into serving pieces	2	10½-ounce cans cream of chicken soup
		1	can water

1. Preheat the oven to 375 degrees.

2. Lay the chicken pieces in a baking dish large enough to hold them in one layer. Mix the soup with the water until the mixture is smooth. Pour the mixture over the chicken and bake for 1 hour, or until the chicken is fork tender.

Note: If your family requires 2 or 3 more pieces of chicken, just add the extra pieces and stir an additional ¼ cup of water into the soup mixture. Bake as above.

Sometimes I add quartered peeled potatoes to the chicken.

MEXICAN CHICKEN   4 Servings

3   *pounds chicken pieces*   1   *16-ounce can mild*
                                           Mexican-style sauce

1. Preheat the oven to 375 degrees.

2. Put the chicken pieces in a baking dish and pour the canned sauce over them. Bake for 1 hour, or until the chicken is fork tender. Serve the chicken on a bed of steamed white rice and garnish with green and/or red pepper rings.

CHICKEN AND NOODLES   4 to 6 Servings
                                                 Freezes Well

1   *2½- to 3½-pound chicken,*   1   *teaspoon salt*
    cut into serving pieces   *Black pepper to taste*
                                       1½ *to 2 cups egg noodles*

1. Put the chicken pieces in a Dutch oven and add salt, pepper, and water just to cover the chicken pieces. Bring the water to a boil, cover the pan, and cook the chicken over fairly high heat for 20 to 30 minutes, or until it is fork tender. Remove the chicken pieces from the broth and let them cool a little.

2. Add enough water to the broth in the pan to make 3 cups. Bring the broth to a boil and add the noodles. Cook, stirring occasionally, until barely tender.

3. While the noodles cook, remove the chicken from the bones, leaving it in large chunks. When the noodles are just tender, return the chicken to the pan and cook over low heat for 5 minutes longer, stirring occasionally. Serve immediately.

PINEAPPLE-CHICKEN SAUTÉ   6 Servings

4   *tablespoons butter or*   1   *20-ounce can unsweetened*
    margarine   *pineapple slices*
6   *boneless and skinless*   1   *teaspoon lemon juice*
    chicken breast halves   1   *4½-ounce box sesame-*
    Salt   *Cheddar stick snacks*
    White pepper, optional   1   *tablespoon flaked or*
                                           shredded coconut

1. Melt the butter in a large frying pan. When the butter is sizzling, add the chicken breast halves and sauté them over medium heat, turning once, until they are lightly browned. Season the chicken with salt and pepper.

2. Drain the juice from the pineapple directly into the frying pan. Add the lemon juice and bring the mixture to a boil. Cover the frying pan, lower the heat, and simmer the chicken for 15 to 20 minutes, turning occasionally and spooning some of the sauce over the pieces.

3. Push the chicken pieces to one side of the frying pan and add the stick snacks to the sauce. Cook for 2 to 3 minutes, or until they are heated through.

4. Add the pineapple slices to the frying pan and heat for 1 to 2 minutes.

5. Put the pineapple slices on a warm serving platter. Lay the chicken pieces on top of the pineapple slices. Pour the sauce with the stick snacks over the chicken and garnish the chicken with the coconut. Serve immediately.

CHICKEN VERONIQUE

4 Servings

6	skinless and boneless chicken breast halves	1	cup seedless white grapes, plus small clusters of grapes for garnish
2	tablespoons butter or margarine	2	tablespoons all-purpose flour
1	cup dry sherry	¼	cup cold water
1	teaspoon salt	1	egg white, beaten
	Pinch of white pepper	1	tablespoon confectioner's sugar
	Pinch of dried tarragon		

1. Cut each chicken breast half into 2 or 3 long strips.

2. Melt the butter in a frying pan. When the butter is sizzling, add the chicken strips and sauté until golden brown on all sides. Add the sherry, salt, pepper, and tarragon and mix well. Cover, lower the heat, and simmer for 8 to 10 minutes.

3. Wash the grapes, including the clusters for garnish. Cut the 1 cup of grapes in half and add to the chicken. Combine the flour and water and stir until smooth. Add the mixture to the frying pan and cook, stirring constantly, until the sauce is thick. (If the sauce is too thick, add a little more sherry or water.) Transfer the chicken and sauce to a serving platter and garnish the platter with the grape clusters after dipping them in the egg white and sugar.

SAUCY VEGETABLE CHICKEN BREASTS   8 Servings

8	*skinless and boneless chicken breast halves*
½	*teaspoon salt*
4	*tablespoons butter or margarine*
1	*15½-ounce jar spaghetti sauce*
½	*teaspoon Italian seasoning*

¼	*teaspoon dried oregano*
1½	*cups diagonally cut celery, or 1 4-ounce can sliced mushrooms*
1	*or 2 diced zucchini*
4	*cups cooked white rice*
¾	*to 1 cup finely grated mozzarella cheese*

1. Sprinkle the chicken breast halves with the salt.

2. Melt the butter in a frying pan and, when it is sizzling, add the chicken pieces. Cook for 4 to 5 minutes, turning once. Pour the spaghetti sauce over the chicken and sprinkle on the Italian seasoning and oregano. Cover the frying pan and cook over low heat for 10 to 15 minutes. Add the celery and zucchini and mix it in well. Cover and cook for about 10 minutes, or until the celery is just crisp. Serve the chicken on a bed of rice, topped with the sauce. Pass the grated mozzarella separately and let people serve themselves.

Note: If you are going to freeze this dish, do not add celery, mushrooms, or zucchini to the sauce. You can add and cook the vegetables when you reheat the dish.

CHICKEN ELYSE   4 Servings

1	*8-ounce bottle light French dressing (not the creamy kind)*
1	*package dry onion soup mix*
1	*16-ounce can jellied or whole cranberry sauce*
1	*tablespoon lemon juice or dry sherry*

1	*or 2 unpeeled baking apples, diced*
2	*navel oranges, sliced ¼ inch thick*
4	*to 6 skinless and boneless chicken breast halves, or 1 3½-pound chicken, cut into serving pieces*

1. Combine the French dressing, onion soup mix, cranberry sauce, lemon juice, diced apples, and orange slices in a large bowl. Add the chicken pieces, cover the bowl, and refrigerate for at least 5 hours, turning the chicken in the marinade occasionally.

2. Preheat the oven to 350 degrees. Transfer the chicken and marinade to a baking dish. Lay the orange slices over the chicken pieces and bake for about 1½ hours. Serve the chicken on a bed of fluffy white rice.

CHICKEN KIEV

4 to 6 Servings
Freezes Well

8	to 12 skinless and boneless chicken breast halves	1	stick (4 ounces) very cold butter
	Salt and black pepper to taste	4	eggs
	Pinch of garlic powder, optional	1	cup all-purpose flour
		2½	cups fine seasoned bread crumbs
2	tablespoons chopped fresh parsley	1½	cups vegetable oil

1. Put the chicken breasts between sheets of waxed paper and pound them with the flat side of a meat mallet until they are ¼ to ⅛ inch thick. Sprinkle the flattened breasts with salt, pepper, garlic powder, and parsley.

2. Cut the butter into 3 equal pieces and then quarter each piece. Put 1 piece of butter on the large end of each piece of chicken. Fold the sides of the chicken over the butter and roll the pieces up. Skewer closed with natural toothpicks.

3. Beat the eggs in a flat soup dish or pie plate. Spread the flour on a sheet of waxed paper. Spread the bread crumbs on a second sheet of waxed paper.

4. Dip each chicken roll first in the flour and then in the beaten eggs. Then coat all over with the bread crumbs, pressing the crumbs on with the palm of your hand. Put the coated chicken rolls on one or two plates so that they do not touch one another. Chill the rolls for at least 1 hour before cooking. (The rolls can be frozen at this point, if you wish, and cooked later.

5. Heat about 1 inch of oil in a deep frying pan. When the oil is very hot, add the chicken rolls a few at a time. (Do not crowd the rolls in the pan.) Fry the rolls, turning them occasionally, until they are golden brown on all sides. Transfer the cooked rolls to a heatproof platter lined with paper towels. Keep them warm in a 225-degree oven while you fry the rest of the rolls. Serve 2 rolls to each person.

CREAMED CHICKEN AND EGG SLICES   8 Servings

½ cup cream
1 cup milk
2 10½-ounce cans cream of
   chicken soup
2½ cups diced cooked chicken

¼ to ½ teaspoon curry
   powder, optional
   Salt and black pepper to
   taste
8 hard-boiled eggs, peeled
   and sliced

1. Mix the cream, milk, and chicken soup in a saucepan. Bring to a boil, stirring constantly. Add the chicken, lower the heat, stir in the curry powder, and remove the pan from the heat. Taste, and season with salt and pepper, if necessary.

2. Arrange the sliced eggs over the bottom of a long serving dish. Pour the hot chicken and sauce mixture over the eggs and serve immediately.

CHICKEN À LA KING   4 to 6 Servings
                                         Freezes Well

4 tablespoons butter,
   margarine, or melted
   chicken fat
3 tablespoons all-purpose
   flour
1½ cups chicken broth
¾ cup milk or cream
2¼ cups diced cooked chicken

1 4-ounce can sliced
   mushrooms or mushroom
   stems and pieces, drained
¼ cup chopped pimiento
1¼ cups frozen peas
½ teaspoon salt (if the
   chicken broth is unsalted)
   Hot toast points, hot
   biscuits, or pastry shells

Melt the butter in a saucepan. When the butter is sizzling, add the flour all at once, stirring it into the melted butter until the mixture is smooth. Add the chicken broth slowly, stirring constantly. When the mixture is smooth, add the milk and stir well. Add the remaining ingredients, except the toast, biscuits, or pastry shells, and cook for 3 to 4 minutes longer. Serve the mixture over the hot toast points.

Note: You can also add sliced olives, chopped green pepper, and a dash or two of dry sherry to the recipe and eliminate the mushrooms, pimiento, or peas, if you wish.

Variation

Turkey à la King: To make Turkey à la King, substitute 2¼ cups diced cooked turkey for the chicken.

CHICKEN POT PIE

4 Servings
Freezes Well

1 *10½-ounce can chicken broth, or an equal amount of homemade broth*
2 *tablespoons all-purpose flour*
2 *cups cubed cooked chicken*
1 *cup cubed potatoes*

1 *cup frozen peas, thawed and drained*
1 *cup cubed carrots*
   Salt and black pepper to taste
1 *recipe piecrust (page 228), rolled out*

1. Preheat oven to 350 degrees.
2. Combine ½ cup of the chicken broth with the flour in a small cup. Mix until smooth. Pour the remaining broth into a saucepan and bring it to a boil. Add the flour-broth mixture and stir over low heat until the mixture thickens. Remove from the heat and set aside.
3. Put the chicken, potatoes, peas, and carrots into the bottom of a deep pie plate or square baking dish. Sprinkle them with salt and pepper. Pour the sauce over all. Then cover the top of the pie plate with the rolled-out crust, sealing the crust to the pie plate. Cut a hole in the center of the crust to allow the steam to escape and bake the pie for 1 hour and 15 minutes. If the crust browns too quickly, cover it with foil.

STUFFED CORNISH HENS

4 Servings
Freezes Well

1 *stick (4 ounces) butter or margarine*
½ *cup slivered almonds*
1 *5- to 7-ounce package wild rice mix, cooked following package directions and cooled*

1 *4-ounce can sliced mushrooms, drained*
4 *1- to 1½-pound Cornish hens, thawed if frozen*
   Salt

1. Melt 4 tablespoons of the butter in a small frying pan. When the butter is sizzling, add the almonds and sauté them, stirring constantly,

until they are golden. (Watch carefully so that they do not burn.) Combine the cooked rice with the almonds and butter and the mushrooms.

2. Preheat the oven to 350 degrees.

3. Sprinkle the Cornish hens with salt inside and out. Stuff the birds with the rice mixture and truss them.

4. Melt the remaining butter in a large frying pan and brown the birds lightly. Transfer the birds to a large roasting pan and roast, uncovered, for 1 hour and 15 minutes, basting occasionally with the remaining melted butter in the frying pan.

5. When the birds have roasted for 1 hour and 15 minutes, raise the oven temperature to 400 degrees and roast the birds for 15 minutes longer, basting occasionally with the melted butter. If the birds brown too much, cover them with aluminum foil.

Note: Cooked brown rice can be substituted for the wild rice.

CORNISH HENS IN WINE SAUCE   2 to 4 Servings

2 *to 3 tablespoons butter or margarine*	*Salt and black pepper to taste*
2 *large Cornish hens, thawed if frozen, and cut in half*	1 *cup dry white wine*

Melt the butter in a large frying pan. When the butter is sizzling, add the Cornish hen halves and brown lightly. When the halves are browned, season them with salt and pepper. Pour in the wine, cover the pan, and cook over low heat for 15 to 20 minutes, or until the hens are tender. Check the pan occasionally to see if more wine should be added.

ROAST TURKEY

Ready to Cook Weight	Number of Servings	Roasting Time
8 to 10 pounds	10 to 20	4 to 5 hours
12 to 15 pounds	20 to 25	5 to 6 hours
20 to 25 pounds	25 to 35	6 to 8 hours

Note: If the turkey is unstuffed, it may take less time to roast. (The celery and onion in the turkey cavity are not considered stuffing. They are used to prevent the turkey from drying out.)

Times for Thawing Turkey	In Refrigerator	In Cold Water*
8 to 10 pounds	1 to 2 days	5 to 6 hours
12 to 15 pounds	2 to 3 days	6 to 8 hours
20 to 25 pounds	3 to 4 days	8 to 9 hours

1   *whole ready-to-cook turkey*
    Salt
1   *medium-sized onion, peeled and quartered (if not stuffing)*
2   *celery stalks, cut in half (if not stuffing)*

    Stuffing (page 155), optional
2   *sticks (8 ounces) butter or margarine*
1   *cup water, optional*

1. Check the turkey over and, if necessary, remove all pinfeathers.

2. Preheat the oven to 325 degrees.

3. Sprinkle the turkey inside and out with salt, remembering to rub salt under the skin at the neck.

4. Put the onion and celery into the cavity of the bird, or stuff the bird cavity and the neck cavity with stuffing. Fasten the neck skin down to the back of the bird with skewers or toothpicks. Close the vent over the cavity of the bird with skewers or toothpicks to keep the stuffing in. Fold the wing tips under the back of the bird and tie the legs together with string.

5. Line a large roasting pan with heavy-duty aluminum foil, making sure there is enough extra foil to enclose the turkey completely. Put the turkey in the pan, breast side up.

6. Melt the butter in a saucepan and baste the turkey all over with the melted butter. Cut a piece of cheesecloth large enough to cover the turkey. Dip the cheesecloth in the melted butter and spread the cloth over the bird, covering the wings and legs as well as the body. Add the water to the foil-lined pan. Close the foil tightly around the turkey and roast following the directions in the chart above.

7. During the last half-hour of roasting time, open the foil and fold it back. Cut off and remove the string around the legs. Remove and discard the cheesecloth. Baste the turkey again with the melted butter and some

---

*Cover the bird in its original wrapping in cold water. Change the water every hour or so. If you do not plan to roast it immediately, refrigerate the turkey thawed in this manner until you are ready to roast it.

of the pan juices. (You may remove the pan juices at this point to chill them and remove the grease from them before making the gravy.) Roast the turkey, watching it carefully so that it does not dry out or become too brown. To check for doneness, squeeze the thickest part of the drumstick between your fingers. It should feel very soft. The drumstick should also move up and down easlily.

8. When the turkey is done, remove it from the oven, cover it loosely with the foil, and let it rest for 15 to 20 minutes before slicing.

COOKED TURKEY GIBLETS AND NECK

Rinse the giblets and neck well under cool running water. Discard any fat. Put the giblets (but not the liver) and neck into a saucepan and cover with cold water. Add a small peeled onion, 1 small scraped carrot, 1 small celery stalk, and salt to taste. Bring the water to a boil, lower the heat, cover the pan, and simmer for 2 to 3 hours, or until the gizzard is tender. (During the first hour or so, scoop off and discard any scum that rises to the top of the stock.) Add the liver during the last half-hour of cooking.

Remove the meat from the stock and let it cool. Then cut the meat into small pieces. You can add them to your stuffing or mix them into the gravy. Put the meat in a container with a cover and cover it with some of the stock. Store in the refrigerator until ready to use.

TURKEY GRAVY   Makes 2 Cups

2 *cups defatted turkey pan drippings or stock (or a combination of both)*	3 *tablespoons all-purpose flour* 3 *tablespoons cold water*

Put the turkey pan drippings into a small frying pan and bring just to the simmering point over low heat. Mix the flour and water to a smooth paste in a small cup. Add the mixture to the simmering stock a drop at a time, stirring constantly. When all the flour-water mixture has been incorporated, stir and cook over low heat for 3 to 5 minutes, or until the gravy is smooth and thickened. At this point, you can drain the giblets and add them to the gravy, if you wish. Serve the gravy in a warm sauceboat.

BREAD STUFFING

Makes Enough for a
12- to 16-Pound Turkey

½	cup butter or margarine	1	to 2 teaspoons salt
2	medium-sized onions, chopped	⅛	teaspoon black pepper
1	cup diced celery	1	tablespoon poultry seasoning
10	to 14 cups soft bread crumbs	½	cup turkey broth, bouillon, or water

1. Melt the butter in a small frying pan. When it is sizzling, add the onions and celery and sauté over low heat, stirring constantly, for 5 to 10 minutes, or until the vegetables are soft but not brown.

2. Transfer the vegetables to a large mixing bowl and add the remaining ingredients. Mix well. The stuffing should be rather moist; if it seems too dry, add more broth.

Note: When you stuff the bird, do not pack the stuffing in tightly. It will expand as the bird roasts.

CORN BREAD STUFFING

Makes Enough for a
12- to 16-Pound Turkey

½	cup butter	1	teaspoon poultry seasoning
2	cups chopped onion	1	teaspoon dried sage, optional
2	cups chopped celery		
5	cups crumbled corn bread	2	teaspoons salt
3	cups bread cubes and/or cubed biscuits	¼	teaspoon black pepper
1	egg, beaten	½	cup turkey broth, bouillon, or water

1. Melt the butter in a small frying pan. When it is sizzling, add the onion and celery and sauté over low heat, stirring constantly, for 5 to 10 minutes, or until the vegetables are soft, but not brown.

2. Transfer the vegetables to a large mixing bowl and add the remaining ingredients. Mix well. The stuffing should be rather moist; if it seems too dry, add more broth.

Note: When you stuff the bird, do not pack the stuffing in tightly. It will expand as the bird roasts.

WILD RICE STUFFING

Makes Enough for a
12- to 16-Pound Turkey

1   *cup wild rice, soaked*
2   *cups water*
4   *tablespoons butter*
½   *cup chopped celery*
½   *cup sliced scallions*
½   *clove garlic, peeled and
    minced*
1   *2¼-ounce package almond
    slivers*
1   *4-ounce can sliced
    mushrooms, drained, or ½
    cup sliced fresh mushrooms*

3   *cups cooked long-grain rice
    (cooked in chicken or
    turkey broth, following
    package directions)*
¼   *cup chopped parsley leaves*
1   *tablespoon poultry
    seasoning*
1   *to 2 teaspoons salt*
⅛   *teaspoon black pepper*

1. Cook the wild rice in the water for 30 minutes, or until tender. Set aside until needed.

2. Melt the butter in a frying pan and, when it is sizzling, add the celery, scallions, garlic, almond slivers, and mushrooms. Cook over low heat for 5 to 10 minutes, stirring constantly, until the vegetables are soft and the almonds are toasted. (Watch carefully so that the almonds do not burn.)

3. Transfer the vegetables and nuts to a large mixing bowl. Add the cooked wild rice, cooked long-grain rice, parsley, poultry seasoning, salt, and pepper. Mix well.

Note: When you stuff the bird, do not pack the stuffing in tightly. It will expand as the bird roasts.

QUICK RICE STUFFING

Makes Enough for a
12-Pound Turkey

2   *small packages wild rice
    mix, or 1 large package*
3   *tablespoons butter or
    margarine*

½   *cup sliced scallions*
½   *cup chopped celery*
½   *cup pecan halves or
    almond slivers*

1. Prepare the wild rice mix, following the package directions. Set aside until needed.

2. Melt the butter in a small frying pan. When it is sizzling, add the scallions, celery, and pecan halves. Sauté over low heat, stirring con-

stantly, for 5 to 10 minutes, or until the vegetables are soft but not brown. (Watch carefully so that the nuts do not burn.)

3. Transfer the vegetables and nuts to a mixing bowl and add the cooked wild rice. Mix well.

Note: When you stuff the bird, do not pack the stuffing in tightly. It will expand as the bird roasts.

TURKEY CROQUETTES
                                                          4 Servings
                                                          Freezes Well

1½ cups finely chopped cooked   *4   eggs*
*   turkey*   *1   tablespoon minced onion*
1   10½-ounce can undiluted   *   Pinch of poultry seasoning*
*   condensed cream of chicken*   *   Pinch of ground nutmeg*
*   soup*   *1   to 2 tablespoons milk*
2   cups crushed herb stuffing   *1   cup all-purpose flour*
*   mix*   *   Cooking oil*

1. Mix the turkey, cream of chicken soup, 1 cup of the crushed herb stuffing mix, 2 eggs, minced onion, poultry seasoning, nutmeg, and milk together in a bowl. Cover and refrigerate the mixture for 1 to 2 hours.

2. When you are ready to cook the croquettes, beat the 2 remaining eggs in a small bowl. Spread the flour on a sheet of waxed paper. Spread the remaining crushed herb stuffing mix on another sheet of waxed paper.

3. Divide the turkey mixture into 8 equal parts and form each part into a cone. Roll the cones in the flour and then in the beaten eggs. Then coat them with the crushed herb stuffing mix. As the croquettes are coated, stand them up on a flat plate.

4. Heat enough oil to deep-fry the croquettes in a deep frying pan. When the oil is hot, add the croquettes a few at a time. (Do not crowd them in the pan.) Fry the croquettes until they are golden brown on all sides, turning them as often as necessary. Drain on paper towels and serve with Creamy Chicken Gravy (page 212).

Note: You can also make gravy by combining 1 can of cream of turkey or cream of chicken soup with half a can of milk. Heat this sauce until it bubbles.

Variation

Chicken Croquettes: To make Chicken Croquettes, substitute 1½ cups of finely chopped cooked chicken for the turkey.

TURKEY LOAF

6 to 8 Servings
Freezes Well

2	cups finely chopped cooked turkey	2	eggs, slightly beaten
1	10½-ounce can undiluted cream of turkey or cream of chicken soup	2	tablespoons minced onion
		¼	cup finely chopped celery
		4	tablespoons milk
2	cups crushed herb stuffing mix		Pinch of poultry seasoning
		6	to 8 crackers, crushed
		2	tablespoons butter, melted

1. Preheat the oven to 375 degrees.

2. Combine the turkey, turkey soup, herb stuffing mix, eggs, minced onion, chopped celery, milk, and poultry seasoning in a mixing bowl and mix well. Transfer the mixture to a buttered 9- by 5- by 3-inch loaf pan. Sprinkle the cracker crumbs over the top of the loaf and drizzle the melted butter over all. Bake for 30 to 45 minutes, or until firm. (Be careful not to overcook, or the turkey will be dry.) Serve with Creamy Chicken Gravy (page 212).

ROAST DUCK

4 Servings

1	4- to 5-pound ready-to-cook duck	2	or 3 celery stalks
	Salt		Amaretto-Orange Sauce (page 207) or Caramel-Orange Sauce (page 207)

1. Preheat the oven to 375 degrees.

2. Cut off the tips of the wings and discard them. Sprinkle the duck cavity with salt and put the celery stalks, cut to fit, into the cavity. Truss the duck, if you wish, and prick the skin all over with a sharp fork. Lay the duck, breast up, in a shallow roasting pan, and roast for 1½ to 2 hours. To test for doneness, wiggle the duck's legs. If the joint moves freely, the duck is done. If the joint is stiff, increase the oven temperature to 400 or 425 degrees, and roast the duck for 15 to 20 minutes longer. Then test again.

3. To serve, cut the duck into quarters and put on a warm serving platter and pass the sauce separately.

Meats

BEEF WELLINGTON

4 Servings

Liver Pâté
1 **pound chicken livers**
2 **tablespoons butter or margarine**
1 **to 2 tablespoons mayonnaise**
2 **tablespoons melted butter**
2 **tablespoons very dry sherry**
2 **to 3 tablespoons lemon juice**
2 **tablespoons minced onion**
1 **teaspoon prepared mustard**
½ **teaspoon prepared horseradish, optional**
   Salt and black pepper to taste

Beef
1 **2-pound fillet of beef**
   Salt and black pepper to taste
1 **large square frozen puff pastry, thawed**
½ **to ¾ cup liver pâté**

Gravy
   Pan drippings
1 **cup cold water**
2 **tablespoons all-purpose flour**
¼ **cup milk**
   Salt and black pepper

1. To make the pâté, rinse the chicken livers in cold water and pat them dry with paper towels.

2. Melt the butter in a frying pan and, when it is sizzling, add the chicken livers. Sauté the livers, turning often, for 3 to 5 minutes, or until they are cooked through. Transfer the chicken livers to a food processor and puree them while they are still warm. (Or put them through a meat grinder.) Add the remaining ingredients for the pâté and combine well.

3. Preheat the oven to 400 degrees.

4. Sprinkle the fillet generously with salt and pepper. Lay the pastry on a large square of waxed paper. Put the fillet in the center of the pastry. Spread the fillet with a ⅛-inch-thick coating of the pâté. Enclose the fillet in the pastry, sealing the edges of the pastry by dampening them and pressing them together.

5. Transfer the pastry-covered meat to a greased baking dish and bake for 30 minutes. Lower the oven temperature to 375 degrees and bake for 45 to 50 minutes longer for well done. If you like your beef rare, bake for 20 to 30 minutes only at 375 degrees. If the crust begins to brown too quickly, cover the baking dish with a loose tent of aluminum foil.

159

6. To prepare the gravy, remove the roast to a serving platter and spoon off the grease from the pan drippings. Pour the pan drippings into a small saucepan and add ¾ cup water. Dissolve the flour in the remaining cold water. Bring the pan drippings to a simmer and add the flour-water mixture to the simmering pan drippings a little at a time, stirring constantly. Stir in the milk and season the gravy with salt and pepper to taste. Cook, stirring constantly for 3 to 5 minutes.

BEEF TENDERLOIN ROAST

6 to 8 Servings
Freezes Well

1	5- to 7-pound beef tenderloin *Vegetable oil*	*Salt and black pepper to taste*

1. Preheat the oven to 425 degrees.

2. Remove any excess fat and connective tissue from the roast. Lay the roast on a rack in a roasting pan and brush it with oil. Sprinkle the roast liberally with salt and pepper and roast for 45 minutes to 1 hour and 15 minutes, depending on whether you like your meat rare or well done. Check the degree of doneness with a meat thermometer. If the meat begins to brown too much, cover it loosely with an aluminum foil tent. Let the meat rest for about 10 minutes before slicing.

SIRLOIN TIP ROAST

4 to 6 Servings
Freezes Well

1	2½- to 3-pound sirloin tip roast *Salt and black pepper to taste*	2	3	to 3 tablespoons cooking oil tablepoons all-purpose flour dissolved in ¼ cup water

1. Preheat the oven to 350 degrees.

2. Sprinkle the meat on all sides with salt and pepper. Heat the oil in a frying pan and, when it is hot, brown the roast on all sides. Transfer the roast to a baking pan or dish. Mix ⅓ cup water with ¼ teaspoon salt and a pinch of pepper and pour the mixture over the roast. Cover the roast tightly and bake for 1 hour.

3. Lower the oven temperature to 325 degrees and bake the roast for 30 minutes longer.

4. Transfer the roast to a serving platter and cover it with foil to keep it warm.

5. Spoon the grease off the pan juices and add enough water to make 2 cups of liquid. Bring the mixture to a simmer on top of the stove. Stir in the flour-water mixture, a little at a time. Let the gravy simmer for 3 to 5 minutes, stirring constantly. Serve the gravy over the sliced meat.

ROLLED RUMP ROAST

6 to 8 Servings
Freezes Well

1 *3- to 4-pound rolled rump roast*
Salt and black pepper to taste
2 *tablespoons cooking oil*

⅓ *to ½ cup hot water*
3 *tablespoons all-purpose flour dissolved in ¼ cup cold water*

1. Preheat the oven to 350 degrees.
2. Sprinkle the roast liberally with salt and pepper. Heat the oil in a frying pan and, when it is hot, add the roast and brown it on all sides.
3. Transfer the browned roast to a baking pan and pour in the water. Add ½ teaspoon salt and a pinch of pepper to the water. Cover the roasting pan tightly with aluminum foil and bake the roast for 1 hour and 20 minutes to 2 hours, depending on the degree of doneness you desire. Test the doneness with a meat thermometer.
4. Remove the roast to a serving platter and let it rest while you make the gravy.
5. Spoon off any grease from the pan juices and add enough water to the pan juices to make 2 cups. Bring the pan juices to a simmer on top of the stove. Add the flour-water mixture to the pan juices a little at a time. Cook, stirring constantly, for 3 to 5 minutes, or until thickened. Serve the gravy spooned over the sliced meat.

BEEF ROAST WITH VEGETABLES

6 Servings
Freezes Well

1 *3- to 4-pound boneless beef roast*
Salt and black pepper to taste
½ *cup all-purpose flour*
3 *tablespoons cooking oil*
1 *cup water*

6 *medium-sized carrots, peeled and cut in half*
6 *small onions, peeled*
6 *medium-sized potatoes, peeled and quartered*
2 *to 3 tablespoons all-purpose flour dissolved in ⅛ to ¼ cup water*

1. Preheat the oven to 375 degrees.

2. Sprinkle the roast with salt and pepper and dust it with the flour. Heat the oil in a frying pan, and, when it is hot, brown the roast on all sides. Transfer the browned roast to a baking pan or dish. Mix the water with 1 teaspoon of salt and ¼ teaspoon of black pepper and pour the mixture over the roast. Cover the roast tightly and bake it for 1½ hours.

3. While the roast is cooking, prepare the vegetables. Put them in a saucepan of cold water to keep them from drying out.

4. When the roast has been in the oven for 1½ hours, lower the oven temperature to 350 degrees and add the drained vegetables to the roasting pan around the roast. Cover the roast again, and return it to the oven for another 1 to 1½ hours, depending on the size of the roast. Uncover the roast during the last few minutes to allow it to brown a little.

5. Remove the roast and vegetables to a serving platter and cover with foil to keep them warm.

6. Spoon the grease off the pan juices. Bring the pan juices to a simmer on top of the stove, and stir in the flour-water mixture a little at a time. Let the gravy simmer for 3 to 5 minutes, stirring constantly. Serve in a warm sauce boat.

BEEF AND POT PIE SQUARES   6 Servings

1 *2- to 3-pound boneless beef roast*	*Salt*
	Pinch of black pepper
2⅓ *cups water*	1 *egg yolk*
	1 *cup all-purpose flour*

1. Put the roast in a Dutch oven or crock pot or pressure cooker with 2 cups of water, ½ teaspoon salt, and a pinch of pepper. Cook until the meat is very tender and can be broken easily into chunks. Set the beef and cooking liquid aside.

2. Mix the egg yolk with ½ teaspooon of the salt in a small mixing bowl. Add the flour and mix lightly with a fork. Then gradually add the remaining ⅓ cup water until a dough is formed.

3. Put the dough on a lightly floured board and roll it out following the directions for noodles on page 187. The dough should be about ⅟₁₆ inch thick and should be cut into squares about 1½ inches wide.

4. When you are ready to serve, bring 2 cups of the beef cooking liquid to a boil. Add the noodle squares one at a time and cook, stirring

constantly, at a boil for 10 minutes. Cut the beef into chunks and add it to the noodles. Cook for 5 minutes longer. If the mixture thickens too much, add a little more of the beef cooking liquid or water. Serve immediately.

BAKED ROUND STEAK

4 Servings

1 2-pound round steak,
   about ½ inch thick
   Salt and black pepper to
   taste

½ cup all-purpose flour
3 tablespoons cooking oil
1 cup water

1. Preheat the oven to 350 degrees.

2. Trim the fat from the steak and score it lightly so that it won't curl. Pound the steak lightly with a flat meat mallet or the bottom of a frying pan to thin it a little.

3. Cut the meat into serving portions and season it with salt and pepper and dust it lightly with flour.

4. Heat the oil in a frying pan and brown the steak pieces on both sides.

5. While the steak is browning, put the water in a roasting pan. Add ½ teaspoon salt, ⅛ teaspoon black pepper, and 1 teaspoon of the flour left over from dusting the steak. Mix well. Transfer the browned steak to the pan and roast for 1¼ to 1½ hours. Serve with the pan juices.

BERNIE'S CHOP SUEY

8 Servings
Freezes Well

1¼ pounds round steak
¾ pound boneless pork
   shoulder
¼ cup solid shortening
⅓ cup all-purpose flour
⅓ cup soy sauce
2 cups diced celery
2 cups diced onions
¼ cup water
1 14-ounce can bean sprouts

1 can chop suey vegetables
1 small can water chestnuts
   or sliced bamboo shoots,
   with liquid
1 4-ounce can sliced
   mushrooms, or 1 cup
   chopped fresh mushrooms
   Salt and black pepper to
   taste

1. Cut the meats into ½- or 1-inch cubes.

2. Heat the shortening until it is completely melted and very hot. Add the cubed meat and cook, stirring and turning, until the meat is

browned on all sides. Sprinkle the flour over the browned meat cubes and stir it in. Then stir in the soy sauce and mix well. Set aside.

3. Combine the celery, onions, and water in a saucepan and cook until the vegetables are just wilted. Strain the vegetables, but keep their cooking liquid. Add the vegetables to the beef mixture.

4. Put a large sieve over the bowl with the celery and onion cooking liquid. Pour the bean sprouts into the sieve, catching the liquid from the can in the bowl. Transfer the bean sprouts to the beef mixture in the frying pan. Drain the mixed vegetables, water chestnuts, and mushrooms in the same way.

5. When all the drained vegetables have been added to the frying pan, add enough of the reserved liquids to make a thick gravy. Taste the mixture and season it with salt and pepper to taste. Cook the mixture over low heat, stirring occasionally, for 20 minutes. Be sure the mixture does not stick. Add more of the reserved liquids if it becomes too thick. Serve the chop suey with rice and chop suey noodles.

MEAT FONDUES

4 Servings

3 *pounds boneless beef, lamb, veal, or chicken, cut into ½- to 1-inch chunks*	*Hot Sauce, Mustard Sauce, Mint Jelly Sauce, and Soy Sauce (see below)*
1 *clove garlic, peeled and cut in half*	*Small bowls of shredded or flaked coconut, toasted*
2 *to 3 cups peanut or vegetable oil*	*sesame seeds, and ground peanuts.*

1. Rub the garlic around the inside of a fondue pot and then discard the garlic. Add the oil to the pot and heat until very hot.

2. Arrange the meat of your choice on a serving platter and provide each guest with a long-handled fondue fork. Let your guests spear pieces of meat and cook them to their desired doneness in the hot oil.

3. Provide small bowls of the various sauces and condiments for guests to dip their cooked meat into.

Hot Sauce: Mix ketchup, Tabasco sauce, and Worcestershire sauce together to obtain a spicy mixture.

Mustard Sauce: Mix prepared yellow mustard and Dijon-style mustard with soy sauce and curry powder.

Mint Jelly Sauce: Heat a small jar of mint jelly until it is melted. Stir in 1 to 2 tablespoons of lemon juice and mix well.

Soy Sauce: Combine ½ to ¾ cup soy sauce with ½ teaspoon sugar and stir until the sugar is dissolved.

ALL-DAY STEW

4 Servings
Freezes Well

2   *pounds stewing beef, cut into cubes*
4   *medium-sized onions, or 8 small onions, peeled*
4   *medium-sized carrots, peeled and cut in chunks*
3   *potatoes, peeled and quartered*
2   *stalks celery, cut in chunks, optional*
2   *10½-ounce cans condensed tomato soup*

¾   *can of water*
1   *teaspoon salt*
    Pinch of black pepper
¼   *cup dry sherry or apple juice*
1   *10-ounce package frozen peas*
    Chopped fresh parsley leaves or dried parsley flakes

1. Preheat the oven to 275 degrees.
2. Combine all ingredients except the peas and parsley in a large casserole with a tight-fitting lid. Do not stir. Bake for 5 to 6 hours, without stirring.
3. Add the peas and parsley to taste, and bake for ½ hour longer. Serve the stew from the casserole.

Note: This recipe can also be made with lamb.

If your oven has an automatic timer, you can assemble the stew before you leave for work in the morning, and dinner will mostly be ready when you get back in the evening.

FANCY MEATBALLS IN GRAVY

6 to 8 Servings
Freezes Well

4   *pounds ground beef*
½   *package meat loaf seasoning mix, or 1 teaspoon seasoned salt*
1   *10½-ounce can cream of mushroom soup*

1   *10½-ounce can cream of chicken-mushroom soup*
¾   *can water*
¼   *to ½ cup dry sherry*

1. Shape the ground beef into 50 to 65 small balls. Brown them

lightly in a nonstick frying pan. Sprinkle the meatballs with the meat loaf seasoning while they are browning.

2. While the meatballs are browning, combine the soups and water in a large saucepan. Heat and stir until smooth. Remove from the heat and add the drained browned meatballs to the soup mixture.

3. When all of the meatballs have been browned and combined with the soup mixture, drain off all of the fat in the frying pan and scrape any remaining browned particles of meat loaf seasoning from the bottom of the frying pan into the saucepan with the meatballs. Mix in well and bring the soup mixture to a simmer. Simmer for 10 minutes and add the sherry. Mix it in well, and simmer the meatballs for 5 to 10 minutes longer. Serve the meatballs and sauce over rice or buttered noodles.

Note: You can add a cup of sliced mushrooms, which have been sautéed in butter, to the saucepan at the same time you add the sherry.

MEAT LOAF

4 Servings
Freezes Well

1½ pounds ground beef	½ cup fine bread crumbs
½ teaspoon salt	½ green pepper, chopped, optional
½ cup chopped onion	
1 egg	½ package meat loaf season-
½ cup milk	ing mix, optional
1 cup ketchup	20 saltines, crushed very fine

1. Preheat the oven to 375 degrees.

2. In a large bowl, mix together the beef, salt, onion, egg, milk, ½ cup of the ketchup, and the bread crumbs. Stir in the green pepper and the meat loaf seasoning mix.

3. Spread the finely crushed saltines on waxed paper. Form the meat mixture into a loaf and roll it in the crushed saltines until it is well coated. Transfer the meat loaf to a baking pan.

4. Mix the remaining ½ cup of ketchup with ¼ cup of water and pour the mixture over the meat loaf. Bake for 1 hour to 1 hour and 15 minutes.

Note: If you do not use the meat loaf seasoning mix, increase the salt to 1 teaspoon. You can add chunks of carrots and potatoes to the pan with the meat loaf. If you do, pour ½ cup of water over the vegetables.

STUFFED GREEN PEPPERS

6 to 8 Servings
Freezes Well

6 to 8 large green peppers
1 pound ground beef
⅓ cup chopped onion
2 cups cooked rice
½ cup grated mild Cheddar
   cheese

Salt and black pepper to
taste
½ *teaspoon Worcestershire*
   sauce
4 *teaspoons packed light*
   brown sugar
3 *8-ounce cans tomato sauce*

1. Cut the tops off the peppers and seed them carefully. Put the peppers in a large pot and cover them with boiling water. Return the water to a boil and then remove from the heat immediately. Let the peppers sit in the water for 10 minutes. Then drain completely, putting the peppers upside down on paper towels.

2. Put the ground beef and the onion in a nonstick frying pan and cook until the beef is browned. Break the beef up with a wooden spoon as it browns. Drain the beef-onion mixture well and transfer it to a mixing bowl. Add the rice, cheese, and salt and pepper to taste.

3. Combine the Worcestershire sauce, brown sugar, and tomato sauce. Pour half of the mixture into the ground beef mixture and combine well.

4. Preheat the oven to 375 degrees.

5. Stuff the drained peppers with the ground beef mixture and stand them in a large baking dish. Pour the remaining sauce over the peppers and bake for 20 to 30 minutes, or until you can pierce the peppers easily with a fork.

CABBAGE ROLLS

6 to 8 Servings
Freezes Well

1 *medium-sized head green*
   cabbage
3 *tablespoons cooking oil*
1 *medium-sized onion,*
   chopped
1 *pound ground beef*
1 *teaspoon salt*

Pinch of black pepper
⅓ *cup raw rice*
1 *egg*
2 *16-ounce cans tomato*
   sauce
2 *teaspoons sugar*
½ *cup cabbage liquid*

1. Cut the core out of the cabbage. Put the head of cabbage, upside down, in a large pot. Pour boiling water over the cabbage until it is completely covered. Bring the water back to a boil and cook the cabbage over medium heat removing each cabbage leaf as it separates from the head. Put the leaves in a colander to drain. Reserve the cabbage cooking liquid.

2. Heat the oil in a small frying pan and, when it is hot, add the onion. Cook the onion for about 5 minutes, but do not let it brown. Drain the onion and transfer it to a mixing bowl. Add the ground beef, salt, pepper, rice, and egg. Mix well.

3. Cut the tough vein out of each cabbage leaf. Lay each leaf flat and put 2 tablespoons of the meat mixture in the center of the leaf. Fold the sides of the cabbage leaves over the stuffing and then roll up the leaves to make compact little bundles. As each cabbage leaf is filled, set it aside, seam side down.

4. Chop any remaining cabbage finely and put it in a layer on the bottom of a large saucepan or frying pan. Lay the cabbage rolls in a single layer, seam side down, over the chopped cabbage.

5. Mix the tomato sauce and sugar together and pour it over the cabbage rolls. Pour the water over all, cover the pan and cook over low heat for 1 hour to 1 hour and 15 minutes. Gently stir the cabbage rolls and chopped cabbage occasionally while they cook to be sure they do not stick to the bottom of the pan.

CHILI

8 Servings
Freezes Well

2 pounds ground beef	3½ cups tomato juice
1 cup chopped onion	3 teaspoons sugar
2 15½-ounce cans kidney beans (do not drain)	1 package chili seasoning mix
1 28-ounce can whole peeled tomatoes, with juice, chopped	¼ teaspoon onion salt
	⅛ teaspoon garlic salt
	½ cup grated Cheddar cheese

1. Put the beef and onion in a frying pan and cook over medium heat until the beef is browned. Break the beef up with a wooden spoon as it cooks.

2. Drain the beef-onion mixture and transfer it to a large pot. Add the remaining ingredients except the cheese and bring to a boil. Lower the

heat to medium and cook for 1 hour, stirring occasionally. Turn the heat very low and simmer for ½ hour longer. Serve with additional grated Cheddar cheese to be sprinkled on each serving.

Note: This is a very thick chili. If you like a thinner chili, add ½ to 1 cup more tomato juice.

LIVER AND ONIONS IN GRAVY   4 Servings

1 pound beef liver	Cooking oil
Salt and black pepper to taste	1 large onion, sliced and ringed
4 to 5 tablespoons all-purpose flour	1 or 2 cups water
	2 cups cooked rice

1. Sprinkle the liver with salt and pepper, then dust it with the flour. Set the remaining flour aside, adding to it to make 2 or 3 tablespoons of flour.

2. Heat ¼ to ½ inch of oil in the bottom of a frying pan until it is very hot, but not smoking. Add the liver and brown it on both sides until crispy.

3. Add the sliced onion rings to the frying pan and sauté for 3 to 5 minutes.

4. Lower the heat and add the reserved flour to the frying pan. Stir it into the oil in the pan and combine it well with the liver and sautéed onions. Pour in enough water to make a gravy as thick or thin as you like. Cover the frying pan and cook over very low heat for 10 to 12 minutes. Serve the liver, onions, and gravy over rice.

ROAST LEG OF LAMB   8 to 10 Servings

1 6- to 7-pound leg of lamb	⅛ teaspoon cayenne pepper
2 cloves garlic, peeled and crushed	1 tablespoon all-purpose flour
½ teaspoon dried rosemary	3 tablespoons fine bread crumbs
½ teaspoon ground cinnamon	
½ teaspoon ground cloves	1 cup finely ground pecans
1½ teaspoons salt	4 tablespoons butter or margarine, melted
¼ teaspoon black pepper	

1. Preheat the oven to 350 degrees.

2. Trim the excess fat from the lamb and remove the fell (the thin, almost transparent skin) from the top portion of the leg. Score the lamb in a diamond pattern and put it in a large roasting pan.

3. Put the garlic, rosemary, cinnamon, cloves, salt, black pepper, cayenne pepper, flour, bread crumbs, and pecans in a blender and blend until well combined. Add the melted butter to the mixture and blend until a paste is formed.

4. Pat the paste over the top of the lamb and score the lamb again. Transfer the roast to the preheated oven and roast for 2 to 2½ hours. The meat will be pink. Roast longer if you like your lamb well done.

LAMB CHOPS SUPREME 6 Servings

6   *thick loin lamb chops*
    Salt and black pepper to taste
½   *cup plus 3 tablespoons all-purpose flour*
3   *tablespoons vegetable oil*
1   *tablespoon butter or margarine*
1   *10½-ounce can cream of celery soup*
¾   *can water*

½   *cup sliced scallions, including green tops*
    Pinch of dried rosemary
    Pinch of dried thyme
1   *4-ounce can sliced mushrooms*
1   *tablespoon chopped parsley*
2   *heaping tablespoons grated Parmesan cheese*

1. Season the chops with salt and pepper and dust them with the flour.

2. Heat the oil and butter in a frying pan large enough to hold the chops in a single layer. When the butter is sizzling, add the chops and brown them on both sides. Remove the chops to a plate and clean the frying pan.

3. Put the soup, water, scallions, rosemary, and thyme into the clean frying pan. Mix well and bring to a simmer. Return the chops to the frying pan and spoon some of the sauce over them. Cover the pan and cook over low heat for 35 to 45 minutes or until the chops are tender.

4. Drain the canned mushroom liquid into a small bowl or cup. Add the 3 tablespoons of flour and mix until a smooth paste is formed.

5. Remove the chops to a plate and cover them with foil to keep them warm.

6. Add the flour paste to the sauce in the frying pan a little at a time, stirring constantly. Cook over low heat, stirring, until the sauce has thickened. Then stir in the drained mushrooms, parsley, and Parmesan cheese. Cook until the mushrooms are heated through. Pour the sauce over the chops and serve immediately.

Note: If the sauce is too thick, it can be thinned with a little milk.

IRISH LAMB STEW

6 to 8 Servings
Freezes Well

2	to 3 pounds boneless lamb, cut into 1-inch cubes	2½	cups water
4	large potatoes, peeled and cut into large cubes	1½	teaspoons salt
			Black pepper to taste
8	small onions, peeled	¼	teaspoon sugar
		¼	cup chopped parsley

1. Trim the fat from the lamb cubes and put the cubes in a large Dutch oven. Add the potatoes, onions, water, salt, and pepper. Mix well and bring to a boil. Lower the heat, cover the pan, and simmer for 1 to 2 hours, or until the lamb is tender.

2. Stir the sugar and parsley into the stew and mix well. Simmer for 5 to 10 minutes longer before serving.

VEAL PARMESAN

4 Servings
Freezes Well

2	tablespoons butter or margarine	1	pound veal cutlets
1	egg	1	8-ounce can tomato sauce
¾	cup seasoned stuffing mix	½	teaspoon dried oregano
¼	cup grated Parmesan cheese	¼	teaspoon sugar
	Salt and black pepper to taste		Pinch of onion salt
		2	thin slices mozzarella cheese, cut in half, or ½ cup shredded mozzarella

1. Preheat the oven to 400 degrees. Put the butter in a baking pan or dish and put the pan in the oven until the butter is melted.

2. Beat the egg in a pie plate or soup bowl. Combine the crushed stuffing crumbs, Parmesan cheese, and salt and pepper on a sheet of waxed paper.

3. Dip the veal cutlets into the beaten egg and then coat them on

both sides in the crumb mixture, pressing the coating on with the palm of your hand. Put the coated cutlets in the baking pan on top of the melted butter. Return the baking pan to the oven and bake the cutlets for 20 minutes.

4. Turn the veal cutlets over and bake them for 15 minutes longer, or until they are tender.

5. Combine the tomato sauce, oregano, sugar, and onion salt in a small saucepan. Heat just to the boiling point, stirring occasionally. Pour the hot sauce over the meat in the baking pan. Lay the sliced cheese on top of the veal and return the pan to the oven for 5 to 10 minutes, or until the cheese has melted.

VEAL SCALLOPINI

4 to 6 Servings
Freezes Well

1½ *pounds veal round steak*
½ *cup all-purpose flour*
Salt and black pepper to taste
½ *teaspoon paprika*
Oil for frying
1 *4-ounce can sliced mushrooms*
1 *teaspoon beef bouillon granules*
1 *8-ounce can tomato sauce*
¼ *cup water*

2 *tablespoons chopped green pepper*
1 *tablespoon minced onion*
½ *teaspoon Italian seasoning*
Grated Parmesan cheese
1 *tablespoon chopped fresh parsley or dried parsley flakes*
4 *ounces noodles, cooked following package directions*

1. Put the veal between sheets of waxed paper and pound it with a flat meat mallet or small frying pan to thin it. Cut the veal into serving pieces.

2. Combine the flour, salt, pepper, and paprika on a sheet of waxed paper. Dust the veal pieces with the mixture. Set any remaining flour aside.

3. Heat ¼ inch of oil in a frying pan and, when it is hot, add the veal and brown it on both sides. Transfer the browned veal to a 9-inch-square baking dish.

4. Preheat the oven to 350 degrees.

5. Drain the liquid from the canned mushrooms into a measuring cup. Add enough cold water to make ¾ cup. Stir in 1 tablespoon of the

reserved flour and mix to make a smooth paste. Transfer the mixture to a small saucepan and bring it to a boil. Stir in the bouillon powder and mix well. Pour the sauce over the veal in the baking dish. Cover tightly and bake for 30-45 minutes.

6. Combine the mushrooms, tomato sauce, water, green pepper, minced onion, salt, pinch of pepper, and Italian seasoning and pour the mixture over the veal. Bake, uncovered, for 15 minutes longer. Just before serving, baste the meat with the sauce and sprinkle it with the grated Parmesan cheese and parsley. Serve with the noodles.

PORK ROAST WITH RAISIN SAUCE   8 to 10 Servings

1   *4- to 5-pound center loin,*   1   *tablespoon cooking oil*
   blade loin, or boned loin   1½ *cups Raisin Sauce (page*
   pork roast   *208)*
   Salt and black pepper to
   taste

1. Preheat the oven to 325 degrees.
2. Sprinkle the roast with salt and pepper, and brown it on all sides in the cooking oil. Transfer the meat to a shallow baking pan and roast for 2½ to 3 hours.
3. When the roast is almost done, pour the Raisin Sauce over it. Roast for 30 minutes longer, basting occasionally.
4. To serve the roast, spoon the fat off the sauce in the bottom of the roasting pan and serve the sauce over the sliced meat.

PORK ROAST WITH GRAVY   8 to 10 Servings

1   *4- to 5-pound center loin,*   1   *tablespoon cooking oil*
   blade loin, or boned loin   1   *cup warm water*
   pork roast   ¼   *cup cold milk or water*
   Salt and black pepper to   2   *tablespoons all-purpose*
   taste   *flour*

1. Preheat the oven to 325 degrees.
2. Sprinkle the roast with salt and pepper, and brown it on all sides in the cooking oil. Transfer the meat to a shallow baking pan. Mix the water with ¼ teaspoon salt and pour the mixture into the baking pan.
3. Roast the meat for 2½ to 3 hours, testing for doneness with a meat thermometer.

4. Remove the roast to a serving platter and cover it with aluminum foil to keep it warm.

5. Pour the pan juices into a small saucepan and put the saucepan in the freezer for a few minutes to chill the juices. Scoop off any fat from the top of the chilled juices.

6. Combine the cold milk or water and the flour to make a smooth paste. Stir the mixture into the pan juices in the saucepan. Bring to a boil over medium heat, stirring constantly. Lower the heat and simmer the gravy, stirring, for 3 to 4 minutes. Serve the gravy over the sliced meat.

PORK ROAST ON SAUERKRAUT

6 Servings
Freezes Well

1	4- to 6-pound pork roast	5	heaping tablespoons light brown sugar
	Salt and black pepper to taste		
		1	tablespoon granulated sugar
3	tablespoons cooking oil		
1	27-ounce can sauerkraut, drained	½	cup water

1. Preheat the oven to 350 degrees.

2. Sprinkle the roast generously with salt and pepper and brown it on all sides in the oil.

3. While the roast is browning, combine the sauerkraut, sugars, and water in a roasting pan. Make a depression in the center of the sauerkraut and put the browned roast into the depression. Cover the pan tightly and bake for 2½ to 3 hours.

CROWN ROAST OF PORK WITH NUTTED PINEAPPLE RICE

6 Servings

1	14-rib crown roast of pork	2	2¾-ounce packages slivered almonds
	Salt and black pepper to taste		
		1	cup small pineapple chunks (made from pineapple rings)
6	cups cooked rice		
6	tablespoons butter or margarine		
		1	cup pineapple juice (from canned pineapple rings)

1. Order the crown roast from your butcher a few days ahead of time. Ask him to tie it into shape for you.

2. Preheat the oven to 325 degrees.

3. Sprinkle the roast inside and out with salt and pepper. Put the roast in a roasting pan and roast for 2½ hours, or until a meat thermometer registers between 170 and 175 degrees.

4. While the roast is in the oven, prepare the rice. Use a fork to stir 2 tablespoons of the butter into the hot rice.

5. Melt the remaining butter in a small frying pan and sauté the slivered almonds until they are golden brown. Watch them carefully so that they do not burn. Add the almonds and the pineapple chunks to the rice along with ½ cup of the pineapple juice. Use a fork to toss the mixture until all the ingredients are incorporated.

6. When the roast has cooked for about 2½ hours, remove it from the oven and pour off the pan juices into a small saucepan. (You can use these juices to make gravy if you wish.) Place the roast meat side down and brush it with the remaining ½ cup of pineapple juice. Spoon the rice mixture into the center of the roast and put any remaining rice mixture in the pan around the roast. Return the roast to the oven for 15 to 20 minutes.

7. To serve, transfer the stuffed roast to a serving platter and garnish with the remaining pineapple slices.

BAKED PORK CHOPS

6 Servings
Freezes Well

6	pork loin blade chops All-purpose flour for dusting Salt and black pepper to taste	2	tablespoons red wine vinegar
1	tablespoon cooking oil	1	teaspoon Worcestershire sauce
½	cup ketchup	2	tablespoons dry sherry
¼	cup finely chopped onion	¼	cup pineapple or apple juice
2	tablespoons light brown sugar		Dash of Tabasco sauce
		1	tablespoon butter or margarine

1. Preheat the oven to 375 degrees.

2. Dredge the chops in a mixture of the flour and salt and pepper. Then brown them lightly in the cooking oil. Transfer the browned chops to a baking pan.

3. Combine the remaining ingredients in a small saucepan and heat just to the boiling point. Remove the sauce from the heat and pour it over

the chops in the baking pan. Turn the chops in the sauce to coat both sides.

4. Bake the chops for 40 minutes, or until tender, basting them occasionally with the sauce.

STUFFED PORK CHOPS

4 Servings
Freezes Well

4	*cups prepared stuffing mix*	2	*teaspoons chicken bouillon*
4	*tablespoons butter or*		*granules*
	margarine	2	*cups warm water*
1	*cup finely chopped celery*	4	*double pork chops with*
½	*cup finely chopped onion*		*slit pockets*
1	*egg*		

1. Preheat the oven to 325 degrees.

2. Put the stuffing mix in a baking dish.

3. Melt 3 tablespoons of the butter in a frying pan and, when it is sizzling, add the celery and onion. Sauté the vegetables for 2 to 3 minutes.

4. Mix the sautéed vegetables with the stuffing mix in the baking dish. Stir in the egg until it is mixed in well. Combine the chicken bouillon granules with the water and mix it with the stuffing mix until the stuffing is moist.

5. Melt the remaining tablespoon of butter in the same frying pan in which the celery and onion were cooked. Add the pork chops and brown them on all sides.

6. Push 1 tablespoon of the stuffing mixture into the pocket in each chop. Rest the stuffed chops at an angle on the remaining stuffing in the baking dish, so the stuffing does not come out of the pockets while the chops cook. Cover the baking dish and bake for 1 hour. Remove the cover and bake for 15 minutes longer, or until the chops are tender.

HAM LOAF

4 to 6 Servings
Freezes Well

1	*pound cooked ham*	½	*cup ketchup*
¾	*pound sausage meat*	1	*tablespoon light brown*
¾	*cup bread crumbs*		*sugar*
1	*egg*	2	*tablespoons minced onion*
1	*teaspoon powdered*	¼	*cup finely chopped celery*
	mustard	20	*saltines, crushed*

1. Preheat the oven to 350 degrees.

2. Grind the ham and mix it with the sausage meat in a bowl. Dampen the bread crumbs with a little water to make them soggy and add them to the meats with the egg, mustard, ¼ cup of the ketchup, the onion, and celery.

3. Spread the crushed crackers on a large sheet of waxed paper. Form the meat mixture into a loaf and coat it on all sides with the crushed crackers. Transfer the loaf to a baking pan. Mix the remaining ¼ cup of ketchup with the brown sugar and pour the mixture over the loaf. Bake for 45 minutes.

Variation

Pineapple Upside-Down Ham Loaf: Pour 2 tablespoons of melted butter over the bottom of an 8-inch-square glass baking dish. Sprinkle 4 heaping tablespoons of light brown sugar over the butter. Top the brown sugar with enough drained canned pineapple rings to cover the bottom of the baking dish. Press the *uncoated* ham loaf mixture into the pan on top of the pineapple slices. Bake at 350 degrees for 45 minutes. This will make 6 to 8 servings and it freezes well.

HAM LOAF–SPINACH ROULADE

6 to 8 Servings
Freezes Well

2	tablespoons butter or margarine	1	recipe Ham Loaf mixture (page 176), *without the cracker crumbs*
1	tablespoon grated onion		
2	10-ounce packages frozen chopped spinach, thawed and drained	¼	cup grated mild Cheddar cheese
		2	hard-boiled eggs, peeled and chopped
2	eggs		
4	tablespoons milk	1	cup ketchup
½	teaspoon salt	½	cup honey
	Pinch of black pepper	1	teaspoon lemon juice
	Pinch of ground nutmeg	¼	to ½ cup drained crushed pineapple
1	cup fine bread crumbs, moistened with water		

1. Melt the butter and, when it is sizzling, add the onion and sauté for 2 minutes. Add the thawed and drained spinach, eggs, milk, salt, pepper, and nutmeg. Mix well and cook over low heat for 1 to 2 minutes.

2. Preheat the oven to 350 degrees.

3. Put the Ham Loaf mixture between two long sheets of waxed paper and roll it into a long rectangle. Remove the top sheet of waxed paper and spread the spinach mixture over the ham mixture. Sprinkle the grated Cheddar cheese and chopped eggs over the spinach. Then roll up the rectangle like a jelly roll, removing the waxed paper as you go.

4. Transfer the roulade to a foil-lined roasting pan, seam side down. Bake for 30 minutes.

5. While the roulade is baking, combine the ketchup, honey, lemon juice, and crushed pineapple in a saucepan. Heat until the sauce just reaches the boiling point. Remove from the heat and set aside until the roulade has baked for 30 minutes.

6. Baste the roulade with one-third of the sauce and return it to the oven for 10 minutes. Baste two more times, using one-third of the sauce each time, and baking the roulade for 10 minutes longer each time.

BAKED HAM

1 6-pound fully cooked ham half with bone in, or 1 8-pound whole boneless ham, or 1 10-pound fully cooked ham with bone in	*Fruit Glaze*
1 cup cola	½ cup fruit syrup
	½ cup loosely packed light brown sugar
	½ teaspoon powdered mustard

1. Preheat the oven to 325 degrees.

2. Score the ham on the fat side and put it fat side up on a large piece of heavy-duty aluminum foil in a large baking pan. Pour the cola over the ham and seal the foil tightly around the ham. Transfer the pan to the oven and roast the ham 1 hour and 15 minutes for the 6-pound ham, 2 to 2½ hours for the 8-pound ham, or 2½ to 3 hours for the 10-pound ham.

3. While the ham bakes, combine the ingredients for the glaze in a small saucepan. Heat the mixture just until it comes to a boil. Remove from the heat and set aside.

4. Open the foil surrounding the ham and pour off the pan juices. Spoon the fruit glaze over the ham and bake the ham for 1 hour longer, no matter what size the ham is.

NAVY BEAN AND HAM CASSEROLE

6 to 8 Servings
Freezes Well

1   *pound navy beans, picked*
    over and washed
    Salt

2   *to 3 cups cubed or sliced*
    ham

1. Soak the beans overnight in cold water to cover them by 1 inch.

2. Drain the beans and cover them again with cold water to a depth of 1 inch above the beans. Add ¼ teaspoon salt and bring the water to a boil. Lower the heat, cover the pan, and cook the beans for 2 hours, stirring occasionally.

3. Preheat the oven to 325 degrees.

4. Pour half the beans into a casserole. Put the cubed or sliced ham in a layer on top of the beans and pour the remaining beans over the ham. Cover the casserole and bake for 35 to 45 minutes, or until the beans are tender.

Note: If you forget to soak the beans overnight, you can just cook them for 30 minutes longer before assembling the casserole, and then bake them for an additional 15 minutes in the oven.

The beans should be rather soupy before they are poured into the casserole. If they are not, add ½ to 1 cup of water to the beans before you assemble the casserole for baking.

BARBECUED SPARERIBS

8 Servings
Freezes Well

6   *to 8 pounds meaty*
    spareribs
    Salt and black pepper to
    taste

2   *cups Spicy Barbecue Sauce*
    (page 211), or see
    Note below

1. Preheat the oven to 425 degrees.

2. Cut the ribs into serving portions and sprinkle them with salt and pepper on both sides. Lay the ribs, curved side up, in shallow baking pans. Roast for 30 to 35 minutes.

3. Lower the oven temperature to 225 degrees and baste the ribs with the barbecue sauce. Continue to roast for 1 to 2 hours longer, depending on the thickness of the ribs. Baste once or twice more with the barbecue sauce. For a crustier coating, run the ribs under the broiler for 2 to 3 minutes before serving.

Note: If you don't want to use the Spicy Barbecue Sauce, you can combine an 8-ounce jar of prepared barbecue sauce with ¼ to ½ cup pineapple juice and brush this mixture over the ribs instead.

Pasta, Noodles, and Rice

SPAGHETTI SAUCE WITH MEAT

6 Servings
Freezes Well

2 pounds ground beef	1½ packages spaghetti
1 teaspoon salt	seasonings with
½ cup chopped onion	mushrooms
¾ cup chopped green pepper	2 4-ounce cans mushroom
1 32-ounce jar prepared	stems and pieces, drained,
spaghetti sauce with meat	or 1 cup chopped fresh
1 8-ounce jar prepared	mushrooms
spaghetti sauce with meat	2 to 3 tablespoons sugar

1. Put the ground beef, salt, and onion in a frying pan and cook over medium heat, breaking up the ground beef with a wooden spoon, until the meat is browned.

2. Drain and put the meat mixture in a saucepan large enough to hold all the ingredients. Add the green pepper, both jars of spaghetti sauce with meat, the spaghetti seasonings with mushrooms, the mushrooms, and the sugar. Stir to combine well and bring to a boil. Cook over medium heat, stirring occasionally, for 30 minutes. Lower the heat to very low, and cook for 15 to 30 minutes longer, or until the sauce has thickened slightly.

Note: If you are going to freeze the sauce, let it cool to room temperature before you put it in freezer containers.

If you cook extra spaghetti when you use this sauce, you can freeze the leftover spaghetti in a freezer bag. Then you will not have to cook spaghetti when you want to serve this sauce again. The defrosted and reheated spaghetti can just be combined with the sauce after it has heated for a little while.

CHEESE-STUFFED PASTA SHELLS

6 Servings
Freezes Well

24 to 30 extra-large pasta shells

12 ounces large-curd cottage cheese

1 pound ricotta cheese, approximately

1 cup shredded processed American cheese

½ cup grated Romano or Parmesan cheese

1 heaping tablespoon parsley flakes

2 eggs

1 teaspoon salt

¼ teaspoon onion salt

¼ teaspoon garlic salt

½ teaspoon sugar

2 heaping tablespoons seasoned bread crumbs, crushed

2 8-ounce cans tomato sauce, or 2 cups Spaghetti Sauce (page 180)

2 tablespoons water

1 teaspoon dried oregano

1. Cook the pasta shells in boiling water, following the package directions. Drain well and run under cool water for a few seconds. Turn each pasta shell upside down on a flat surface and let drain while you prepare the remaining ingredients.

2. Combine the cottage cheese, ricotta, American cheese, Romano cheese, parsley flakes, eggs, salts, sugar, and bread crumbs in a mixing bowl. Beat together with a fork until the mixture is smooth.

3. Preheat the oven to 375 degrees.

4. Pour half the spaghetti sauce over the bottom of a baking dish large enough to hold the pasta shells comfortably. Stir in the water and mix well.

5. Use a teaspoon to stuff the cooked shells with the cheese mixture. As they are filled, put the shells in the baking dish. When all the shells are filled and in the dish, pour the remaining sauce over the top of the shells.

6. Sprinkle the oregano over the stuffed shells and bake for 35 to 40 minutes. Serve immediately.

CHICKEN-FILLED PASTA SHELLS

4 Servings
Freezes Well

12   *extra large pasta shells*
2   *cups minced cooked*
     skinless chicken
¼   *cup very fine unseasoned*
     bread crumbs (made in
     blender)
3   *teaspoons minced onion*
½   *cup chicken broth*
1   *egg*
     Salt and black pepper to
     taste

Cheese Sauce

2   *tablespoons all-purpose*
     flour
1¼ *cups cold milk*
¼   *to ½ teaspoon salt*
1   *cup grated processed*
     American cheese
1   *cup grated Swiss cheese*
     Pinch of ground nutmeg
½   *teaspoon sugar*
1   *tablespoon butter or*
     margarine

1. Cook the pasta shells in boiling water, following the package directions. Drain well and run under cool water for a few seconds. Turn each pasta shell upside down on a flat surface and let drain while you prepare the remaining ingredients.

2. Put the chicken in a mixing bowl and sprinkle the bread crumbs and onion over it. In another small bowl, combine the chicken broth, egg, and salt and pepper. Mix together very well and then pour over the chicken and mix well again.

3. Use a teaspoon to stuff the cooked shells with the chicken mixture. As you fill them, put the shells in a buttered baking dish just large enough to hold them.

4. Preheat the oven to 350 degrees.

5. To make the Cheese Sauce, put the flour in a small saucepan. Gradually add the milk, stirring with a wire whisk, until the flour is completely dissolved. Stir in the salt and put the saucepan over medium heat. Bring to a boil, stirring occasionally. Then add the remaining sauce ingredients. Lower the heat and stir until the cheeses have melted and the sauce is smooth. (If the sauce seems too thick, thin it with a little more milk, added a tablespoon at a time.) Pour the sauce over the filled pasta shells and bake for 15 to 20 minutes. Remove from the oven just before the cheese begins to brown.

ALENE DREXLER'S MEATBALL LASAGNE

8 Servings
Freezes Well

Meatballs

1   pound ground beef
½   pound ground pork
2   cloves garlic, peeled and
     finely chopped
1   egg
1   teaspoon salt
¼   teaspoon black pepper
4   saltine crackers

Sauce

1   pound Italian sausages
3   28-ounce cans tomato
     puree
1   28-ounce can whole peeled
     tomatoes
2   tablespoons dried basil
     Salt and pepper to taste

Ricotta Mixture

1   pound ricotta cheese,
     approximately
4   eggs
1   teaspoon salt
½   teaspoon black pepper
     Oil for frying
1   package lasagne noodles
1   pound mozzarella cheese,
     sliced

1. Put the ground meats, garlic, egg, salt, black pepper, and saltines in a mixing bowl. Mix well, using your hand or a spoon. Form the mixture into small balls, approximately 1 inch in diameter. (You will find it easier to form the balls if you dampen the palms of your hands before you roll each ball.)

2. Heat some cooking oil in a frying pan and, when it is hot, add the meatballs. Brown them on all sides, turning them gently as they brown. Transfer the meatballs to a plate as they are browned. When all the meatballs have been cooked, add the sausages to the frying pan and brown them on all sides. Transfer them to the plate with the meatballs.

3. Combine the tomato puree, peeled tomatoes, and basil in a large Dutch oven. Stir to mix well. Bring to a boil over medium heat, stirring occasionally. When the sauce is boiling, season with salt and pepper and add the meatballs and sausages. Lower the heat, cover, and cook for 3 hours, stirring occasionally so the meats do not stick to the bottom of the pan. (After the sauce has cooked for about an hour, you may want to skim off and discard any fat that has risen to the top of the sauce.)

4. While the sauce is cooking, combine the ricotta with the eggs, salt, and pepper in a mixing bowl. Beat together with a fork until the eggs

are completely mixed with the ricotta. Cover the bowl tightly and re-frigerate until needed.

5. Just before the sauce is finished, cook the lasagne noodles, following the package directions. Drain the noodles well and let them stand in a pot of cold water until needed.

6. Preheat the oven to 375 degrees.

7. Remove the meatballs and sausages from the sauce. Break the meatballs into small pieces with a fork. Cut the sausages into thin slices with a knife.

8. To assemble the lasagne, cover the bottom of a 9- by 13-inch baking dish with a thin layer of sauce. Drain enough lasagne noodles to cover the bottom of the baking dish and lay them in the dish, overlapping them slightly. Spread about one-third of the ricotta mixture over the noodles. Spread about one-third of the meatball and sausage pieces over the ricotta. Lay one-third of the mozzarella slices over the pieces of meat. Spoon a thin layer of sauce over the mozzarella and continue making layers of lasagne noodles, ricotta, meat, and mozzarella until all are used up. Top the last layer of mozzarella with a thin layer of sauce, add a top layer of overlapping lasagne noodles, and spread the noodles with a generous amount of sauce.

9. Bake the lasagne for 1 hour. Let sit for about 15 minutes before cutting and serving with the remaining sauce which has been heated through.

MEAT LASAGNE

8 Servings
Freezes Well

12	lasagne noodles	1	teaspoon sugar
1½	pounds ground beef	1	32-ounce jar spaghetti
	Salt		sauce with mushrooms
¼	cup chopped onion		Butter
12	ounces large-curd cottage		Dried basil
	cheese		Dried oregano
1	pound ricotta cheese,	24	ounces shredded mozzarella
	approximately		cheese
2	eggs		Grated Parmesan cheese
	Black pepper to taste		

1. Cook the lasagne noodles in boiling water, following the package directions. Drain the noodles well and let them stand in a pot of cold water until needed.

2. Put the ground beef, salt to taste, and the onion in a frying pan and cook over medium heat, breaking up the ground beef with a wooden spoon, until the beef is browned. Drain the fat from the meat mixture and transfer the meat to a small bowl.

3. Combine the cottage cheese, ricotta, eggs, salt to taste, and pepper in a mixing bowl. Beat together with a fork until the mixture is smooth. Set aside until needed.

4. Stir the sugar into the spaghetti sauce.

5. Preheat the oven to 350 degrees.

6. Butter the bottom and sides of a 9- by 13-inch baking dish. Spoon a thin layer of sauce over the bottom of the dish. Drain 4 lasagne noodles and lay them over the sauce, overlapping them slightly. Spread one-third of the cheese mixture over the noodles and sprinkle it with some basil and oregano. Sprinkle on about a third of the ground beef mixture. Then sprinkle a third of the mozzarella over the ground beef. Spoon a thin layer of sauce over the mozzarella and continue making layers as above, ending with a layer of mozzarella on top. Sprinkle grated Parmesan cheese generously over the mozzarella and bake the lasagne for 45 minutes to 1 hour. Let sit for about 15 minutes before cutting. Serve with any remaining sauce, heated through.

EASY VEGETABLE LASAGNE

8 to 10 Servings
Freezes Well

12	lasagne noodles	3	large zucchini, trimmed, washed, and sliced thin
	Butter		
1	32-ounce jar spaghetti sauce with mushrooms	24	ounces shredded mozzarella cheese
1	24- or 30-ounce container cottage cheese		Dried basil
			Dried parsley flakes
			Grated Parmesan cheese

1. Cook the lasagne noodles in boiling water, following the package directions. Drain the noodles well and let them stand in a pot of cold water until needed.

2. Preheat the oven to 375 degrees.

3. Butter the bottom and sides of a 9- by 13-inch baking dish. Spoon a thin layer of sauce over the bottom of the dish. Drain 3 lasagne noodles and lay them over the sauce, overlapping them slightly. Spread one-third of the cottage cheese over the noodles. Then make a layer of one-third of

the zucchini slices. Sprinkle about a third of the mozzarella over the zucchini and then sprinkle some basil and parsley over the mozzarella. Spoon a thin layer of sauce over the mozzarella and spices and continue making layers, ending with a layer of noodles topped with mozzarella. Sprinkle the grated Parmesan cheese generously over the top.

4. Bake for 45 minutes to 1 hour. Remove from the oven and let sit for about 15 minutes before cutting and serving with any remaining sauce which has been heated through.

Note: You can substitute chopped, well-drained spinach for the zucchini. Ricotta can serve as a substitute for the cottage cheese.

IRISH SPAGHETTI

8 Servings
Freezes Well

Spaghetti
4   to 6 cups water
1   tablespoon butter,
    margarine, or oil
½   teaspoon salt
2   cups elbow macaroni

Meat Mixture
1   pound ground beef
½   cup chopped onion

2   16-ounce cans peeled
    tomatoes, chopped, with
    liquid
1   cup tomato juice
4   to 5 teaspoons sugar
1   tablespoon butter or
    margarine
    Salt and pepper to taste

1. To cook the macaroni, put the water, butter, and salt in a saucepan and bring to a boil. Add the elbow macaroni, return to a boil, and cook for 8 to 10 minutes, stirring occasionally. Drain well and set aside.

2. Put the ground beef and onion in a frying pan and cook over medium heat, breaking up the ground beef with a wooden spoon, until the beef is browned.

3. Drain and put the meat mixture in a saucepan large enough to hold all the ingredients. Add the tomatoes with their liquid, the tomato juice, sugar, butter, cooked, drained macaroni, and salt and pepper. Stir to mix well and bring to a boil over high heat. Lower the heat and simmer, stirring occasionally for 10 to 15 minutes longer. Serve immediately.

Note: This can be served immediately or can be turned into a buttered baking dish and baked in a 350-degree oven for 30 to 45 minutes.

MACARONI AND CHEESE

8 Servings
Freezes Well

2 cups elbow macaroni
2 cups grated American cheese
2 tablespoons butter, melted

½ pound (8 ounces) mild Cheddar cheese, diced
2½ cups milk
1 teaspoon salt

1. Cook the macaroni in boiling water, following the package directions. Drain well and transfer to a large mixing bowl to cool.

2. When the macaroni is cool, preheat the oven to 350 degrees. Add the remaining ingredients to the macaroni in the bowl and mix thoroughly. Transfer to a large buttered casserole and bake for 1 hour to 1 hour and 15 minutes. Let sit for a few minutes before serving.

EGG NOODLES

4 Servings

1½ cups all-purpose flour
2 egg yolks

⅓ cup water
Pinch of salt

1. Put the flour in a mixing bowl. Make a depression in the center of the flour and add the egg yolks, water, and salt to the depression. Use a fork to stir the flour gradually into the yolks and water. When the flour is completely moistened, form the dough into a ball.

2. Put the dough in the center of a well-floured board and roll it out, turning it over a few times, flouring the top of the dough as you go. Roll the dough out as thin as possible. (You may also find it necessary to flour the board and rolling pin to keep the dough from sticking.) Let the rolled-out dough dry on the floured board for 30 minutes to 1 hour.

3. Fold the dough in half and then roll it up tightly. Cut the rolled dough in very thin slices with a sharp knife, separating as you go. Let the noodles dry on a flat surface for 2 to 3 hours.

Note: You can store the noodles in an airtight container in the refrigerator, or freeze them in a plastic bag.

Cook the noodles in salted broth, using 2 cups broth to 1 cup noodles. Cook for 10 to 15 minutes, or until the noodles are tender.

Tuna-Noodle Casserole

4 Servings
Freezes Well

2 cups cooked noodles
1 7-ounce can tuna, drained
1 can cream of mushroom
  soup
½ cup half-and-half
½ cup milk
  Salt, optional

2 tablespoons chopped
  parsley, optional
½ cup crushed potato chips,
  or ¼ cup unseasoned bread
  crumbs
2 tablespoons butter, melted

1. Preheat the oven to 400 degrees.

2. Combine the noodles, tuna, soup, half-and-half, milk, salt, and parsley in a large mixing bowl. Pour the mixture into a large buttered casserole and bake for 20 to 25 minutes. Remove from the oven and stir. Sprinkle the potato chips over the top of the casserole and drizzle the melted butter over the potato chips. Return to the oven and bake for 5 to 7 minutes longer.

Note: If you use bread crumbs for a topping instead of crushed potato chips, toss the crumbs with the melted butter before you sprinkle them over the top of the casserole.

Variation

Chicken-Noodle Casserole: Substitute 1 cup of diced cooked chicken for the tuna and 1 can of cream of chicken soup for the mushroom soup.

Rice Pilaf

4 Servings
Freezes Well

3 tablespoons butter
1 cup raw rice
2 cups chicken or beef broth,
  heated
¼ cup sliced scallions

1 2½-ounce jar sliced
  mushrooms, drained
½ teaspoon salt (if broth is
  unsalted)

Melt the butter in a saucepan. Add the rice and sauté, stirring constantly, for 2 to 3 minutes. Stir in the hot broth and bring to a boil. Lower the heat to very low, add the scallions, mushrooms, and salt, and cover tightly. Cook for 10 to 15 minutes, or until the broth has been absorbed and the rice is tender. Stir with a fork once or twice during the cooking time.

RICE SOUFFLÉ   4 Servings

4 tablespoons butter or margarine	1 cup cold cooked instant rice
1 cup milk	½ teaspoon salt
4 tablespoons all-purpose flour	4 eggs, at room temperature, separated
¼ cup grated Parmesan cheese	2 egg whites, at room temperature
½ cup shredded mild Cheddar cheese	

1. Preheat the oven to 300 degrees.

2. Melt the butter in a small saucepan. While the butter is melting, mix ¼ cup of the milk with the flour until the flour is completely dissolved. Then add the remaining milk until smooth.

3. When the butter is melted, stir the milk mixture into the butter, stirring constantly until it thickens slightly. Stir in the Parmesan cheese and mix well. Then stir in the Cheddar cheese, rice, and salt. Cook, stirring constantly, until the cheeses are melted and the sauce is smooth and thick. Remove from the heat and let cool for 5 minutes.

4. Beat the egg yolks in a medium-sized mixing bowl until they are thick. Add the cheese sauce to the beaten egg yolks a little at a time, stirring constantly. When all the sauce is combined, set the mixture aside until needed.

5. Beat the egg whites in a bowl with an electric mixer until soft peaks form. Fold half of the beaten egg whites into the egg yolk–cheese mixture until they are completely incorporated. Then fold the remaining egg whites in gently until they are just incorporated. (Do not fold too much or too vigorously.)

6. Pour the mixture into a buttered 2-quart soufflé dish. Bake for 55 to 60 minutes, or until lightly browned on top. A knife inserted near the center should come out clean. Serve immediately.

RICE AND PEAS ORIENTAL   6 to 8 Servings

1 *cup raw rice*	1 *10-ounce package frozen*
2½ *cups boiling water*	*peas, thawed*
½ *cup butter*	2 *tablespoons soy sauce*
¼ *cup minced onion*	1 *cup sliced water chestnuts*
½ *cup sliced fresh*	
mushrooms, or ½ cup	
canned sliced mushrooms,	
drained	

1. Preheat the oven to 350 degrees.

2. Heat a frying pan and add the rice. Stir constantly until the rice is lightly browned. Transfer the rice to a 1½-quart casserole. Pour in the boiling water and stir to separate the rice grains. Cover tightly and bake for 30 minutes.

3. Melt the butter in a frying pan. When it is sizzling, add the onion and mushrooms. Sauté over medium heat for 5 minutes, stirring constantly. Remove from the heat and add the peas, soy sauce, and water chestnuts. Add the baked rice and toss to mix well. Return the mixture to the casserole and bake 15 to 20 minutes longer.

CHEESE BAKED RICE   4 to 6 Servings

2 *cups water*	1¼ *cups grated mild Cheddar*
3 *tablespoons butter or*	*cheese or processed*
margarine	*American cheese*
1 *teaspoon salt*	*Paprika*
1 *cup raw rice*	

1. Put the water, 1 tablespoon of the butter, and the salt in a saucepan. Bring to a boil and stir in the rice. Return to a boil, cover the pan, and lower the heat to very low. Cook the rice for about 15 minutes, or until all the water has been absorbed and the rice is tender.

2. Preheat the oven to 350 degrees.

3. Use a fork to toss the remaining 2 tablespoons of butter with the rice. Then toss the rice with 1 cup of the grated cheese. Transfer the rice to a buttered casserole. Sprinkle the remaining ¼ cup of grated cheese over the top of the rice. Sprinkle with paprika and bake for 15 minutes, or until the top of the casserole begins to brown.

Vegetables

ZESTY BAKED BEANS

Add grated onion, dark brown sugar, and crisp diced fried bacon to taste to canned pork and beans or vegetarian beans. Mix well, heat, and add salt if necessary. Serve cooked beans or bake them in a 350 degree oven 45 minutes to 1 hour.

LEMON-BUTTERED BROCCOLI   4 to 6 Servings

4   to 6 large stalks fresh   Pinch of sugar
    broccoli   Pinch of salt
4   tablespoons butter or   Pinch of white pepper,
    margarine   optional
2   teaspoons fresh lemon juice   1   small lemon, sliced

1. Trim the broccoli ends and remove all leaves. Put the broccoli stalks in a steamer basket, and cook in a covered pot over boiling salted water until the stalks are just tender-crisp.

2. While the broccoli is steaming, melt the butter in a small saucepan. Add the lemon juice, sugar, salt, and white pepper. Bring just to the boiling point and add the lemon slices. Reduce the heat and cook for 1 minute, to heat the lemon slices through.

3. When the broccoli is cooked, transfer it to a serving plate and pour the warm sauce over it.

Note: You might find that the sauce will be too lemony if you use all the lemon slices. I use only about three-quarters of the best slices when I prepare this sauce.

BRUSSELS SPROUTS WITH NUTS   4 Servings

1   pint Brussels sprouts, or 1   4   tablespoons butter or
    10-ounce package frozen   margarine, melted
    Brussels sprouts, thawed   ½   cup chopped walnuts or
2   cups water   pecans
    Salt

191

1. If you are using fresh Brussels sprouts, remove any damaged leaves from the sprouts and cut a cross in the bottom of each sprout. (This will make them cook faster and more evenly.)

2. Bring 2 cups of salted water to a boil and add the sprouts. Cover, lower the heat, and cook the sprouts for about 10 minutes, or until they are tender. Drain well and transfer the sprouts to a serving bowl. Drizzle the melted butter over the sprouts and toss the sprouts gently in the butter with a wooden spoon, so that they are coated with the butter. Add the nuts and toss gently again. Serve immediately.

HOT SLAW WITH APPLE SLICES   4 Servings

½	*head cabbage, shredded*	2	*tablespoons butter or*
2	*apples, cored, peeled, and*		*margarine*
	sliced	1	*teaspoon white vinegar*
½	*teaspoon salt*	1	*tablespoon sugar*

Put the cabbage, apples, and salt in a medium-sized saucepan. Add water just to cover the mixture. Bring to a boil, lower the heat, cover, and simmer for about 5 minutes, or until the cabbage and apples are tender. Pour off all but ½ to 1 cup of the cooking water. Add the butter, vinegar, and sugar to the saucepan and cook for 3 to 5 minutes longer, stirring occasionally. Serve immediately.

SAUERKRAUT

Use a can or package of sauerkraut large enough to make the number of servings you will need. Put the sauerkraut with the liquid it is packed in into a saucepan. Sweeten the sauerkraut with a mixture of brown and white sugar to taste, using 3 parts brown sugar to 1 part granulated sugar. Bring to a boil and cook over moderately high heat for 5 to 7 minutes, stirring occasionally so the sauerkraut does not stick to the pan.

DILLED CARROTS   2 to 4 Servings

1	*package baby carrots*	1	*teaspoon dillweed*
4	*tablespoons butter*		

1. Trim and scrape or peel the carrots. Steam the carrots in a covered saucepan over boiling water until they are barely tender. Remove the pan from the heat immediately.

2. Melt the butter in a frying pan and add the dill and carrots. Stir and toss with a wooden spoon until the carrots are coated with the butter and dill mixture. Serve immediately.

Note: You can substitute 1 16-ounce jar or can of carrots or 1 10-ounce package frozen carrots (cooked following package directions) for the baby carrots.

GLAZED CARROTS
4 Servings
Freezes Well

6	to 8 carrots, or 12 to 16 baby carrots	1	tablespoon granulated sugar
2	tablespoons butter		Pinch of salt
½	cup light brown sugar		

1. Trim and scrape or peel the carrots and cut them into 2- or 3-inch lengths. (If you are using the baby carrots, do not cut them into pieces.) Steam the carrots in a covered saucepan over boiling salted water for 5 to 10 minutes, or until they are barely tender. Remove from the pan immediately.

2. Melt the butter in a frying pan. Add the sugars and stir to blend with the butter. Add the cooked carrots and the salt and mix carefully with a wooden spoon, until the carrots are all glazed. Cook over medium heat, stirring occasionally, for 3 to 5 minutes. Remove from the heat and serve immediately.

Note: If you substitute canned carrots, cook the glaze together for 3 to 5 minutes and then add the drained canned carrots. Stir with a wooden spoon to glaze the carrots and cook only until they are all heated through.

CAULIFLOWER WITH CHEESE SAUCE

Remove the green leaves from a head of cauliflower. Cut the center of the core of the cauliflower out, but be careful not to remove all of the core or the cauliflower will fall apart. Put the head of cauliflower in a steamer basket, core side down. Steam the cauliflower in a covered pot over salted water or broth for 15 to 25 minutes, or until the cauliflower is just tender. Remove the whole cauliflower from the steamer basket and put it in a serving dish. Pour Cheese Sauce (page 210) over the whole head and sprinkle with some chopped parsley before serving.

Note: The cauliflower with cheese sauce can be used as the center of a vegetable platter if you surround it with such vegetables as buttered peas, buttered carrots, parsleyed potatoes, or buttered string beans.

CORN FRITTERS

6 to 8 Servings
Makes 30 to 40 Fritters
Freezes Well

1	cup milk	½	teaspoon salt
1	egg	1	12-ounce can whole kernel
1	tablespoon sugar		corn, drained
1½	cups all-purpose flour		Oil for deep frying
3	tablespoons baking powder		Maple syrup

1. Beat the milk and egg together in a mixing bowl. Mix together the sugar, flour, baking powder, and salt and gradually stir it in to the egg-milk mixture, stirring constantly until the flour mixture is completely incorporated. Stir in the corn. (The batter will be thinner rather than thicker — much like cake batter.)

2. Heat the oil in a deep frying pan until it is very hot. Drop the fritter mixture by tablespoonfuls into the hot oil. Fry, turning once, for 3 to 4 minutes, or until they are golden brown. Drain on paper towels and keep warm until all the fritters are made. Serve warm with syrup.

SCALLOPED CORN

6 to 8 Servings
Freezes Well

2	15-ounce cans whole kernel	2	small eggs
	corn, drained	3	tablespoons butter or
1	15-ounce can cream-style		margarine, melted
	corn	8	saltine crackers, crushed
1	teaspoon salt		into fine crumbs
½	to ¾ cup milk		

1. Preheat the oven to 350 degrees.

2. Put the corn and salt into a mixing bowl. Beat the milk and eggs together and add the mixture to the corn. Stir to mix well. Add the melted butter and cracker crumbs and mix well again. Pour the corn mixture into an 8-inch-square or 2-quart baking dish and bake for 1 hour to 1 hour and 15 minutes.

GRILLED CORN ON THE COB

Remove the husks and silk form the ears of corn. Lay each ear of corn on a sheet of heavy-duty aluminum foil and brush it all over with Herb-Lemon Butter (page 207) or plain butter. Wrap the foil tightly around each ear and grill over white-hot charcoal for 15 to 20 minutes, turning frequently.

To grill corn in its husks, carefully pull the husks back from each ear of corn and remove the silk within. Brush the corn all over with butter and smooth the husks back over the ears. Tie the husks in place at the top of each ear with string. Grill over white-hot charcoal for approximately 20 minutes, turning frequently.

TASTY FRIED EGGPLANT   4 to 6 Servings

1 **large unpeeled eggplant**	1½ **cups bread crumbs or**
1 **cup milk**	**cracker crumbs**
¾ **cup all-purpose flour**	½ **cup grated Parmesan**
¼ **teaspoon salt**	**cheese**
2 **eggs**	**Cooking oil for frying**

1. Trim the ends off the eggplant and cut it into round slices ¼ inch thick.

2. Pour the milk into a bowl. Combine the flour and salt on a sheet of waxed paper. Put the eggs in a bowl and beat them with a fork until the yolks and whites are well combined. Put the bread crumbs on a second sheet of waxed paper. Pour about ¼ inch cooking oil into a frying pan and heat it.

3. When the oil is hot, dip each slice of eggplant in the milk, then in the flour mixture, then in the beaten eggs. Then coat with the bread crumbs, pressing the crumbs on with the palm of your hand. Put the coated slices of eggplant in the hot oil and fry until golden brown on one side. (This will happen very quickly, so you will have to watch them carefully.) Turn the eggplant slices over and brown them on the second side. Sprinkle the browned side of each slice with Parmesan cheese. As the slices brown on the bottom, transfer them to paper towels to drain.

Note: Zucchini, tomatoes, cucumbers, and pumpkin blossoms can also be prepared in this way.

EGGPLANT PARMESAN

6 Servings
Freezes Well

1 *large unpeeled eggplant*	½ *cup grated Parmesan cheese*
2 *eggs*	
1 *cup all-purpose flour*	1 *16-ounce can tomato sauce*
½ *teaspoon salt*	2 *cups shredded mozzarella cheese*
¼ *to ½ cup cooking oil*	

1. Trim the ends off the eggplant and cut it into round slices ⅛ to ¼ inch thick.

2. Put the eggs in a bowl and beat them with a fork until the yolks and whites are well combined. Spread the flour and salt on a sheet of waxed paper. Heat the cooking oil in a frying pan.

3. When the oil is hot, dip each slice of eggplant in the beaten eggs and then in the flour, coating both sides. Put the coated slices into the hot oil and fry until golden brown on both sides. (If you have to add more oil to the frying pan, make sure it is hot before adding more eggplant slices.) Drain the browned eggplant slices on paper towels.

4. Preheat the oven to 375 degrees.

5. Put a layer of eggplant in the bottom of a medium-sized baking dish. Sprinkle the eggplant with some Parmesan cheese and spoon some tomato sauce over it. Then sprinkle a layer of mozzarella over the tomato sauce. Continue making layers, ending with a layer of mozzarella, until all the ingredients are used. (If you have any empty spaces in the eggplant layers, cut up a slice or two to fill them.) Bake for 30 to 35 minutes.

COLLARD GREENS

4 servings

½ *cup chopped raw bacon or salt pork*	¼ *to ½ cup water* *Salt and black pepper to taste*
2 *tablespoons minced onion*	
1 *10-ounce package frozen collard greens, thawed*	

Put the chopped bacon in a small heavy saucepan. Sauté over low heat for about 2 minutes, stirring occasionally. Add the onion and sauté for 1 minute longer. Add the collard greens and water and bring to a boil. Separate the greens with a fork, cover the pan, and simmer for 35 to 45 minutes. Do not overcook the greens. Drain and serve.

Note: You can substitute ½ cup chopped cooked ham for the bacon or salt pork. If you do, sauté the onion in 1 or 2 tablespoons of butter before you add the ham and collard greens.

CREAMED ONIONS

6 Servings
Freezes Well

4 **to 6 cups very small white onions**	1 **cup thinned Medium White Sauce (page 209)**
1 **to 1½ cups water**	2 **tablespoons butter, melted**
1½ **teaspoons salt**	1 **cup shredded mild Cheddar cheese**

1. To peel the onions, put them in a saucepan and cover them with boiling water. Let sit in the water for 8 to 10 seconds, then drain and run under cold water. The skins should slip off easily. When you have peeled the onions cut a shallow cross in the bottom (stem end) of each onion.

2. Pour 1 to 1½ cups of water into a saucepan and add the salt. Bring the water to a boil, add the peeled onions, cover, and cook over medium heat for 25 minutes, or until the onions are just tender. Stir occasionally while the onions are cooking.

3. Preheat the oven to 350 degrees.

4. Drain the onions and transfer them to a baking dish. Pour the thinned sauce and melted butter over the onions and stir to mix well. Sprinkle the cheese over the top, cover the dish, and bake for 20 to 25 minutes.

Note: If you are going to freeze this dish, do not sprinkle the cheese over the top before you bake it. *And* cut the baking time to only 15 minutes. Then, when the baked onions have cooled, sprinkle the cheese on top and freeze.

CREAMED PEAS AND ONIONS

Put 1½ tablespoons all-purpose flour in a medium-sized saucepan. Stir in 1 cup of cold water with a wire whisk until the flour is completely dissolved. Season the mixture with ¼ teaspoon of salt and a pinch of black pepper. Put the saucepan over low heat and bring to a boil, stirring constantly. Add 1 10-ounce package of frozen peas, cooked according to package directions and drained, and 1 large can of small onions, drained, to the mixture in the saucepan. Heat, stirring occasionally, until the vegetables are warmed through.

BLACK-EYED PEAS

8 Servings
Freezes Well

1	16-ounce package black-eyed peas	½	cup honey
8	slices bacon, diced	1	tablespoon lemon juice
2	tablespoons minced onion		Salt and black pepper to taste

1. Pick the peas over to remove any stones or dirt. Wash well and cook, following the directions on the package.

2. When the peas are tender, preheat the oven to 325 degrees.

3. Pour the peas and any liquid in the pot into a large casserole. Add the remaining ingredients, cover the casserole, and bake for 1½ hours, stirring occasionally. Uncover the casserole for the last 10 to 15 minutes of baking.

MASHED POTATOES

6 to 8 Servings
Freezes Well

6	to 8 medium-sized potatoes	Milk or half-and-half
1	teaspoon salt	Black pepper, optional
4	to 6 tablespoons butter or margarine	

1. Peel the potatoes and cut them in quarters. Put the potato pieces in a large saucepan and cover them with water. Add the salt and bring the water to a boil. Cover the pan, lower the heat, and cook for 20 to 30 minutes, or until the potatoes can be pierced easily with a fork.

2. Drain the potatoes, pouring the cooking water into a large glass measuring cup or a bowl. Add the butter to the potatoes and mash it into the potatoes with the blades of an electric mixer (do not turn on the mixer until after you have done this). Beat the potatoes for 1 minute and then begin to add ⅓ cup of the reserved cooking water and enough milk to give you the consistency you want. Taste for salt and pepper and add, if necessary. Beat the potatoes for 2 or 3 minutes longer, or until they are nice and fluffy.

Note: The secret to good mashed potatoes is to add lots of butter *and* the cooking water.

Shredded mild Cheddar cheese can also be added to the potato mixture for a little variety.

Variation

Mashed Potato Flowerets: Choose a large cake-decorating tube fitted with a star tip and fill it with seasoned mashed potatoes. Press out dollops of potatoes to form stars on a buttered baking sheet. Run under the broiler until nicely browned. These flowerets look nice arranged in a ring around a roast.

AU GRATIN POTATOES

4 to 6 Servings
Freezes Well

4   to 6 medium-sized potatoes
    Butter or margarine
    Flour
    Salt and black pepper

1½ cups shredded mild
    Cheddar or longhorn cheese
2½ cups milk
    Paprika, optional

1. Preheat the oven to 375 degrees.
2. Peel the potatoes and slice them about ¼ inch thick. Butter the bottom and sides of an oval baking dish. Put a layer of potato slices in the bottom of the dish. Sprinkle the potatoes with a little flour, salt, and pepper. Dot the potatoes with some butter and sprinkle on some cheese. (Set aside about ¼ cup of the cheese for topping). Continue making layers in this manner until the dish is almost completely filled. Pour the milk over the potato layers and sprinkle the remaining cheese over the top.
3. Put the baking dish in the oven and bake for about 1 hour, or until the potatoes are tender. If desired, you may sprinkle some paprika over the top of the dish during the last 10 minutes of baking.

CHANTILLY POTATO CASSEROLE

4 Servings

2¼ cups Mashed Potatoes
    (page 198) or instant
    mashed potatoes
½ cup heavy cream

⅓ cup grated Parmesan
    cheese
¼ teaspoon salt

1. Preheat the oven to 350 degrees.
2. Put the mashed potatoes into a 1-quart casserole.
3. Beat the cream until it is stiff. Then fold in the grated cheese and salt. Spread the mixture over the top of the mashed potatoes.
4. Put the casserole in the oven and bake for 10 minutes, or until the top is lightly browned. Serve immediately.

SCALLOPED POTATOES

4 to 6 Servings

4   to 6 medium-sized potatoes
Butter or margarine
All-purpose flour

Salt and black pepper
Milk

1. Preheat the oven to 350 or 375 degrees.

2. Peel the potatoes and slice them about ¼ inch thick. Butter the bottom and sides of a deep baking dish. Put a layer of potato slices in the bottom of the dish. Sprinkle the potatoes with a little flour and salt and pepper and dot generously with butter. Continue making layers in this manner until the dish is almost completely filled. (You might want to stop layering about ½ inch from the top of the baking dish.) Pour in enough milk to come just to the top layer of potatoes. Dot the top layer of potato slices with butter.

3. Put the baking dish in the oven and bake for about 1 hour, or until the potatoes are tender.

Note: Finely minced onion and/or bacon bits can also be sprinkled over the potato layers for added flavor.

MOLDED POTATO BAKE

6 Servings

6   medium-sized baking
potatoes
Butter or margarine

1   teaspoon salt
Black pepper, optional
6   tablespoons butter or
margine, melted

1. Preheat the oven to 400 degrees.

2. Cut the unpeeled potatoes into very thin slices. Butter the bottom and sides of a glass pie plate, baking dish, or soufflé dish. Make layers of the potatoes, sprinkling each layer with salt and pepper. When you have finished layering the potatoes, pour the butter over the top of the potatoes and bake for 45 to 50 minutes.

3. Remove the potatoes from the oven and use a rubber spatula to loosen the potatoes from the sides of the baking dish. Put a serving platter over the baking dish and reverse it so that the potatoes are bottom-side up on the platter. Cut in wedges or slices to serve.

BAKED POTATOES OR SWEET POTATOES   4 Servings

4   *medium-sized to large*
     potatoes

Wash the potatoes under cold running water and then dry them with paper towels. Stick a fork into each potato in several places. Heat the oven to 350 degrees and lay the potatoes on the rack in the middle of the oven. Bake the potatoes for 1 hour to 1 hour and 15 minutes, or until you can easily stick a fork into them. (If the potatoes are very large, you may have to cook them a little bit longer.) To serve the potatoes, split them open and top them with butter or sour cream or both.

TWICE-BAKED POTATOES   8 Servings
                                                        Freezes Well

4   *large baking potatoes*   4   *tablespoons butter or*
8   *ounces mild Cheddar*   *margarine*
     cheese, in one piece   *Salt to taste*
                                     ½   *cup milk*

1. Preheat the oven to 375 or 400 degrees.

2. Wash the potatoes, dry them carefully, and wrap them tightly in heavy-duty aluminum foil. Bake for about 1½ hours, turning them every so often, or until they are soft to the touch.

3. Remove the potatoes from the oven and unwrap them. Let them cool slightly, until they can be handled. Then cut the potatoes in half lengthwise. Use a spoon to scoop out most of the potato flesh, making sure you do not break the potato skins. Put the potato flesh in a mixing bowl and put the skins in a baking dish.

4. Cut the cheese in half. Cut one half into very thin slices. Grate the other half. Set aside until needed.

5. Add the butter and salt to the potatoes in the mixing bowl and mash, adding the milk a little at a time. When the potatoes are creamy, stir in the grated cheese and mix well.

6. Spoon equal amounts of the potato mixture into the potato skins in the baking pan. Put the cheese slices over the top of each potato. Bake in a 350-degree oven for 5 to 10 minutes, or until the cheese is melted and the potato stuffing is hot. Serve immediately or cool and freeze.

Note: If you want to top the stuffed potatoes with grated cheese instead of the cheese slices, grate the whole piece of cheese, but remember to use only half in the mashed potato mixture.

POTATO PANCAKES
4 Servings

2 cups grated raw potatoes	1 teaspoon baking powder
2 eggs, beaten	2 tablespoons all-purpose
2 tablespoons minced onion, optional	flour
	½ teaspoon salt

Mix the potatoes, eggs, and onion together in a bowl. Combine the baking powder, flour, and salt and stir into the potato mixture. Drop by tablespoons onto a well-greased griddle and brown on both sides. Serve with hot applesauce.

POTATO BASKETS

Line a wire potato basket with well-drained grated potatoes. Close the basket and deep-fry until golden brown. Potato nests can be used as serving containers for other vegetables, such as peas, carrots, Brussels sprouts, mushrooms, or onions.

BAKED ACORN SQUASH
6 Servings

3 acorn squash	3 tablespoons light brown
3 tablespoons butter or margarine	sugar

1. Preheat the oven to 350 degrees.
2. Cut each squash in half lengthwise. Scoop out the seeds with a spoon. Put the squash halves in a baking pan, cut side up. Dot each squash half with about half a tablespoon of butter. Sprinkle about half a tablespoon of brown sugar over the top and down into the center of each squash half. Pour about ½ inch of boiling water into the baking pan around the squash halves. Bake for 1 hour, or until the squashes are tender and nicely glazed.

ACORN SQUASH RINGS
4 Servings

2 acorn squash	4 to 6 tablespoons light
4 tablespoons butter or margarine, melted	brown sugar

1. Preheat the oven to 350 degrees.
2. Cut each squash lengthwise into ½-inch-thick slices. Remove the seeds from the center of each slice and lay the slices in a single layer in a

large baking dish. Drizzle the melted butter over the slices and sprinkle the sugar over the butter. Bake for 50 minutes to 1 hour.

BAKED SPAGHETTI SQUASH

Place a whole spaghetti squash in a shallow baking dish or pan and pour 1 cup of water around the squash. Bake in a 350-degree oven for 45 minutes to 1 hour, or until the squash is tender. (If you are baking more than 1 squash, add more water to the dish.) When the squash is tender, cut it in half lengthwise and remove the seeds. Put on a plate and loosen the flesh with a serving spoon. Season with butter or margarine, salt, and pepper to taste.

CANDIED SWEET POTATOES

4 to 6 Servings
Freezes Well

4   *to 6 large sweet potatoes*
½   *cup loosely packed light*
    brown sugar

3   *tablespoons granulated*
    sugar
¼   *teaspoon salt*

1. Peel the sweet potatoes and cut them into large chunks. Put the chunks into a saucepan and add enough water barely to cover the potatoes. Bring the water to a boil, cover the pan, and cook over medium heat until the potatoes are just tender. Drain the potato chunks, but save the cooking water.

2. Preheat the oven to 350 degrees.

3. Put the potatoes in a shallow baking dish and sprinkle them with the sugars and salt. Pour ¼ cup of the reserved cooking water over the potato chunks and bake, uncovered, for 35 to 45 minutes, or until the potatoes are glazed. Stir the potatoes once or twice while they bake so that all sides are coated with the sugar mixture.

Note: You can substitute a 16-ounce can of sweet potatoes for the fresh potatoes, if you wish. Begin the recipe, then, with step 2 and use the liquid in the can in place of the potato cooking water.

Drained canned pineapple chunks can be baked with the potato chunks, if desired. And miniature or cut-up marshmallows can be added to the plain potato chunks for the last few minutes of baking.

STRING BEANS AMANDINE   2 to 4 Servings

1   13- to 16-ounce can string   3   to 4 tablespoons butter or
    beans   margarine
                                      ¼   cup slivered almonds

1. Pour the beans and their liquid into a small saucepan. Place over medium heat.

2. Melt the butter in a small saucepan and, when it is sizzling, add the almonds and stir them until they are lightly browned.

3. Drain the beans well and put them in a serving dish. Pour the butter and almonds over the beans and toss to mix well. Serve immediately.

Note: Sautéed sliced scallions and/or bacon bits can be added to the dish or used to replace the almonds, if desired.

BAKED STRING BEANS   6 to 8 Servings

2   13-ounce cans string beans,   2   heaping cups shredded
    or 3 cups cooked fresh or   American cheese
    frozen string beans   2   tablespoons minced onion
1   can cream of celery soup   1   2.8-ounce can French-fried
½   can milk   onion rings, optional
2   2½-ounce cans sliced
    mushrooms

1. Preheat the oven to 350 degrees.

2. Drain the string beans and spread them on the bottom of an oblong baking dish. Mix the soup and milk together in a bowl until very smooth. Drain the mushrooms and add them to the soup mixture along with 1½ cups of the shredded cheese and the minced onion. Stir to mix well. Pour the mixture over the beans and mix well. Sprinkle the remaining ½ cup of shredded cheese over the top and bake for 45 to 50 minutes.

3. Serve with the canned onion rings on the side. Do not mix them with the beans or they will lose their crunchiness.

Note: This recipe can be halved or doubled quite easily. Remember to adjust the baking time accordingly.

BROILED TOMATOES

Use 1 tomato for each serving. Remove the stems from the tomatoes and cut each tomato in half. Place the tomato halves on a broiler pan and sprinkle each of them with 1 heaping tablespoon of fine bread crumbs. Drizzle 1 teaspoon of melted butter over each tomato half and then sprinkle with grated Parmesan cheese. Broil the tomatoes for 3 to 5 minutes, or until they just start to brown. You will have to watch them carefully so they do not burn.

DILLED VEGETABLE MEDLEY   4 to 6 Servings

4	*large long carrots*	½	*teaspon dillweed*
4	*large long zucchini*		*Salt and black pepper to*
1	*pound string beans*		*taste*
4	*tablespoons butter or*		
	margarine		

1. Trim the ends off the carrots and zucchini and then cut them into julienne strips. Trim the ends off the string beans, but leave the beans whole.

2. Put the vegetables in layers in a steamer basket. (The zucchini will probably cook more quickly, so put them on top.) Steam the vegetables in a covered pot over boiling salted water until they are tender-crisp. (Check the zucchini, and remove it as soon as it is done.)

3. Transfer the vegetables to a serving bowl and keep them warm.

4. Melt the butter and, when it is sizzling, stir in the dill. Pour the mixture over the vegetables and season them with salt and pepper. Toss to coat the vegetables with the butter and serve immediately.

MIXED VEGETABLES WITH BACON
AND ONION SAUCE   6 Servings

3	*large zucchini*	6	*slices bacon, diced*
3	*medium-sized onions*	½	*cup chopped onion*
3	*large yellow squash*		*Salt and black pepper,*
	Water, beef broth, or		*optional*
	chicken broth		

1. Trim the zucchini and wash them well. Then slice them ½-inch-thick rounds. Peel the onions and slice them into ¼-inch-thick slices. Trim the yellow squash, wash them well, and slice them into ½-inch-thick rounds. Put the sliced vegetables in a steamer basket and steam them over boiling water or broth in a covered pan until they are tender-crisp.

2. While the vegetables are steaming, fry the bacon in a frying pan until it is crisp. Use a slotted spoon to transfer the bacon to a paper towel to drain. Add the chopped onion to the frying pan and sauté until light golden brown. Remove the onion from the bacon fat with a slotted spoon and set it aside.

3. When the vegetables have steamed, transfer them to the frying pan with the warm (not hot) bacon grease and roll them around until they are coated with the bacon grease. Use a slotted spoon to transfer the vegetables to a serving dish (so you don't transfer too much of the bacon grease) and sprinkle with the reserved bacon and sautéed onion. Season with salt and pepper, if desired.

Note: Brussels sprouts, string beans, and carrots can also be used in this dish. The important thing is to have a good variety of vegetables and enough to make 6 servings.

Butters, Sauces, and Gravies

HERB-LEMON BUTTER

Makes 1 Cup

½ pound butter, softened
1 teaspoon freeze-dried
chives
1 teaspoon dried basil,
optional
2 tablespoons lemon juice

Combine all the ingredients in a small mixing bowl. Cover and refrigerate to allow the flavors to blend.

HONEY BUTTER

Mix equal amounts of honey and softened butter together in a small bowl. The mixture should be creamy and smooth. Serve with hot biscuits, muffins, toast, waffles, pancakes, or French toast.

AMARETTO ORANGE SAUCE

4 Servings
Freezes Well

½ cup butter or margarine
½ cup granulated sugar
½ cup dark brown sugar
6 ounces orange juice
concentrate
1 teaspoon lemon juice
1 navel orange, sliced in half
and cut into ⅛-inch-thick
slices
Dash of Amaretto or your
favorite brandy

Melt the butter in a small saucepan. Add the sugars and juices and bring to a boil. Then add the orange slices and liqueur and cook for 1 minute longer. This sauce complements roast duckling nicely.

Note: If you freeze the sauce, the orange flavor will be intensified.

CARAMEL-ORANGE SAUCE

4 Servings
Freezes Well

½ cup lightly packed light
brown sugar
2 tablespoons butter or
margarine
Pinch of salt
4 heaping tablespoons (about
8 ounces) orange
marmalade
1 navel orange, sliced

Put the brown sugar, butter, and salt into a small saucepan or frying pan. Heat over low heat until the butter and sugar are melted and combined. Add the orange marmalade and bring to a boil, stirring constantly. Boil for 2 minutes, add the orange slices, and remove from the heat. This sauce complements roast duckling nicely.

Note: You can garnish the roast with the orange slices when you serve it, or you can put the orange slices on the duck for the last few minutes it is in the oven.

CHERRY SAUCE

Pour a large can of cherry pie filling into a saucepan. Mix in ⅛ teaspoon white vinegar or lemon juice and 1 tablespoon butter. Heat over low heat, stirring occasionally, until bubbling. This sauce is very good with grilled or pan-fried ham steaks.

HEAVY RAISIN SAUCE   Makes 1½ Cups

1	*cup water*	¼	*teaspoon salt*
¼	*cup packed dark brown sugar*	¼	*teaspoon lemon juice, or ⅛ teaspoon white vinegar*
1	*tablespoon cornstarch*	1	*cup golden or dark raisins*

Combine all the ingredients except the raisins in a saucepan. Cook over low heat, stirring occasionally, until the sugars dissolve. Then bring to a boil and cook until the bubbles look glassy. Add the raisins and cook for 2 or 3 minutes longer. Remove from the heat and allow the sauce to cool and thicken. When ready to serve, warm the sauce over very low heat, stirring occasionally so that it does not stick to the pan. If you are using the sauce as a glaze, do not let it cool, but pour it over the meat to be glazed, and continue to roast.

LIGHT RAISIN SAUCE   Makes 1½ Cups

1	*cup water*	¼	*teaspoon salt*
⅓	*cup granulated sugar*	¼	*teaspoon lemon juice*
1	*tablespoon dark brown sugar*	¾	*to 1 cup golden or dark raisins*
1	*tablespoon cornstarch*		

Combine all the ingredients except the raisins in a saucepan. Cook over low heat, stirring occasionally, until the sugars dissolve. Then bring to a boil and boil until the bubbles look glassy. Add the raisins and cook for 2 or 3 minutes longer. Remove from the heat and allow the sauce to cool and thicken. When ready to serve, warm the sauce over very low heat, stirring occasionally so that it does not stick to the pan. If you are using the sauce as a glaze, do not let it cool, but pour it over the meat to be glazed, and continue to roast.

CAPER SAUCE   6 to 8 Servings

6 tablespoons butter or margarine	1 tablespoon dry mustard
4 tablespoons flour	1 2½-ounce jar capers
2½ cups beef broth	1½ to 2 tablespoons caper juice
1 teaspoon lemon juice	½ cup dry sherry

Melt the butter in a small saucepan. Add the flour and mix until it is well combined. Add the beef broth slowly, stirring until the sauce is smooth. Stir in the lemon juice, mustard, capers, caper juice, and sherry. Bring to a simmer and simmer for 3 to 5 minutes to combine the flavors. Serve with broiled steak or sautéed veal or chicken cutlets.

MEDIUM WHITE SAUCE   Makes 1 Cup

1 tablespoon cornstarch or 2 tablespoons all-purpose flour	2 tablespoons butter or margarine
1 cup cold milk	¼ teaspoon salt
	Pinch of white pepper

Put the cornstarch into a small saucepan. Gradually add the cold milk, stirring with a wire whisk, until the cornstarch is completely dissolved. Put the saucepan over medium heat and add the butter, salt, and pepper, stirring constantly. Bring to a boil and boil for 1 minute. Serve with vegetables, fish, meat, or poultry.

Variations

À la King Sauce: Use the 2 tablespoons of butter in the Medium White Sauce recipe to sauté the poultry for á la king. Then combine the remaining sauce ingredients and add to the frying pan and cook, following the directions above.

Dill Sauce: Add ¼ to ½ teaspoon dillweed and a dash of Worcestershire sauce to the Medium White Sauce.

Mustard Sauce: Add 2 tablespoons prepared mustard and 1 tablespoon lemon juice to the Medium White Sauce.

Cheese Sauce: Add 1 cup of your favorite grated cheese to the Medium White Sauce. Experiment with different herbs and spices, too.

Mustard-Cheese Sauce: Add 2 tablespoons prepared mustard, a dash of Worcestershire sauce, and ¼ cup grated mild Cheddar cheese to the Medium White Sauce. Stir until smooth over medium heat.

CHEESE SAUCE
Makes 1½ Cups

2   tablespoons butter or
    margarine
2   tablespoons all-purpose
    flour
½   teaspoon salt
    Pinch of white pepper,
    optional
    Pinch of cayenne pepper

1   cup milk
¼   pound mild Cheddar
    cheese, grated
    Dash of dry white sherry,
    optional

Melt the butter in a saucepan. When the butter is sizzling, add the flour and stir it in with a whisk. As soon as the flour is incorporated into the butter, remove the pan from the heat. Add the salt, pepper, cayenne, and milk and mix until smooth. Return the pan to the heat and bring to a boil, stirring constantly with the whisk. Lower the heat and add the cheese. Cook, stirring constantly, until the cheese is melted. Add the sherry to thin the sauce if necessary.

CHEESE SAUCE SUPREME
Makes 1½ Cups

1¼ cups cold milk
2   tablespoons all-purpose
    flour
¼   to ½ teaspoon salt
1   cup grated processed
    American cheese

1   cup grated Swiss cheese
    Pinch of nutmeg
½   teaspoon sugar
1   tablespoon butter or
    margarine

Put the milk, flour, and salt in a small saucepan. Stir until the flour is completely absorbed. Bring the mixture just to a boil and add the remaining ingredients, stirring until the sauce is smooth and thick. If the sauce is too thick, thin it by adding milk, a tablespoon at a time, until the sauce is the proper consistency. For dishes that are going to be baked, the sauce should be thinner.

SPICY BARBECUE SAUCE

Makes 1½ Cups
Freezes Well

½ cup grated onion
1 teaspoon salt
1 teaspoon white vinegar
1 tablespoon granulated sugar
4 tablespoons packed light brown sugar

1 teaspoon Worcestershire sauce
¼ teaspoon chili powder
¼ teaspoon black pepper
½ cup ketchup
½ cup pineapple juice

Combine all the ingredients in a saucepan. Bring to a simmer, and cook for 15 to 20 minutes.

HOLLANDAISE SAUCE

Makes About ¾ Cup

¼ pound (1 stick) butter
3 egg yolks

½ teaspoon salt
2 teaspoons lemon juice

1. Melt the butter slowly in a small saucepan.
2. While the butter is melting, put the egg yolks, salt, and lemon juice in the container of a blender and blend until smooth. (You can also use an electric mixer to do this.)
3. When the butter is bubbling, pour the egg mixture into the butter all at once. Stir until thick and smooth. Serve at once, or keep warm in a covered pot over hot water.

TARTAR SAUCE

In a jar with a tight-fitting lid, mix a large scoop of mayonnaise with a little grated onion, some pickle relish, a few drops of lemon juice, 4 finely chopped green olives, a pinch of salt, and sugar to taste. Cover tightly and refrigerate for at least 1 hour before serving.

CREAMY CHICKEN GRAVY

4 to 6 Servings
Freezes Well

1 cup milk
½ cup all-purpose flour
1 egg yolk, slightly beaten
3 cups chicken broth

1 cup cold water
Salt and black pepper to taste

1. Pour the milk into a small bowl. Gradually add the flour, stirring with a wire whisk to make a smooth thin paste. Stir in the egg yolk and set the mixture aside.

2. Bring the chicken broth to a boil in a saucepan. Pour in the cold water and *immediately* add the milk-flour paste. Simmer for a few minutes, stirring occasionally, until the gravy has thickened. Season with salt and pepper to taste. If the gravy is too thick, you can thin it with more chicken broth.

Note: You can add diced chicken or turkey to the gravy and serve it over biscuits.

MUSHROOM GRAVY   4 Servings

4 **tablespoons butter or margarine**	**¾** **to 1 cup beef or chicken broth**
1 **tablespoon all-purpose flour**	**Salt and black pepper to taste**
1 **4½-ounce can whole or sliced mushrooms, drained**	

1. Melt the butter in a saucepan. When the butter is sizzling, add the flour and stir well. Add the mushrooms and cook until the mushrooms and the flour begin to brown.

2. Add the broth a little at a time, combining it well with the mushroom-flour mixture. Cook for 3 to 4 minutes. The gravy will be thin but not watery. Gravy made with beef broth will be very good with London broil. Gravy made with chicken broth will go very good with plain roasted chicken.

Note: You can substitute an equal amount of dry sherry for the broth, or use a mixture of broth and sherry.

CINNAMON SUGAR

In a jar with a tight-fitting lid, mix 4 parts of sugar with 1 part of cinnamon. Cover the jar and shake until well combined. Transfer the mixture to a large shaker and use on applesauce or buttered toast, or when glazing fruit.

QUICK MEAT MARINADE

Use bottled Italian salad dressing as a marinade for beef steaks or cubes, pork chops or cubes, or chicken parts before grilling.

Sandwiches and Other Lunch Dishes

HAM AND CHEESE CROISSANTS

4 Servings
Freezes Well

8   croissants
    Butter
1   8-ounce package sliced
    mozzarella or Muenster
    cheese

1   pound sliced boiled ham

Slice the croissants almost in half along the inside curve. (Be careful not to cut all the way through; you only want to make a pocket.) Spread the inside of the croissant with butter. Lay a slice of cheese over the butter and a slice or two of ham over the cheese. (Don't worry if the filling sticks out a little.) Close the croissants and put them on a broiler pan. Broil for 3 or 4 minutes, or until the cheese melts. Watch them carefully so they don't burn or get too crusty.

Note: If you want, you can sprinkle some grated mozzarella over the top of each stuffed croissant.

These can be made ahead, frozen, and broiled just before you serve them. They make a good snack after the theater and go very well with champagne and a bowl of fresh strawberries.

HAM AND CHEESE SANDWICH MELTS

4 Servings

8   slices of bread
    Softened butter

Sliced boiled ham
Sliced Muenster cheese

Butter one side of each slice of bread. Lay 4 slices of bread buttered side down on a griddle or frying pan. Top each slice with 1 or 2 slices of ham and 1 slice of cheese. Lay the reamining 4 slices of bread on top of the cheese buttered side up. Cook over low to medium heat for 2 to 4 minutes on the first side. Turn the sandwiches over and cook on the other side until golden brown. Slice on the diagonal and serve while warm.

213

QUEEN AND KING SANDWICHES   4 to 6 Servings

1	12- to 24-inch loaf of unsliced Italian or French bread Mayonnaise Butter or mustard	1	pound sliced turkey or chicken loaf
1	pound sliced boiled ham	4	medium-sized tomatoes, washed, cored, and sliced thin
½	pound sliced Italian salami	2	medium-sized onions, peeled and sliced thin
		½	pound sliced Swiss cheese Pickles and relish

Cut the loaf of bread in half lengthwise. Spread the inside of the top of the loaf with mayonnaise and spread the inside of the bottom with butter or mustard. Layer the remaining ingredients, except the pickles and relish, over the bottom half of the loaf. Replace the top and cut in thick slices to serve. Serve with pickles and relish on the side.

PITA VEGGI MELT SANDWICHES

For each serving, use a 6-inch pita, cut in half crosswise. Open the halves and fill with 1 slice of salted tomato, 3 parboiled carrot slices, 3 parboiled or raw zucchini slices, 1 green pepper ring, 1 thin onion ring, 2 tablespoons grated mozzarella cheese. Sprinkle with your favorite herbs, if you want. Put the filled pita halves on a cookie sheet and bake in a preheated 400-degree oven for 3 to 5 minutes, or until the cheese melts and the filling is heated through.

REUBEN SANDWICHES   4 Servings

	Softened butter	4	slices Swiss cheese
8	slices rye bread	1	17-ounce can sauerkraut, well drained
14	to 16 thin slices cooked corned beef		Sour cream or horseradish

Butter one side of each slice of bread. Grill or toast the bread (on the buttered side only) under the broiler. Put 4 slices of the bread, buttered side down, on a baking sheet or griddle. Place the corned beef, Swiss cheese, and sauerkraut on the bread in layers. Top with the remaining bread slices, buttered side up. Broil or toast on both sides until browned. Serve with sour cream or horseradish on the side.

QUICK SLOPPY JOES

4 Servings
Freezes Well

1	*pound ground beef*	2	*tablespoons light brown*
¾	*teaspoon salt*		*sugar*
¼	*cup finely chopped onion*	1	*teaspoon granulated sugar*
1	*heaping tablespoon finely*	2	*or 3 drops white vinegar*
	chopped green pepper,	1	*teaspoon Worcestershire*
	optional		*sauce*
1	*cup ketchup*	¼	*cup water*
6	*ounces tomato juice*		

1. Combine the ground beef, salt, onion, and green pepper in a frying pan. Cook over medium heat, stirring occasionally, until the beef is browned. Drain well and return to the frying pan.

2. Add the ketchup and tomato juice to the frying pan and mix well. Stir in the remaining ingredients and simmer over medium heat for 15 minutes. Lower the heat and simmer for 5 minutes longer. Serve as hand-held sandwiches or over bread on a plate.

Note: If the mixture is too thick, you can add some water a little at a time to thin it to your liking.

You can substitute 1 8-ounce can tomato sauce and ½ cup water for the ketchup and tomato juice, if you wish.

QUICHE LORRAINE

6 Servings
Freezes Well

	Pastry for a single-crust	2	*cups half-and-half*
	pie (page 228)	2	*tablespoons all-purpose*
6	*slices bacon*		*flour*
1½	*tablespoons butter or*	¼	*teaspoon salt*
	margarine		*Pinch of ground nutmeg*
1	*medium-sized onion,*	1½	*cups shredded Swiss*
	chopped		*cheese*
4	*eggs*		

1. Preheat the oven to 450 degrees. Roll the pastry out and fit it into a deep-dish pie plate or a quiche pan. When the oven is hot, bake the pie shell for 5 to 10 minutes.

2. Cook the bacon until it is crisp. Drain on paper towels. Then crumble and set aside.

3. Melt the butter in a small frying pan and, when it is sizzling, add the onion. Sauté for 5 minutes, stirring occasionally. Drain and set aside.

4. Remove the pie shell from the oven after it has baked and lower the oven temperature to 325 degrees.

5. Put the eggs, half-and-half, flour, salt, and nutmeg in a mixing bowl and beat until well combined. Stir in the bacon, onion, and Swiss cheese.

6. Pour the filling into the baked pie shell and bake for 50 to 55 minutes, or until a knife inserted near the center comes out clean. Remove from the oven and let stand for about 10 minutes before serving.

Note: If the crust begins to brown too fast, cover the quiche with aluminum foil.

BACON-ONION QUICHE

6 Servings
Freezes Well

1	9-inch unbaked pie shell (page 228)	⅔	cup milk
6	slices bacon	1	cup half-and-half
1	small- to medium-sized onion, peeled and sliced thin	2	tablespoons all-purpose flour
		½	teaspoon salt
			Pinch of ground nutmeg
4	eggs	1	cup shredded Swiss cheese

1. Preheat the oven to 450 degrees. When the oven is hot, bake the pie shell for 7 to 10 minutes.

2. Cook the bacon until it is crisp. Drain on paper towels. Then crumble and set aside.

3. Pour off all but 2 tablespoons of the bacon fat in the frying pan and add the onion slices. Sauté, breaking the onion slices into rings, for 5 to 7 minutes. Drain the onion rings and set them aside.

4. Remove the pie shell from the oven after it has baked and lower the oven temperature to 375 degrees.

5. Put the eggs, milk, half-and-half, flour, salt, and nutmeg in a mixing bowl and beat until well combined. Stir in the bacon, onion rings, and Swiss cheese.

6. Pour the filling into the baked pie shell and bake for 30 to 35 minutes, or until a knife inserted near the center comes out clean. Remove from the oven and let stand for about 10 minutes before serving.

Note: If the crust begins to brown too fast, cover the quiche with aluminum foil.

CHEESE FONDUE   6 Servings

1	clove garlic, peeled and cut in half	½	teaspoon salt
			Pinch of black pepper
2	cups shredded Gruyère cheese		Small pinch of ground nutmeg
2	cups shredded Swiss cheese	1	loaf Italian or French bread, cut into bite-sized cubes
1	tablespoon cornstarch		
1	cup dry white wine		
1	teaspoon lemon juice		
3	tablespoons kirschwasser or dry sherry		

1. Rub the inside of the fondue pot with the cut garlic. Then discard the garlic. Toss the cheeses with the cornstarch and set aside.

2. Pour the wine into the fondue pot and put it over low heat. When the wine begins to warm, stir the cheeses and lemon juice into the wine and cook, stirring constantly, until the cheese melts and the mixture is smooth. Add the kirschwasser, salt, pepper, and nutmeg and stir to combine well. Serve immediately with the bread cubes.

BROCCOLI SOUFFLE′   4 to 6 Servings

1	10-ounce package frozen chopped broccoli	½	teaspoon salt
		1	cup milk
4	tablespoons butter or margarine	½	cup grated Parmesan cheese
4	tablespoons all-purpose flour	4	eggs, separated
		2	egg whites

1. Cook the broccoli, following the package directions. Drain the cooked broccoli well and return it to the pan. Add the butter and cook over medium-high heat until the butter is melted and any remaining liquid in the broccoli has evaporated. Remove from the heat and stir in the flour and salt. Mix well. Add the milk and ¼ cup of the Parmesan cheese to the broccoli and mix well. Cook over medium heat until the mixture thickens and begins to boil. Remove from the heat and stir in the remaining Parmesan cheese.

2. Preheat the oven to 350 degrees. Butter the bottom and sides of a 2-quart souffle′ dish.

3. Beat the egg yolks until they are slightly thick. Stir the broccoli mixture into the egg yolks and mix well.

4. Beat the egg whites until they form soft peaks. Gently fold half of the beaten egg whites into the broccoli mixture. Then fold the remaining egg whites into the mixture. Pour the soufflé mixture into the prepared soufflé dish and bake for 40 to 45 minutes. The soufflé is done when a knife inserted near the center comes out clean. Serve immediately.

SPINACH SOUFFLÉ CREPES   4 Servings

2	*packages frozen spinach*	1	*Cheese Sauce Supreme*
	soufflé		*recipe (page 210)*
1	*Crepes recipe (page 219)*		

1. Bake the spinach soufflé, following the package directions.

2. Turn the oven temperature to 325 degrees. Fill the crepes with the hot spinach soufflé, folding the crepes over the filling. Put the filled crepes in a buttered baking dish. Bake for 5 to 7 minutes, or until the crepes are heated through. Serve immediately with the hot cheese sauce poured over the crepes.

CHICKEN CREPES   4 Servings

1½	*cups finely chopped cooked*		*Pinch of poultry seasoning*
	chicken		*or seasoned salt*
¼	*cup fine fresh bread crumbs*	1	*Crepes recipe (page 219)*
½	*cup chicken broth*		*Creamy Chicken Gravy*
1	*tablespoon grated onion*		*(page 212) or Mushroom*
1	*egg, beaten*		*Gravy (page 212)*

1. Preheat the oven to 325 degrees.

2. Mix the chicken, bread crumbs, chicken broth, onion, egg, and poultry seasoning together in a bowl. Fill the crepes with the mixture, folding the crepes over the filling. Put the filled crepes in a buttered baking dish. Bake for 5 to 7 minutes, or until heated through. Serve with the hot gravy of your choice.

Note: If you don't have time to make gravy, you can heat 1 can of undiluted cream of chicken soup to serve over the crepes.

HAM CREPES

4 Servings

1   *cup finely chopped cooked*   1   *Crepes recipe (page 219)*
     ham   *Dill Sauce (page 209) or*
½   *cup Medium White Sauce*   *Mustard Sauce (page 209)*
     (page 209)
½   *cup cooked green peas*
     Pinch of dillweed

1. Preheat the oven to 325 degrees.

2. Mix the ham, Medium White Sauce, peas, and dillweed together in a bowl. Fill the crepes with the mixture, folding the crepes over the filling. Put the filled crepes in a buttered baking dish. Bake for 5 to 7 minutes, or until heated through. Serve with the hot sauce of your choice.

CREPES

6 Servings
12 8-inch Crepes
Freezes Well

4   *eggs*   ½   *teaspoon salt*
2   *cups milk*   2   *tablespoons melted*
1½   *cups sifted all-purpose*   *shortening*
      flour

1. Put all the ingredients into the container of a blender and blend until smooth. Pour the batter into a mixing bowl, cover tightly, and chill for at least 1 hour.

2. Butter a crepe pan and heat it over medium heat. Pour 3 to 4 tablespoons of the crepe batter into the hot pan and swirl it around so that it coats the bottom of the pan evenly and thinly. Brown on both sides, turning the crepe once. Continue making crepes until all the batter has been used. Use immediately or place between layers of waxed paper and freeze. The crepes can also be filled and frozen with or without sauce.

QUICK PIZZA

Grease a pizza pan and sprinkle salt lightly over the surface of the pan. Form the biscuits from a large cylinder of prepared biscuit dough into a sheet and line the pizza pan with this crust. Spread the dough generously with canned tomato or pizza sauce. Sprinkle sliced mushrooms, chopped onions, chopped or sliced green peppers, sliced cooked sausages, or browned and drained chopped beef in any combination you wish over the sauce. Sprinkle generously with grated mozzarella and Parmesan cheese and oregano. Bake the pizza in a 500- to 550-degree oven for 30 to 45 minutes, or until the crust is well browned. The cheese topping should be melted and creamy.

PAN CORN BREAD

8 Servings
Freezes Well

1	cup yellow cornmeal	1¼	cups milk
1¼	cups all-purpose flour	¼	cup salad oil
½	cup sugar	1	tablespoon melted butter
2	teaspoons baking powder		or margarine
½	teaspoon salt	1	egg

1. Preheat the oven to 375 degrees. Butter the bottom and sides of an 8-inch-square baking pan or dish.

2. Put the cornmeal, flour, sugar, baking powder, and salt in a mixing bowl. Combine the milk, oil, melted butter, and egg in a small mixing bowl and beat to mix well. Pour the mixture into the dry ingredients and stir until the ingredients are just combined.

3. Pour the batter into the prepared pan and bake for 25 minutes, or until a toothpick inserted near the center comes out clean.

BUTTERED FRENCH BREAD

Cut a long loaf of French bread into slices, but do not cut all the way through the bottom of the loaf. Melt 1 or 2 sticks of butter or margarine and brush both sides of each slice with the melted butter. Press the loaf together again and lay it on a large sheet of aluminum foil. Brush the top of the loaf with the remaining butter and seal the loaf in the foil. Heat in a 325-degree oven for 8 to 12 minutes, depending on the size of the loaf.

Note: The bread can be buttered, wrapped in foil, and frozen ahead. But do not bake until you are ready to serve it.

A thin cheese spread can also be brushed over the bread slices, instead of the butter.

Sweets

PINEAPPLE UPSIDE-DOWN CAKE   8 to 10 servings

6 tablespoons butter or
   margarine
1 cup lightly packed brown
   sugar
1 20-ounce can sliced
   pineapple, drained
1 small jar maraschino
   cherries, or 10 to 12
   walnut or pecan halves
1 heaping cup all-purpose
   flour

1 cup granulated sugar
1 heaping teaspoon baking
   powder
   Pinch of salt
4 tablespoons solid
   shortening
2 eggs
1 teaspoon vanilla extract
⅓ cup milk

1. Preheat the oven to 375 degrees. When the oven is hot, put the butter in an 8-inch-square baking pan and put the pan in the oven until the butter is melted.

2. Remove the pan from the oven and add the brown sugar to the pan, stirring the sugar until it dissolves. Lay the pineapple slices in a single layer over the bottom of the pan. Put maraschino cherries or walnut or pecan halves in the center of each pineapple slice.

3. Combine the flour, granulated sugar, baking powder and salt in a mixing bowl. Cut the solid shortening in with a pastry cutter or two knives until the mixture resembles coarse meal. Then stir in the eggs, vanilla, and milk. Mix well. Pour the batter into the prepared pan and bake for 45 to 50 minutes. Remove from the oven and cool for a few minutes. Invert the cake onto a serving platter and serve warm.

Note: To make Apricot Upside-Down Cake, substitute drained canned apricot halves for the sliced pineapple. Put the cherries or nuts between the apricot halves and continue with the recipe as above.

CARAMEL-BANANA-BUTTER PECAN CAKE   12 to 14 Servings

1 butter pecan cake mix
1 stick (4 ounces) butter or
   margarine
½ cup packed light brown
   sugar
   Pinch of salt

½ cup milk
1 to 2 boxes confectioner's
   sugar
2 ripe bananas
   Lemon juice

221

1. Prepare the butter pecan cake mix, following the package directions. Bake in two layers. Cool the layers completely.

2. When the cake layers are cool, prepare the frosting. Melt the butter in a saucepan. When the butter is sizzling, add the brown sugar and salt. Cook for 2 to 3 minutes until the mixture bubbles, stirring often. Remove from the heat and let stand at room temperature for 10 to 15 minutes to cool.

3. When the sugar mixture is cool, return the saucepan to the heat and add the milk. Cook, stirring occasionally, for 2 to 3 minutes. Remove from the heat and stir in sifted confectioner's sugar until the icing is the desired consistency. Allow the icing to stand for 15 to 20 minutes. If the icing becomes too stiff to spread, add milk a tablespoon at a time to thin it slightly.

4. Peel and slice the bananas on the diagonal. Dip the banana slices in lemon juice so they will not discolor.

5. Put a cake layer on a serving plate and spread the icing over the top of the layer about ¼ inch thick. Make a layer of the banana slices on top of the icing. Add the second cake layer and spread the remaining icing over the sides and top of the cake, swirling it into an attractive pattern. Use the remaining banana slices to form a layered flower in the center of the top of the cake. Serve immediately.

EASY COFFEE CAKE   6 to 8 Servings

Streusel Topping
¾ cup light brown sugar
2½ tablespoons all-purpose
    flour
2½ teaspoons ground
    cinnamon
8 tablespoons butter or
    margarine
½ to ¾ cup chopped nuts

Cake
1½ cups sifted all-purpose
    flour
1½ tablespoons baking powder
¼ teaspoon salt
⅔ cup granulated sugar
¼ cup solid shortening
⅔ cup milk
1 egg, lightly beaten
1 teaspoon vanilla

1. Make the streusel topping first. Combine the sugar, flour, cinnamon, and butter in a small bowl. Add the nuts and stir well. Set aside until needed.

2. Preheat the oven to 375 degrees. Grease the bottom and sides of an 8-inch-square baking pan and set aside until needed.

3. Sift the flour, baking powder, salt, and sugar together into a bowl. Cut in the shortening using a pastry blender or two knives until the mixture resembles coarse meal. Stir in the milk, egg, and vanilla until they are just mixed in. Do not beat the batter or stir it too much.

4. Pour half the batter into the prepared pan and sprinkle half of the streusel topping over it. Pour in the remaining batter and sprinkle it with the remaining topping. Bake for 25 to 30 minutes, or until a toothpick inserted near the center comes out clean.

DELUXE GINGERBREAD

8 Servings
Freezes Well

2 cups all-purpose flour	¼ cup lightly packed light brown sugar
1 teaspoon baking soda	
½ teaspoon salt	1 egg
½ to 1 teaspoon ground ginger	¾ cup cark molasses
	1 cup buttermilk
1 teaspoon ground cinnamon	Whipped cream or applesauce
½ cup solid shortening	
½ cup granulated sugar	

1. Preheat the oven to 325 degrees. Grease the bottom and sides of an 8-inch-square or 9- by 12-inch baking pan and set aside.

2. Sift the flour, baking soda, salt, ginger, and cinnamon together on a piece of waxed paper. Set aside until needed.

3. Cream the shortening and sugars together until they are light and fluffy. Beat in the egg and molasses until they are well combined.

4. Add the sifted dry ingredients to the batter alternately with the buttermilk until they are all combined. Pour the batter into the prepared pan and bake for 45 to 50 minutes, or until a toothpick inserted near the center comes out clean. Serve warm or cooled with whipped cream or applesauce.

CREAMY CHOCOLATE ICING

Makes Enough to Ice
2 9-inch Layers

3½ cups confectioner's sugar	½ cup unsweetened cocoa powder
3 tablespoons butter or margarine, melted	⅓ cup milk

Sift the confectioner's sugar into a mixing bowl. Then add the remaining ingredients and stir well.

Note: If the icing is too thick, you can thin it by adding milk a half teaspoon at a time, until the desired consistency is reached.

CARAMEL ICING

Makes Enough to Ice
2 9-inch Layers

4   tablespoons butter or
    margarine
2   cups lightly packed light
    brown sugar

2   cups confectioner's sugar
    (approximately)
1   teaspoon vanilla extract
    Pinch of salt

1. Melt the butter in a saucepan. When the butter is sizzling, add the brown sugar and stir until it has dissolved. Then bring the mixture to a boil. Remove from the heat and cool.

2. Transfer the sugar mixture to a mixing bowl and sift in the confectioner's sugar a little at a time until the mixture is spreadable. Stir in the vanilla and salt and mix well.

Note: If the icing is too thick, it can be thinned by adding milk a little at a time.

PETIT FOURS FROSTING

Makes Enough for
about 12 Petit Fours

2   cups granulated sugar
⅛   teaspoon cream of tartar
1   cup boiling water

½   teaspoon vanilla extract
2   cups confectioner's sugar
    (approximately)

Combine the sugar, cream of tartar, and boiling water in a saucepan. Bring to a boil and cook until the syrup reaches 226 degrees on a candy thermometer. Remove from the heat and cool to lukewarm (110 degrees on a candy thermometer). Add the vanilla and mix well. Sift in enough confectioner's sugar to make the mixture pourable. Tint with food coloring if you wish. Pour a thin coating of this icing over the prepared cakes and let dry. Then pour on a second thin coating.

Note: To make the petit fours, prepare a white or yellow cake from scratch or from a mix and bake it in a 9- by 13-inch pan. Let the cake cool completely before cutting it into diamonds, squares, and/or rounds.

APPLE PIE

6 Servings
Freezes Well

½ *cup granulated sugar*
¼ *cup all-purpose flour*
¼ *teaspoon salt*
1 *unbaked 9-inch piecrust*
   (top and bottom), page 228
5 *to 6 cups peeled and sliced*
   apples

½ *cup packed light brown*
   sugar
1 *teaspoon ground cinnamon*
⅛ *to ¼ cup water*
4 *tablespoons butter or*
   margarine

1. Preheat the oven to 400 degrees.

2. Sprinkle the granulated sugar, flour, and salt over the bottom of the piecrust in the pie dish.

3. Combine the apples with the brown sugar and cinnamon in a mixing bowl, tossing to coat the apples well. Transfer the apples to the piecrust in the pie dish. Pour the water over the apples and dot the butter on top of the apples. Fit the top crust to the top of the pie, moistening the edges so they stick together. Cut slashes in the top crust to allow the steam to escape. Bake for 50 to 60 minutes, or until both crusts are golden.

Note: This pie is wonderful served warm and topped with slices of cheese.

CHERRY PIE

6 Servings
Freezes Well

1¼ *cups granulated sugar*
1½ *tablespoons all-purpose*
    flour
1½ *tablespoons cornstarch*
⅔   *cup cherry juice (from*
    canned cherries), or ½ cup
    water plus 5 drops red
    food coloring, if using
    fresh pitted cherries

1 *tablespoon butter or*
   margarine
½ *teaspoon lemon juice*
2 *16-ounce cans pitted red*
   cherries, or 4 cups pitted
   fresh red cherries
1 *recipe piecrust (page 228)*

1. Combine the sugar, flour, cornstarch, cherry juice, and butter in a saucepan. Cook over medium heat, stirring occasionally, until thickened. Remove from the heat and add the lemon juice. Cool to room temperature.

2. Preheat the oven to 400 degrees.

3. When the syrup has cooled, add the cherries and mix them in well.

4. Roll out the bottom crust for the pie and fit it in the pie dish. Roll out the top crust and leave it in one piece or cut it into lattice strips.

5. Pour the filling from the saucepan into the bottom piecrust. Fit the top crust or the lattice crust to the top of the pie, moistening the edges so they stick together. If you are using the top crust, be sure to cut a hole in the center to allow the steam to escape. Bake the pie for 50 to 60 minutes, or until both crusts are golden.

PECAN PIE
6 Servings

1	cup granulated sugar	1	teaspoon vanilla extract
¼	cup butter or margarine, softened	3	eggs, well beaten
	Pinch of salt	1	cup chopped or whole pecans
½	cup light or dark corn syrup	1	unbaked 9-inch pie shell (page 228)

1. Preheat the oven to 400 degrees.

2. Mix the sugar, butter, salt, and corn syrup until a smooth batter is formed. Add the vanilla and beaten eggs and mix well. Stir in the pecans and pour the filling into the prepared pie shell.

3. Bake the pie in the preheated oven for 10 minutes. Then lower the oven temperature to 300 degrees and bake for 35 minutes longer.

PUMPKIN PIE
6 Servings
Freezes Well

2	eggs, lightly beaten	¼	teaspoon salt
1	16-ounce can pumpkin	1	teaspoon ground cinnamon, optional
2	tablespoons light brown sugar	1	13-ounce can evaporated milk
¾	cup granulated sugar		
¾	teaspoon pumpkin pie spice	1	unbaked 9-inch pie shell (page 228)

1. Preheat the oven to 425 degrees.

2. Combine the eggs, pumpkin, sugars, pumpkin pie spice, salt, cinnamon, and evaporated milk in a large mixing bowl. Beat until smooth.

Pour into the prepared pie shell and bake for 20 minutes. Lower the oven temperature to 350 degrees and bake for 40 minutes longer, or until a knife inserted near the center of the pie comes out clean.

Note: If you really like the taste of cinnamon, you can eliminate it from the pie filling and sprinkle it on top while the pie is baking or sprinkle it on top right after you remove the pie from the oven.

Variation

Pumpkin Tarts: To make the tarts, roll the piecrust out and cut it to fit tart pans. (Or purchase prepared graham cracker tart shells.) Fill them with the pumpkin mixture and bake at 325 degrees for 25 to 30 minutes, or until a knife inserted near the center comes out clean.

SWEET POTATO PIE

6 Servings
Freezes Well

1½ cups mashed sweet potatoes	1 cup evaporated milk or half-and-half
½ cup firmly packed dark brown sugar	½ cup butter or margarine, melted
½ teaspoon salt	1 tablespoon molasses
Pinch of ground nutmeg	1 unbaked 9-inch pie shell (page 228)
½ teaspoon ground cinnamon	
½ teaspoon pumpkin pie spice	1 cup heavy cream, whipped, for garnish
3 eggs	

1. Preheat the oven to 450 degrees.
2. Combine the mashed sweet potatoes, brown sugar, salt, nutmeg, cinnamon, pumpkin pie spice, and eggs and mix well. Stir in the milk and then the melted butter and molasses. Beat with a hand mixer until smooth.
3. Pour the filling into the prepared pie shell and bake in the preheated oven for 10 minutes. Reduce the oven temperature to 350 degrees and bake for 35 to 45 minutes longer, or until a knife inserted near the center comes out clean. Serve the cooled pie garnished with whipped cream.

PIECRUST

Makes Enough Crust
for Top and Bottom
of 9-inch Pie

2   *cups all-purpose flour*
½   *teaspoon salt*
1   *teaspoon sugar*

¾   *cup solid shortening*
4   *tablespoons water*

Mix together the flour, salt, and sugar in a bowl. Cut in the shortening using a pastry blender or 2 knives until the mixture resembles coarse meal. Add the water gradually, tossing it in with a fork, until the dough can be formed into a ball.

BROWNIES

12 Brownies

1   *cup light brown sugar*
1   *egg*
    Pinch of salt
½   *cup all-purpose flour*
2   *tablespoons unsweetened cocoa*

¼   *cup butter, melted and cooled slightly*
1   *teaspoon vanilla extract*
1   *cup chopped nuts*

1. Preheat the oven to 350 degrees. Grease the bottom and sides of an 8-inch-square baking pan and set aside until needed.

2. Combine the sugar, egg, and salt in a mixing bowl. Mix well. Add the flour, cocoa, melted butter, and vanilla. Stir to mix well. Stir in the nuts and pour the batter into the prepared pan. Bake for 20 minutes and remove from the oven. Let cool for a few minutes before cutting.

Note: To make Double Fudge Brownies, add 1 to 1½ cups semisweet chocolate chips to the batter instead of the nuts.

SOFT SUGAR COOKIES

Makes 4½ to 5 Dozen
Freezes Well

4½ *cups all-purpose flour*
1   *teaspoon baking soda*
½   *teaspoon salt*
½   *cup solid shortening*
½   *cup plus 1 tablespoon butter or margarine*

2½ *cups granulated sugar*
3   *eggs*
1   *tablespoon vanilla extract*
¾   *cup milk*

1. Sift together the flour, soda, and salt onto a piece of waxed paper. Set aside until needed.

2. Preheat the oven to 350 degrees.

3. Put the shortening, butter, sugar, eggs, and vanilla into a mixing bowl. Beat with an electric mixer until smooth and creamy.

4. Add the flour mixture to the creamed mixture alternately with the milk, beating after each addition.

5. Drop by teaspoonfuls onto greased baking sheets. Bake for 10 to 12 minutes. Transfer to racks to cool.

Note: For variety, you can add semisweet chocolate or peanut butter chips to the batter. You can also brush the top of the hot cookies with melted butter and then sprinkle them with granulated sugar.

FILLED ANGEL FOOD CAKE   8 to 10 Servings

1 *angel food ring cake*	*Sugar*
1 *to 2 pints strawberry ice*	*Red food coloring*
cream	24 *to 30 large fresh*
1 *pint heavy cream*	*strawberries with stems*

1. Slice off the top of the cake about 1 inch from the top. Set the top aside.

2. Hollow out the inside of the bottom of the cake, leaving a shell about ½ inch thick on the bottom and sides. Fill the shell with tiny ice cream balls, packing them down on each other. Replace the top of the cake.

3. Whip the cream until it is almost stiff and sweeten it with sugar to taste. Whip until stiff and then add red food coloring until the cream turns a delicate pink. Spread the cream over the top and sides of the cake, swirling it in an attractive pattern. Freeze the cake and remove it from the freezer 5 to 10 minutes before you are ready to serve it. Serve each portion garnished with 3 strawberries.

ANGEL CONFETTI LOAF

12 Servings
Freezes Well

1   12- to 14-ounce angel food
    loaf cake
1   pint lime sherbet
1   pint pineapple or lemon
    sherbet
1   pint raspberry sherbet

1   pint vanilla ice cream (in
    square box)
2   10-ounce packages frozen
    raspberries in syrup,
    slightly thawed

1. Tear the angel food cake into bite-sized pieces and spread the pieces in a 3-quart oblong dish.

2. Add the sherbet to the dish one flavor at a time by dropping rounded tablespoonfuls of each sherbet randomly in among the pieces of cake. When all of the sherbet has been used, wrap a piece of aluminum foil over the tips of your fingers and press down on the cake bits and sherbet to compact them a little.

3. Remove the vanilla ice cream from the carton and cut it into ½-inch-thick slices. Lay the slices over the cake and sherbet in the dish. Let stand at room temperature for about 5 minutes, or until it softens slightly. Then smooth the ice cream out as you would an icing. Cover the dish tightly and freeze until firm.

4. Cut in squares to serve. Top each serving with slightly thawed raspberries.

Note: If you do not use the entire dessert for a meal, you can return the remainder to the freezer for use another time.

CUPCAKE-ICE CREAM SURPRISE

12 Servings
Freezes Well

1   package cake mix (any
    flavor)

½   gallon ice cream (any
    flavor to go with the cake)
    Whipped cream

1. Prepare the cake mix, following the package directions, and bake as cupcakes. When cool, cut off the top of each cupcake about ½ inch down.

2. Hollow each cupcake leaving a shell about ¼ to ½ inch thick. Fill the shell with tiny ice cream balls and replace the top of the cupcakes.

3. Ice the cupcakes with whipped cream (tinted with food coloring, if you wish) and serve immediately.

Note: These desserts can be made in advance and frozen until just about 10 minutes before you serve them.

PEPPERMINT ICE CREAM DESSERT

Put peppermint ice cream, crushed peppermint candy, and a little milk in a blender and blend until smooth. Add a large scoop or two of whipped topping and blend again. Pour into tall stemmed glasses and stick a candy cane in each serving (if you are serving this around Christmastime), or top with crushed peppermint candy. If you are making this for a large crowd, you can serve it in a pretty glass bowl instead.

AMARETTO-ICE CREAM WHIP   4 Servings

Blend 1 pint of vanilla ice cream and 6 tablespoons of Amaretto in a blender until smooth. Pour into 4 stemmed glasses and freeze until thick. Serve with very thin chocolate or vanilla cookies.

Note: You can also add 1 to 2 tablespoons of chocolate syrup to the mixture before you blend it. If you do, decrease the Amaretto to only 4 tablespoons.

DOUBLE STRAWBERRY MERINGUE   16 Servings
                                            Freezes Well

6 *egg whites at room temperature*	½ *gallon strawberry ice cream*
1½ *teaspoons lemon juice, or ½ teaspoon cream of tartar*	1 *16-ounce package frozen strawberries, partially thawed*
2 *cups granulated sugar*	

1. Put the egg whites and lemon juice into a large mixing bowl. Beat on high speed until the egg whites are frothy. Then begin adding the sugar a little at a time, continuing to beat at high speed until the egg whites are stiff and glossy. (This may take from 15 to 30 minutes.)

2. Preheat the oven to 400 degrees. Line a baking sheet with plain brown paper. Draw a large circle on the brown paper the size you want the meringue to be. (A good size is 9 to 10 inches in diameter.) Then draw a smaller circle inside to form a ring. Drop spoonfuls of meringue between the two circles to form a ring. Pile the meringue up high and smooth it over with a spatula.

3. Put the baking sheet in the oven, close the door, and turn the oven off. Let the meringue stand overnight in the oven. (Don't peek!)

4. While the meringue is baking, make ice cream balls from the strawberry ice cream. Put the ice cream balls on a baking sheet and put them in the freezer, covered with aluminum foil, until you are ready to assemble the dessert.

5. To serve, fill the meringue shell with the prepared ice cream balls and spoon the partially thawed strawberries over the whole dessert. Cut into wedges to serve.

INDIVIDUAL MERINGUES

8 Servings
Freezes Well

3   egg whites at room
    temperature
½   teaspoon cream of tartar

1   cup granulated sugar
1   teaspoon vanilla extract

1. Put the egg whites and cream of tartar into a mixing bowl. Beat on high speed until the egg whites are frothy. Then begin adding the sugar a little at a time, continuing to beat at high speed until the egg whites are stiff and glossy. (This may take as long as 15 minutes.) Beat in the vanilla.

2. Preheat the oven to 275 degrees. Line a baking sheet with plain brown paper. Draw 8 circles, each 3 to 4 inches in diameter, on the paper.

3. Put ⅓ cup of the meringue in the center of each circle. Gently spread the meringue out to the edges of the circles, forming a depression in the center of each circle with the back of a spoon.

4. Transfer the baking sheet to the oven and bake for 1 hour. For a crunchier meringue, turn the oven off after the meringues have baked for 1 hour, and leave them in the oven for 1 hour longer with the door closed.

Note: This recipe can also be used to make 1 large meringue.

CHOCOLATE CHARLOTTE RUSSE

6 Servings
Freezes Well

2   *packages ladyfingers*
2   *cans ready-to-serve*
    chocolate fudge pudding
½   *teaspoon vanilla extract*
½   *cup water*

2   *envelopes unflavored*
    gelatin
2   *cups chilled whipped*
    topping

1. Line an 8- by 4- by 2-inch baking dish with waxed paper, leaving a border of waxed paper extending over the top of the dish. Line the bottom and sides of the dish with ladyfinger halves.

2. Combine the pudding and vanilla extract in a large mixing bowl.

3. Put the water in a small saucepan, bring to a boil, and sprinkle the gelatin over it. Lower heat and stir until the gelatin is dissolved. Remove the pan from the heat and stir the dissolved gelatin into the pudding.

4. Fold the whipped topping into the pudding.

5. Pour the pudding mixture into the prepared baking dish. Top with the remaining ladyfinger halves. Cover tightly and chill until firm. (Overnight is best, but 3 to 4 hours might do.)

6. To unmold, pull the dessert out of the dish by the extended waxed paper. Put the dessert on a serving platter and remove the paper carefully.

RICE PUDDING

6 to 8 Servings

1   *package instant vanilla*
    pudding mix
¾   *cup raw rice*
¼   *cup light brown sugar*
2   *tablespoons butter or*
    margarine, melted

1   *cup whipped topping*
1   *cup raisins*
    Ground cinnamon

1. Prepare the pudding mix, following the package directions. Cover and chill in the refrigerator until needed.

2. Prepare the rice, following package directions. While the rice is still warm, stir in the brown sugar and melted butter. Cool to room temperature.

3. Fold the rice mixture into the prepared pudding. Then fold in the whipped topping, and then the raisins. Transfer the pudding to a serving bowl and sprinkle with cinnamon. Chill before serving.

BAKED APPLES

6 Servings
Freezes Well

6   *large baking apples*
½   *to ¾ cup raisins or*
     miniature marshmallows
½   *to ¾ cup walnut or pecan*
     pieces
1   *cup water or apple juice*
½   *cup light brown sugar*

½   *cup honey*
2   *tablespoons butter*
¼   *teaspoon ground cinnamon*
     Pinch of ground nutmeg
2   *teaspoons cornstarch*
     Pinch of salt
     Vanilla ice cream

1. Preheat the oven to 350 degrees.
2. Core the apples, but leave them unpeeled. Fill the centers with the raisins or walnut pieces. Put the apples in a baking pan.
3. Combine the water, ¼ cup brown sugar, honey, butter, ¼ teaspoon of the cinnamon, the nutmeg, cornstarch, and salt in a saucepan. Bring to a boil, stirring occasionally. Pour the hot syrup over the apples and sprinkle them with the remaining brown sugar and cinnamon. Bake for about 1 hour, or until the apples are tender, basting them occasionally with the syrup. Serve warm, topped with a scoop of ice cream.

Note: The apples can be stuffed as described above, or you can add marshmallows to the stuffing along with the raisins and nuts.

CREAM CHEESE-STUFFED APPLES

4 Servings

4   *red Delicious apples*
1   *8-ounce package cream*
     cheese, softened
½   *cup raisins or chocolate*
     chips

¼   *cup chopped walnuts*
     Lemon juice, optional

1. Cut the entire core out of the apples so that they resemble very thick doughnuts.
2. Mix the softened cream cheese, raisins, and walnuts together until well combined. Divide the mixture into fourths, and stuff the apples equally. The stuffed apples can be cut in halves or fourths to serve, if you wish. If you do cut them, brush the cut surfaces with lemon juice to prevent the apples from turning brown.

Note: This goes nicely with a cheese tray.

STACKED BLUEBERRY DESSERT   4 Servings

1½ *cups packaged pound cake mix*	1 *large can blueberry pie filling*
Pinch of salt	3 *teaspoons butter*
Pinch of ground nutmeg or ground allspice	½ *teaspoon white vinegar, lemon juice, or lime juice*
2 *eggs*	1 *teaspoon granulated sugar*
½ *cup water*	*Vanilla ice cream*
1 *tablespoon milk*	

1. Combine the pound cake mix, salt, nutmeg, eggs, water, and milk in a mixing bowl. Mix until smooth. The batter will be thin.

2. Heat a griddle until hot and butter it (if you are not using a nonstick griddle). Drop the batter by tablespoonfuls onto the hot griddle and brown on both sides. As the pancakes brown, remove them to paper towels or a plate to cool.

3. Heat the pie filling with the butter, vinegar, and sugar in a saucepan. Stir occasionally and when the mixture begins to bubble, remove it from the heat.

4. To make the stacks, put a pancake on a dessert plate and top it with 1 tablespoon of the hot filling. Continue making layers in this way until the dessert is as high as you want it. Top each stack off with a dip of vanilla ice cream and serve at once.

Note: The pancakes can be prepared in advance and stacked with waxed paper between them, wrapped tightly, and frozen until needed. If the pancakes are frozen, reheat them in a 400-degree oven for 15 to 20 minutes before preparing the dessert.

CHERRIES JUBILEE   2 to 4 Servings

1 *16-ounce can dark pitted sweet cherries*	2 *tablespoons cold water*
	Pinch of salt
⅓ *cup granulated sugar*	¼ *cup brandy or kirschwasser*
2 *tablespoons cornstarch*	*Vanilla ice cream*

1. Drain the juice from the cherries into a saucepan. Set the cherries aside until needed. Combine the cornstarch and water and add it to the cherry juice along with the salt. Cook over medium heat until the mixture is thickened. Remove from the heat and stir in the cherries.

2. Transfer the cherries and sauce to a heatproof bowl or a metal pan with a long handle. Pour the brandy into a metal ladle and ignite it. Pour the flaming brandy over the cherries. Serve immediately over scoops of vanilla ice cream.

AMARETTO-GLAZED ORANGES

4 Servings

4   *navel oranges*
⅔   *cup light corn syrup*
⅔   *cup orange juice*
3   *tablespoons Amaretto*
    Pinch of salt

1   *cup whipped cream or*
    whipped topping
¼   *cup toasted almond slivers*

1. Peel the oranges and slice them into ¼- to ½-inch slices. Stack the slices together to re-form the oranges. Put the re-formed oranges in a flat serving dish and set aside until needed.

2. Combine the corn syrup, orange juice, Amaretto, and salt in a small saucepan. Stir well and bring to a boil, stirring constantly. Boil for 1 to 2 minutes. Remove from the heat and cool for 5 minutes. Then pour the syrup over the oranges. Serve the oranges topped with whipped cream and sprinkled with the toasted almonds.

AMBROSIA DESSERT SALAD

4 to 6 Servings

1   *cup canned mandarin*
    orange sections, drained
    well
1   *cup miniature marsh-*
    mallows
1   *cup pineapple chunks,*
    drained

1   *cup white seedless grapes,*
    halved
1½ *cups whipped topping*
¼   *cup mayonnaise*
¼   *cup flaked or shredded*
    coconut

1. Combine the orange sections, marshmallows, pineapple chunks, and grape halves in a bowl. Mix well and chill for at least 1 hour.

2. Combine the whipped topping and mayonnaise and fold into the fruit mixture. Chill for at least 1 hour before serving. Serve in dessert glasses, garnishing each serving with coconut.

Note: Fresh orange sections and fresh pineapple chunks can be used instead of the canned fruits.

AMARETTO PEARS

4 Servings

8   *canned pear halves, well*
    drained

10 *tablespoons Amaretto*
4   *mint sprigs*

Put 2 pear halves in each of 4 long-stemmed glasses. Pour 2½ tablespoons of Amaretto over the pears in each of the glasses. Put the glasses in the freezer just before you serve dinner, and let chill until you are ready to serve them. Garnish each serving with a mint sprig before serving.

Variation

Amaretto Cream Pears: Add 4 tablespoons of cream to the Amaretto before you pour it over the pear halves in the glasses.

PEACH FRUIT FLUFF   4 to 6 Servings

6 *canned peach halves, drained and cubed*	¾ *cup white seedless grapes*
	1½ *cups whipped topping*
1 *cup miniature marshmallows*	*Extra chopped pecans for garnish*
6 *tablespoons chopped pecans*	

Put the cubed peaches, marshmallows, 6 tablespoons of chopped pecans, grapes, and whipped topping in a mixing bowl and fold together gently. Transfer the mixture to individual stemmed glasses and chill. Top each serving with 1 to 2 tablespoons chopped pecans before serving.

LEMON-LIME GELATIN FRUIT SALAD   8 to 12 Servings

1 *6-ounce box lemon gelatin*	1 *6-ounce box lime gelatin*
4 *cups hot water*	*Pinch of salt*
2 *3-ounce packages cream cheese, softened*	1 *cup pineapple juice (from canned pineapple)*
2½ *cups cold water*	1 *20-ounce can crushed pineapple, drained*
3 *cups whipped topping*	

1. Dissolve the lemon gelatin in 2 cups of the hot water. While the gelatin is still warm, stir in the softened cream cheese until it is well combined. Add 1½ cups of cold water and mix well. Add 1 cup of whipped topping and stir until the mixture is smooth. Pour into a 3- to 4-quart oblong dish and refrigerate until set.

2. When the lemon gelatin mixture is just about set, prepare the lime gelatin mixture. Dissolve the lime gelatin in 2 cups of the hot water. Stir in 1 cup of pineapple juice, 1 cup of water, and a pinch of salt and mix well. Cool to room temperature and add the drained crushed pineapple. Refrigerate until the mixture is syrupy, then pour over the set lemon gelatin and refrigerate until set.

3. To serve, spread the top of the gelatin with the remaining whipped topping and cut into squares.

Chocolate Dessert Cups

Melt bittersweet or milk chocolate over simmering water until it is smooth. Use a pastry brush to brush the melted chocolate over the inside of foil cupcake tin liners. Brush on the melted chocolate until it is at least ⅛ inch thick. Chill the cupcake liners until just before you are ready to use them. Then peel away the liners and fill the chocolate cups with sliced fresh fruit, pudding, or ice cream.

Note: These can be frozen ahead, but do not remove the cupcake liners until you are ready to use them.

Dessert Fondues

Chocolate Cream

Combine an 8-ounce chocolate bar with a pinch of salt and ½ cup heavy cream. Cook over low heat until the chocolate is melted and the mixture is smooth.

Semisweet Chocolate

Combine ½ cup light corn syrup, a pinch of salt, 1 teaspoon of vanilla extract, and 1 6-ounce package semisweet chocolate chips in a fondue pot. Cook over low heat until the chocolate is melted and the mixture is smooth.

Peanut Butter

Combine 1 cup creamy peanut butter, 1 cup half-and-half, and ½ cup honey in a fondue pot. Cook over low heat until the mixture is smooth.

Use these dessert fondues for dipping banana chunks, pineapple cubes, strawberries, pear chunks, apple slices, marshmallows, angel food cake cubes, pound cake cubes, or whatever fruit or cake takes your fancy.

Chocolate Chip-Cheese Spread

Mix ¼ to ½ cup semisweet chocolate chips with 8 ounces of soft cream cheese (or mix with 8 ounces of regular cream cheese, softened, and combined with 1 to 2 tablespoons of milk) for an hors d'oeuvres spread for crackers or for hot muffins, biscuits, or bagels.

BUTTERSCOTCH SAUCE   Makes 2 Cups

1 *cup light brown sugar*	½ *cup cream*
4 *tablespoons butter or margarine*	*Pinch of salt*
	2 *egg yolks, lightly beaten*

1. Put the sugar and butter into the top of a double boiler. Beat until they are creamy.

2. Add the cream and salt to the egg yolks and mix well. Then sitr the mixture into the sugar and butter in the top of the double boiler. Cook over simmering water until thickened. Serve hot or cold.

CARAMEL SAUCE   Makes 1 Cup

1 *cup granulated sugar*	2 *tablespoons half-and-half*
½ *cup boiling water*	

Put the sugar in a heavy pan or a cast-iron skillet. Cook over very low heat, stirring constantly, until the sugar melts and turns brown. Add the boiling water very slowly, stirring constantly. (Be careful when you add the water; it will cause the sugar to boil up and give off a lot of very hot steam.) When all the water has been added and the sugar has all melted, remove the pan from the heat. Stir in the half-and-half and mix well. Serve the sauce hot or cold.

CARAMEL-MARSHMALLOW SAUCE   Makes 1½ Cups

1 *cup light brown sugar*	¼ *cup cream*
½ *cup light corn syrup*	⅓ *cup cream*
½ *cup water*	
4 *tablespoons butter or margarine*	

Put the sugar, corn syrup, and water in a small saucepan and mix until well combined. Bring to a boil and boil, stirring constantly, until the bubbles look glassy. Add the butter and cook until the butter has melted. Remove from the heat and cool to room temperature. Stir in the cream and marshmallows.

HOT FRUIT SAUCE

4 to 6 Servings
Freezes Well

2¼ tablespoons all-purpose
   flour, or 1¼ tablespoons
   cornstarch
6 tablespoons granulated
   sugar
   Pinch of salt
¾ cup water

½ cup diced and peeled fresh
   fruit
1½ tablespoons butter or
   margarine
¼ teaspoon lemon juice,
   optional

Mix the flour, sugar, salt, and water together in a small saucepan. Stir until the flour and sugar are dissolved. Add the fruit and cook over low heat, stirring constantly, until the sauce has thickened. Remove from the heat and add the butter and lemon juice. Stir well and cool to room temperature before using.

LEMON DESSERT SAUCE

4 Servings
Freezes Well

4 tablespoons granulated
   sugar
   Pinch of salt
   Pinch of ground nutmeg
1½ tablespoons cornstarch

1½ cups water
2 tablespoons butter or
   margarine
1 tablespoon lemon juice
   Grated rind of 1 lemon

Put the sugar, salt, nutmeg, cornstarch, and water in a small saucepan. Stir until well combined and then bring to a boil. Add the butter and cook until the butter has melted. Remove the mixture from the heat and stir in the lemon juice and grated lemon rind. Mix well and cool the sauce to room temperature before serving.

HOMEMADE CHOCOLATE SYRUP

Makes about 2 cups

1 cup granulated sugar
⅓ cup unsweetened cocoa
   powder
2 tablespoons all-purpose
   flour

1 cup boiling water
2 tablespoons butter or
   margarine
½ teaspoon vanilla extract

Combine the sugar, cocoa, and flour in a heavy glass bowl. Pour in the water and mix until smooth. Add the butter and vanilla and stir until the butter has melted. Cool to room temperature and pour the syrup into a jar with a tight-fitting lid. Cover tightly and refrigerate until chilled and thickened. This syrup is good over ice cream or cake.

INDEX

241